PENTON-KTM
WORKSHOP MANUAL
1972 to 1975

PENTON Jackpiner - Hare & Mint
KTM MC & GS Models
(Motocross & Gelande Sport)

Includes Illustrated
Engine Parts Manual &
Frame & Chassis Parts Manual

A Floyd Clymer Publication - 2025 VelocePress.com

CONTENTS

Preface & Introduction

Workshop Manual .... page 1

Frame & Chassis Parts Manual .... page 47

KTM Engine Parts Manual .... page 85

PREFACE

TRADEMARKS & COPYRIGHT

Penton® is the registered trademark of Penton, Inc. This publication is not sponsored by or endorsed by the trademark owner. We recognize that some words, model names and designations, for example, mentioned herein are the property of the trademark holder. We use them for identification purposes only. This is not an official publication however; it may include non-copyright works of the trademark holder.

INTRODUCTION

Welcome to the world of digital publishing ~ the book you now hold in your hand was printed using the latest state of the art digital technology. The advent of print-on-demand has forever changed the publishing process, never has information been so accessible and it is our hope that this book serves your informational needs for years to come. If this is your first exposure to digital publishing, we hope that you are pleased with the results. Many more titles of interest to the classic automobile and motorcycle enthusiast, collector and restorer are available via our website at www.VelocePress.com. We hope that you find this title as interesting as we do.

NOTE FROM THE PUBLISHER

The information presented is true and complete to the best of our knowledge. All recommendations are made without any guarantees on the part of the author or the publisher, who also disclaim all liability incurred with the use of this information.

INFORMATION ON THE USE OF THIS PUBLICATION

This manual is an invaluable resource for those interested in performing their own maintenance. However, in today's information age we are constantly subject to changes in common practice, new technology, availability of improved materials and increased awareness of chemical toxicity. As such, it is advised that the user consult with an experienced professional prior to undertaking any procedure described herein. While every care has been taken to ensure correctness of information, it is obviously not possible to guarantee complete freedom from errors or omissions or to accept liability arising from such errors or omissions. Therefore, any individual that uses the information contained within, or elects to perform or participate in do-it-yourself repairs or modifications acknowledges that there is a risk factor involved and that the publisher or its associates cannot be held responsible for personal injury or property damage resulting from the use of the information or the outcome of such procedures.

WARNING!

One final word of advice, this publication is intended to be used as a reference guide, and when in doubt the reader should consult with a qualified technician.

Penton 175-250-400 Service Manual

INTRODUCTION

Congratulations on becoming the proud owner of the Penton Sport Cycle. You now join the growing number of owners and riders throughout the world who depend on the Penton cycle to bring them the rewards of the sport of cycling.

The Penton is unique in that it was designed and manufactured exclusively for the American competition scene by one of the country's greatest cycle competitors, John Penton, whose name the cycle bears. His knowledge of the sport and industry have revolutionized the sport of small bore racing in the United States.

The Pentons competitive edge over other cycles is maintained by us at the factory who are riding every weekend in the same competitions that you, the rider and owner, are competing in. This continuous testing in conjunction with the International Six Days Trials has enabled us to provide you with a highly dependable and competitive cycle you will be proud to own and ride.

This manual is designed to give you the knowledge necessary to keep your Penton in competitive shape and carry out needed maintenance and repair. This manual is complete in its service to the Penton cycle and should be carried out in the most professional of ways. You, the owner, may prefer to let the dealer who sold you the Penton make needed engine repairs, as this should be carried out only with the proper tools and a good knowledge of mechanics. You, the owner, have a special job in seeing that the Penton is maintained in perfect operating condition. With this, you will always have a competitive cycle and concentration will be on winning rather than finishing.

TECHNICAL DATA

ENGINE	175cc JACKPINER	250cc HARE SCRAMBLER	400cc MINT
Type	Single cylinder/two-stroke piston-port/air cooled		
Bore	63.5mm	71mm	81mm
Stroke	54mm	62mm	69mm
Displacement	171cc	245cc	355.5cc
Max. H.P.	28 H.P.	34 H.P.	42 H.P. DIN
Cylinder	Aluminum cylinder with cast-in iron liner	Aluminum cylinder with pressed-in iron liner	
Piston	Forged aluminum piston with one L-ring and one square ring		
Distance from top of cylinder to top of L-ring at top dead center (adjusted by base gaskets)	.028"–.032"	piston EK 1274 .040 EK 1274A .047	.051"
Piston Clearance	set at .003"	set at .0025	
Ring Gap	set at .011, maximum gap .018"		
Connecting rod bearings	Needle bearings top and bottom		
Lubrication	Oil and gas mixture (see text)		
Exhaust pipe	Performance tuned expansion chamber with integrated muffler		
CARBURETOR			
Type	30mm Bing	36mm Bing	38mm Bing
*Main jet	150	165	185/190
*Pilot jet	30	40	35
*Needle jet	276	283	285
*Needle position	3	2	2
*Vaporizer	51-596 (shielded full body type)		
Air Filter	oiled foam		
*Check with dealer to be sure you are current and for fine tuning carb			
ELECTRICAL			
Type	Motoplat, transistor, solid state, magneto ignition with 35 watt main lighting coil		
Timing	3.00mm btdc	2.55mm btdc	2.4mm btdc
Spark plug	Bosch W-280-MI	Bosch W-290-T16	Bosch W-290
TRANSMISSION			
Gearbox	six-speed/drum selector/dog-shift gears		
Primary drive	straight-cut gear drive ratio 25/69		
Gear ratios	1st, 14/36, 2nd, 18/32, 3rd, 21/28, 4th, 24/25; 5th, 26/23, 6th, 28/21		
Clutch	Multi-disc wet clutch, 5 plate	Multi-disc wet clutch, 7 plate	
Countershaft	12 tooth		
Rear sprocket	52 tooth		
Chain	3/8 x 5/8"		
Transmission Capacity	1–1.1/2 quarts		
CHASSIS			
Type	Double-down cradle/Chrome molybden steel/Special Hi-Breather air intake on down tube		
Suspension front	Ceriani-hydraulically dampened telescopic fork (approx. 180cc of fork oil each leg)		
Suspension rear	Ceriani		
Swing arm	Swing arm mounted on needle bearings (see text)		
Hubs	All magnesium/full width front, conical rear, full drum brake shoes		
Tires	3.00x21 front, 4.00x18 rear	3.00x21 front, 450x18 rear	
Gas tank	1.8 or 2.9 gallon fiberglass		

NOTE: Specifications are subject to change ... be sure to consult dealer for such things as timing, spark plugs, carb changes or any critical measurements which may be made.

SPECIFICATIONS

LUBRICATION CHART – CAPACITY AND QUALITY

ENGINE Mixture of 95 octane, 100% leaded gasoline with Hi-Point Deluxe two-stroke concentrate (follow label instructions).

FRONT FORKS 185cc of Hi-Point fork oil or Hi-Point Silicone fluid in each leg.

GEARBOX 1 quart of Hi-Point Gear Lube transmission lubricant.

CABLES Good quality penetrating oil or "Dry - Slide".

WHEEL BEARINGS Lithium base grease high quality Hi-Point chain oil.
CHAIN

TIGHTENING TORQUES FOR NUTS AND BOLTS

Used On	Dimensions	Tightening Torque in Foot Pounds
Crankshaft Pinion	M 18 x 1.5	40
Crankshaft Magneto	M 12 x 1 (left-hand)	35
Inner Clutch Hub	M 22 x 1.5	45-50
Sprocket Nut	M 20 x 1.5	35
Cylinder Screws	M 8 x 40 (Allen)	18-20
Cylinder Studs	M 8 (in Crankcase)	12
Cylinder Studs Nuts	M 8	18-20
Seal Retaining Plate	M 5	4.5
Bearing Cover	M 6 (Studs)	4.5
	M 8 (Studs)	6
	M 8 (Nut)	18
*Kickstarter Stop Bolt		18-20
Kickstarter Assembly	Screw Bushing	30
Screws in Housing	M 6 (Allen)	5.5-6
Intake Manifold	M 6	5.5-6
Exhaust Adapter	M 6	5.5-6

*Never remove this bolt while engine is assembled. It is located under the engine and is identifiable because of its strange head configuration.

SPECIFICATIONS

DECIMAL EQUIVALENTS OF MILLIMETERS

mm.	Inches	mm.	Inches	mm.	Inches	mm.	Inches	mm.	Inches
.01	.00039	.41	.01614	.81	.03189	21	.82677	61	2.40157
.02	.00079	.42	.01654	.82	.03228	22	.86614	62	2.44094
.03	.00118	.43	.01693	.83	.03268	23	.90551	63	2.48031
.04	.00157	.44	.01732	.84	.03307	24	.94488	64	2.51968
.05	.00197	.45	.01772	.85	.03346	25	.98425	65	2.55905
.06	.00236	.46	.01811	.86	.03386	26	1.02362	66	2.59842
.07	.00276	.47	.01850	.87	.03425	27	1.06299	67	2.63779
.08	.00315	.48	.01890	.88	.03465	28	1.10236	68	2.67716
.09	.00354	.49	.01929	.89	.03504	29	1.14173	69	2.71653
.10	.00394	.50	.01969	.90	.03543	30	1.18110	70	2.75590
.11	.00433	.51	.02008	.91	.03583	31	1.22047	71	2.79527
.12	.00472	.52	.02047	.92	.03622	32	1.25984	72	2.83464
.13	.00512	.53	.02087	.93	.03661	33	1.29921	73	2.87401
.14	.00551	.54	.02126	.94	.03701	34	1.33858	74	2.91338
.15	.00591	.55	.02165	.95	.03740	35	1.37795	75	2.95275
.16	.00630	.56	.02205	.96	.03780	36	1.41732	76	2.99212
.17	.00669	.57	.02244	.97	.03819	37	1.45669	77	3.03149
.18	.00709	.58	.02283	.98	.03858	38	1.49606	78	3.07086
.19	.00748	.59	.02323	.99	.03898	39	1.53543	79	3.11023
.20	.00787	.60	.02362	1.00	.03937	40	1.57480	80	3.14960
.21	.00827	.61	.02402	1	.03937	41	1.61417	81	3.18897
.22	.00866	.62	.02441	2	.07874	42	1.65354	82	3.22834
.23	.00906	.63	.02480	3	.11811	43	1.69291	83	3.26771
.24	.00945	.64	.02520	4	.15748	44	1.73228	84	3.30708
.25	.00984	.65	.02559	5	.19685	45	1.77165	85	3.34645
.26	.01024	.66	.02598	6	.23622	46	1.81102	86	3.38582
.27	.01063	.67	.02638	7	.27559	47	1.85039	87	3.42519
.28	.01102	.68	.02677	8	.31496	48	1.88976	88	3.46456
.29	.01142	.69	.02717	9	.35433	49	1.92913	89	3.50393
.30	.01181	.70	.02756	10	.39370	50	1.96850	90	3.54330
.31	.01220	.71	.02795	11	.43307	51	2.00787	91	3.58267
.32	.01260	.72	.02835	12	.47244	52	2.04724	92	3.62204
.33	.01299	.73	.02874	13	.51181	53	2.08661	93	3.66141
.34	.01339	.74	.02913	14	.55118	54	2.12598	94	3.70078
.35	.01378	.75	.02953	15	.59055	55	2.16535	95	3.74015
.36	.01417	.76	.02992	16	.62992	56	2.20472	96	3.77952
.37	.01457	.77	.03032	17	.66929	57	2.24409	97	3.81889
.38	.01496	.78	.03071	18	.70866	58	2.28346	98	3.85826
.39	.01535	.79	.03110	19	.74803	59	2.32283	99	3.89763
.40	.01575	.80	.03150	20	.78740	60	2.36220	100	3.93700

SPECIFICATIONS

DECIMAL EQUIVALENTS

8ths	32nds	64ths	64ths
1/8 = .125	1/32 = .03125	1/64 = .015625	33/64 = .515625
1/4 = .250	3/32 = .09375	3/64 = .046875	35/64 = .546875
3/8 = .375	5/32 = .15625	5/64 = .078125	37/64 = .578125
1/2 = .500	7/32 = .21875	7/64 = .109375	39/64 = .609375
5/8 = .625	9/32 = .28125	9/64 = .140625	41/64 = .640625
3/4 = .750	11/32 = .34375	11/64 = .171875	43/64 = .671875
7/8 = .875	13/32 = .40625	13/64 = .203125	45/64 = .703125
16ths	15/32 = .46875	15/64 = .234370	47/64 = .734375
1/16 = .0625	17/32 = .53125	17/64 = .265625	49/64 = .765625
3/16 = .1875	19/32 = .59375	19/64 = .296875	51/64 = .796875
5/16 = .3125	21/32 = .65625	21/64 = .328125	53/64 = .828125
7/16 = .4375	23/32 = .71875	23/64 = .359375	55/64 = .859375
9/16 = .5625	25/32 = .78125	25/64 = .390625	57/64 = .890625
11/16 = .6875	27/32 = .84375	27/64 = .421875	59/64 = .921875
13/16 = .8125	29/32 = .90625	29/64 = .453125	61/64 = .953125
15/16 = .9375	31/32 = .96875	31/64 = .484375	63/64 = .984375

CONVERSION TABLE

Millimetres (mm) to Inches (in)	1 cm = 10 mm
1 mm = 0.0394 in	Conversion factor 0.0394
e. g. 15.003 mm x 0.0394 = 0.5911182 in	

Square centimetre (cm²) to Square inch (sq in)	
1 cm² = 0.155 in	Conversion factor 0.155
e. g. 1.5 cm² x 0.155 = 0.2325 sq in	

Cubic centimetre (cc) to Cubic inch (cu in)	
1 cc = 0.06102 cu in	Conversion factor 0.06102
e. g. 135 cc x 0.06102 = 8.2377 cu in	

Kilograms (kg) to Pounds (lb)	
1 kg = 2.205 lb	Conversion factor 2.205
e. g. 92 kg x 2.205 = 202.86 lb	

Kilopondmetres (mkp) to Foot pounds (ftlb)	
1 mkp = 7.233 ft lb	Conversion factor 7.233
e. g. 1.3 mkp x 7.233 = 9.4029 ft lb	

Litres (l) to US-gallons (US-gall)	
1 l = 0.2642 US-gall	Conversion factor 0.2642
e. g. 9.3 l x 0.2642 = 2.45706 US-gall	

Kilograms/square centimetre (kg/cm² = atu) to Pounds/square inch (lb/sqin = psi)	
1 atu = 14,22 psi	Conversion factor 14. 22
e. g. 1.2 atu x 14.22 = 17.064 psi	

Kilometres (km) to Miles (mil)	
1 km = 0.621 mil	Conversion factor 0.621
e. g. 100 km x 0.621 = 62,1 mil	

Litres/100 Kilometres (l/100 km) to Miles/US-gallon (mil/US-gall)	
$\text{mil/US-gall} = \dfrac{235}{\text{l/100 km}}$	e. g. $\dfrac{235}{7 \, l} = 33.57$ mil/US-gall

CONTROLS

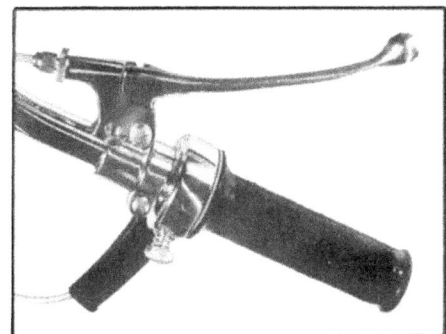
fig. 1

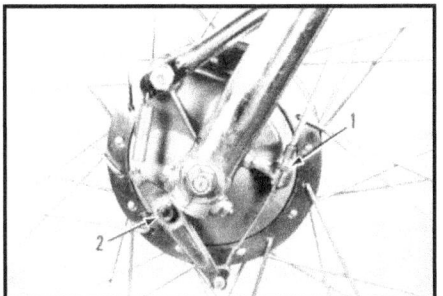
fig. 2

Front Hand Brake Lever

To adjust the brake use the cable adjuster on the hand lever (fig. 1). If the hand lever is impossible to adjust use the adjuster on the brake plate cover (fig. 2/1). Before setting the brake plate adjuster set the hand lever adjuster to approximately mid-position so later adjustment may be made. Due to wear of the brake lining and stretching of the cable both adjusters may no longer tighten the brake. If the lining is in proper condition, the brake plate lever (fig. 2/2) may be moved forward one tooth. To have a good lever effect, the position of the lever must not be understepped or moved forward too far. Be sure return spring tension is tight so brake drag does not occur.

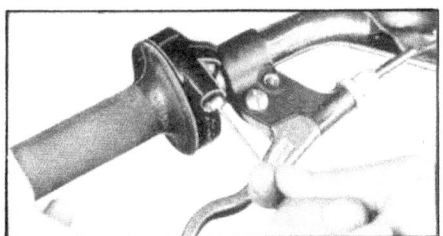
fig. 3

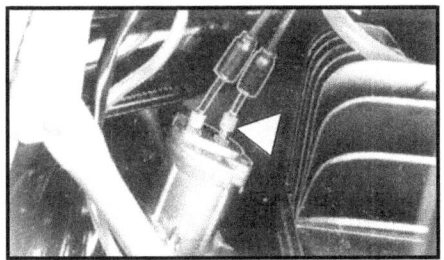
fig. 4

Throttle Twist Grip

The throttle twist grip is located on the right side of the handlebar and is made out of nylon. By removing the threaded screw bushing and rotating the throttle to full close you can remove the cable without taking the throttle apart. You can put in a new throttle the same way. NOTE: The threaded screw bushing should be screwed in all the way in the throttle as this acts as a stop bushing. (Do not make throttle adjustment here.) The throttle cable should have a slight play in it when in the closed position. The play is correct if the cable can be pulled out of the carburetor approximately 1/8" without pulling up the slide. Adjustment of the throttle cable is made by the adjusting screw on top of the carburetor, (1, fig. 4). Secure the locking nut when the proper adjustment is made. Always check this play after adjusting the idle. The throttle cable should be free of binding and routed so as not to catch on anything. Use dry-slide to lubricate cable and throttle.

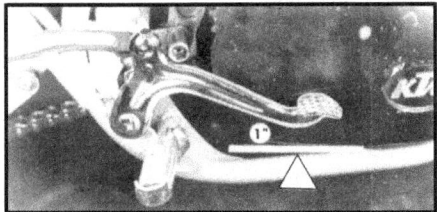
fig. 5

fig. 6

Foot Brake Pedal

The play of the foot brake pedal should be approximately 1" (fig. 5). To adjust the play use the brake rod wing nut (fig. 6). If the play is excessive and the adjusting nut can no longer reset the pedal, reset the brake plate lever (fig. 6/1) backward one notch. Make sure the position of the lever does not over or understep or lever action will be impaired. Before adjusting the brake plate lever check the state of the brake lining. When the rear wheel is adjusted re-check the brake pedal adjustment. Be sure the return spring tension is tight so brake drag does not occur.

5

CONTROLS

Clutch Lever, Adjusting and Refitting the Cable

The play of the clutch lever, measured at the lever outside (fig. 7) should be approximately 1/2 in. For this adjustment use the cable adjuster (fig. 7). If this adjuster is no longer able to take up the play, use the cable adjuster where the clutch cable goes into the cases (fig. 8). No other adjustments are possible to make to the clutch cable and replacement must be made if cable becomes too stretched.

The clutch arm at the engine is not adjustable. The ideal clearance is shown in figure 4. It is very important that there be clearance between the clutch arm and the mag case (x), otherwise the clutch will be partially thrown out, causing it to slip. If, through worn clutch plates or clutch pushrods, distance O is much too small, causing improper clutch throwout, this distance can be obtained by adding another ball bearing between the two pushrods. It will probably then be necessary to grind the end of a pushrod to obtain distance O.

If slipping of the clutch occurs when riding, the tightening of the clutch stud nuts (fig. 111, Pg. 43) will usually cure the problem.

The clutch should be used as often as possible, with a positive movement of the gearshift lever. However, if clutchless shifts are necessary, ALWAYS turn off the throttle when upshifting and "Blip" the throttle to give it a little gas on the downshift.

There is a screw on the center of the clutch pressure plate that looks like a push rod adjuster nut, but is not. Do not adjust that screw as it is for taking the pressure from the clutch rod only and should be kept tight.

To change the clutch cable remove the mag side cover, loosen clutch lever and case adjusting screws and remove cable. Replace with new clutch cable, being sure that the cable is secure in the brass barrel nipple at the engine lever. Be sure the cable has no sharp bends or kinks in it. Readjust lever and engine case adjusters.

For more info and work on the clutch, see engine sections.

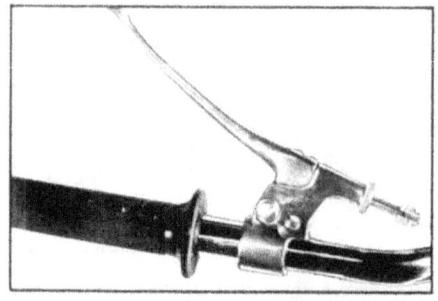

fig. 7

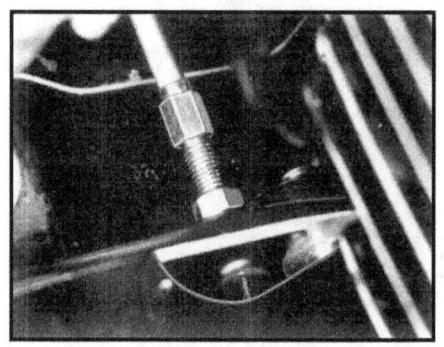

fig. 8

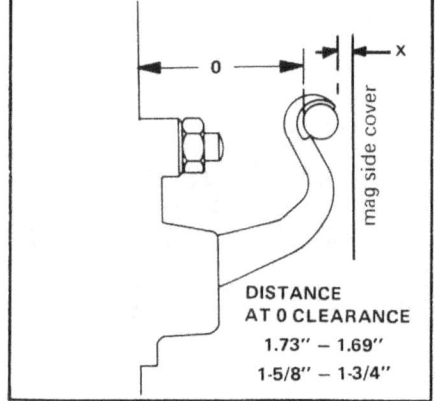

fig. 9

Foot Gear Shift Lever

Gear changes are made as shown in fig. 10. Pedal position may be changed by loosening the fixing screw, removing the pedal and fitting to a new position. The clutch should be used at all times when shifting and a positive movement should be made when changing gears.

With proper clutching, shifting, and treatment in general, you can use this Penton for several years on the same clutch and transmission.

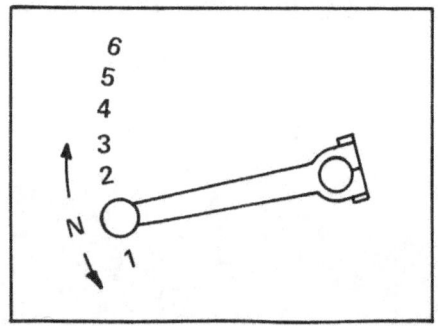

fig. 10

CONTROLS

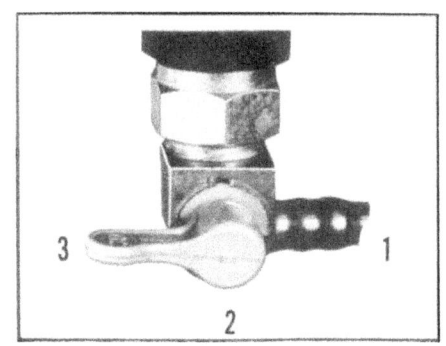
fig. 11

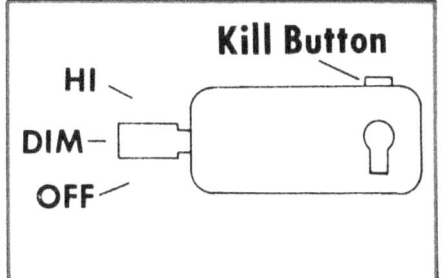
fig. 12

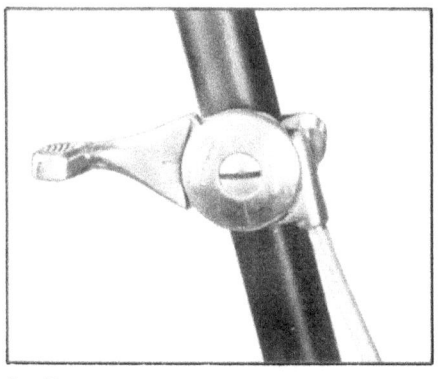
fig. 13

fig. 14

Fuel Cocks

The fuel cocks are located on both sides at the rear of the gas tank. They should both be open when the cycle is running. The fuel cocks have 3 positions: 1-off, 2-on, 3-reserve (fig. 11).

When the cycle is not running, keep fuel cocks closed!

Light Switch

Located on the left handlebar, the control handles all the auxiliary electrical controls. See page 20 for electrical wiring diagram.

Choke Lever

Located on the left side of the handlebar, the choke lever is on when moved to position shown in fig. 13. In order to assure that the choke is out of operation during normal running, the carburetor has an adjusting screw (fig. 14). When choke is moved to off position, no part of the choke slide should show in the carburetor throat when throttle is wide open.

It is a good idea to put a heavy rubber band holding the choke lever closed so during operation, vibration or accidentally bumping the lever will not close the choke making the bike run rich.

Handlebar

The handlebar may be adjusted by the rider as his requirements may need. Loosen the nuts beneath the top fork crown, adjust the handlebar and retighten up the nuts securely. After adjusting the handlebars, check all controls and correct if necessary.

OPERATION AND MAINTENANCE

Fuel

The fuel for the Penton should be pre-mixed in a separate gas can. The proper fuel is a 95% octane, 100% leaded gasoline only mixed with Hi-Point 2-cycle engine oil with a ratio of 20 to 1 or with Hi-Point 2-cycle Concentrate at a ratio of 40 to 1. If other oil is used be sure it is 2-cycle air cooled motorcycle engine oil and follow label instructions. Do not run without an oil gas mixture, or use outboard engine oil. The proper oil will eliminate plug fouling, smoke, carbon build-up and prolong your engine life. We recommend Hi-Point 2-Cycle Concentrate available from your Penton Dealer.

Starting Procedure for the Penton

Open both fuel cocks to the open position. Push carburetor tickler until fuel flows from the overflow hole. Close choke lever. With cycle in neutral, kick the starter crank sharply. Use the throttle control for engine speed. Once the engine is running cleanly the choke may be turned off. Keep from overrevving the engine while in neutral.

Breaking In

In breaking in your Penton it is important to follow this procedure: Do not ride on full throttle from the beginning. Gradually increase the stress to the engine and close the throttle entirely for short intervals. In the first hour of riding use only half throttle, gradually work up to full throttle over a several hour period. This will insure proper seating of the rings and a smoother running engine. This will also give you time to get used to riding the Penton. If a new piston or cylinder is fitted follow the same procedure. Be sure to check over the cycle thoroughly after riding and tighten any loose nuts and bolts and make any necessary adjustments to the controls. When subjecting your machine to long stretches of high speed highway or extreme engine stress, we find it useful to close the choke slightly so the bike will run a little richer to eliminate any possibility of seizing, if the engine leans out.

Carburetor, Maintenance and Tuning

The carburetor fitted to the Penton and the choice of jet sizes are all determined by means of extensive testing at the factory. The carb setting determined in this way represent the optimum setting, and for this reason it is advisable not to make arbitrary adjustments on your own.

If conditions of climate or altitude cause the bike to run rich (blubbering, won't clean out, especially at low end) or lean (pinging), fine adjustments can be made by varying the jet needle position: .... raising the needle produces a richer air-fuel mixture, lowering it produces a leaner mixture. It must be pointed out that varying the jet needle position alters the richness of the mixture only at low and medium engine speeds.

fig. 18

if, while riding your Penton it is obvious, through bad pinging, that the bike is lean in a portion of the power band, refrain from running there until proper carb adjustment can be made, as hard riding while pinging can cause engine seizure.

With correct carburetor setting, the air filter functioning satisfactorily, and a suitable spark plug, the insulator of the spark plug will be stained brown by burning. If carbon collects on the plug or the plug is wet, it means that the air-fuel mixture is too rich. On the other hand, when the plug becomes white, it is an indication that the mixture is too lean. Of course, the thermal value of the spark plug must be as specified. (See spark plug maintenance)

Tuning the Carburetor

Tune the carburetor while the engine is warm. Unscrew throttle valve stop (3, fig. 18) and set the control cable in such a position that the throttle is completely closed.

Screw in the throttle stop valve (3, fig. 18) until the engine (operating at its normal temperature) runs at an increased idling speed when the twist-grip is closed.

Screw in air adjusting screw (4, fig. 18) until a slightly perceptible stopping occurs, and screw it out (by approximately half a turn) until the engine runs very smoothly.

Unscrew stop screw (3, fig. 18) until the required idling is obtained. We recommend no or little idling if the cycle is used in competition. Check the throttle cable for proper play (see controls section).

OPERATION AND MAINTENANCE

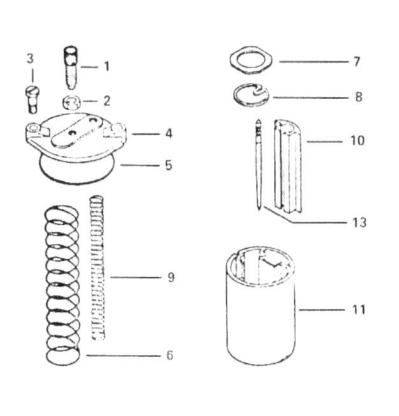
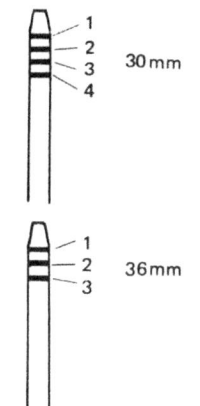

30mm

36mm

1. Cable adjusters
2. Cable adjuster lock nuts
3. Top screws
4. Mixing chamber top
5. Rubber washer
6. Spring
7. Washer
8. Needle clip
9. Choke spring
10. Choke slide
11. Throttle slide
12. Gas fitting
13. Jet needle
14. Carb body
15. Tickler assy.
16. Adjusting screw
17. Spring
18. Air adjusting screw
19. Spring
20. Float needle
21. Float
22. Pin for float
23. Vaporizer
24. Needle jet
25. Mixing device
26. Main jet
27. Idling jet
28. Screen
29. Float chamber
30. Gasket
31. Spring clip
32. Float nut

The Bing Comes with this Set-up

CARBURETOR

Type	30mm Bing	36mm Bing	38mm Bing
*Main jet	150	165	185-190
*Pilot jet	30	35	35
*Needle jet	276	283	285
*Needle position	3	2	2
*Vaporizer	51-596 (shielded full body type)		
Air Filter	Twin Air		

This is what the carburetor jetting is at the time of publication, and it may be changed. We have found this to be the best at the present time. If any different set-ups occur, we will inform you through your dealer. If you or your dealer are good at carb tuning, proceed with the utmost care, checking all throttle ranges for suitability to your area of the country.

Stripping and Cleaning the Carburetor

It is to your advantage to clean the carburetor from time to time especially after a long endurance run where the carb was subject to a lot of dirt or water.

When disassembling and cleaning, be extra careful not to scratch or nick parts. Clean only with gas or solvent and dry with compressed air. (Do not run wires through parts.) Clean all parts meticulously.

Before reassembling check that all parts are in working condition. Worn float needles, needle jets, jet needles and throttle valves must be replaced by new ones as they have an adverse effect on engine performance and fuel consumption. Check also that all seals and gaskets have been fitted and are in good condition.

Replace the carburetor on the engine, hook up control cables and adjust properly. (See Controls section.)

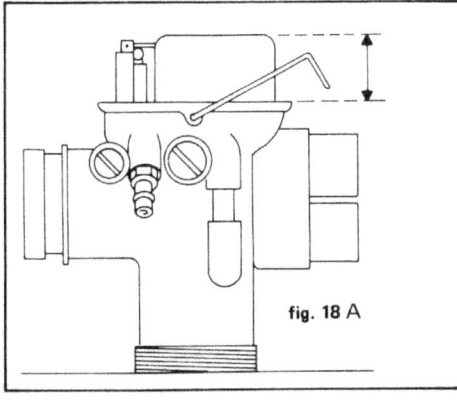

fig. 18 A

Checking the Float Level of the Bing

Before reassembling, the float level should be checked. Place the carb on a level surface as shown in fig.18 A. Be sure the float needle is at the bottom of its seat. The level is correct if the float is parallel with the carb body as shown in fig.18 A. The brass float tab must just be touching on the spring loaded needle ball. The needle ball must not be pressed down. The level is corrected by bending the brass tab on the float.

OPERATION AND MAINTENANCE

Checking the Chain and Sprockets for Wear and Tension

The easiest way to check and see if the chain can still be used is shown in fig. 19. Press the chain by hand upwards to tension it. If the chain can be lifted from the sprocket by more than 1/2 the diameter of the rollers, the chain must be replaced.

If the sprockets are worn as shown in fig. 20 have them replaced.

See page 13 for the correct chain tension according to the shock position. Both excessive and insufficient chain tension will cause unnecessary loading on the chain, sprockets and bearings.

Check to see the chain lines up evenly with both the engine and rear wheel sprockets. Be sure the master link is properly fitted with the closed part in the direction the chain moves. Oil the chain before every event and never run it dry.

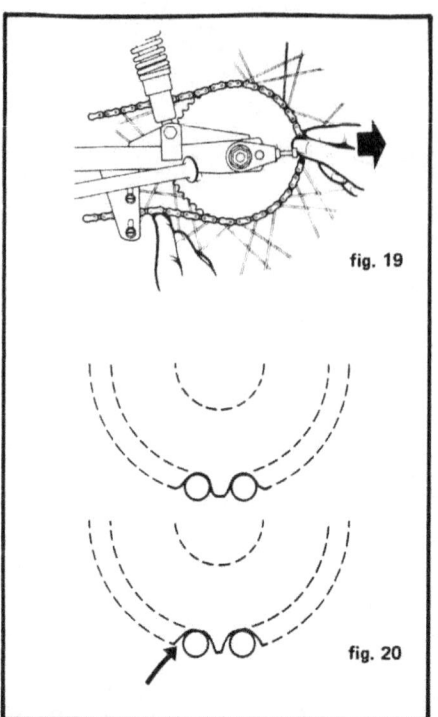

fig. 19

fig. 20

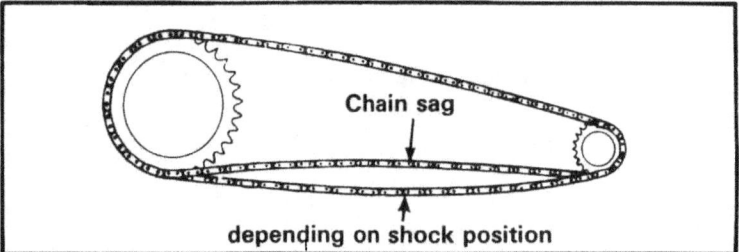

fig. 21

Changing the Gearbox Oil and Maintaining the Level

The gearbox oil should be changed regularly and after every big race or enduro. To drain the oil follow this procedure: Warm the engine up. Remove mag side cover. Remove drain plug (1, fig. 22). Have a large enough container to collect the drained oil. Tilt the machine to be sure all oil is drained off. Replace the oil drain plug. <u>CAUTION: Do not remove odd-shaped bolt on bottom of engine, as this is the kick starter stop bolt.</u>

To fill, use either of the two plugs on top of the engine cases (1, fig. 23) and put in two quarts of Hi-Point Gear Lube. Check crankcase vent (2, fig. 23) for obstructions. ATF (automatic transmission fluid) will facilitate clutch release.

There is a level check plug located underneath the kick starter. Oil must flow from this; however, we are adding more oil than just to the level plug. The transmission will work with 1400cc filled to level plug.

Oil Capacity: Old style clutch cover 1.4 Liter (1.5 qt.) New style profile case 12. Liter (1.3 qt.)

fig. 22

fig. 23

OPERATION AND MAINTENANCE

Front Fork Maintenance and Service

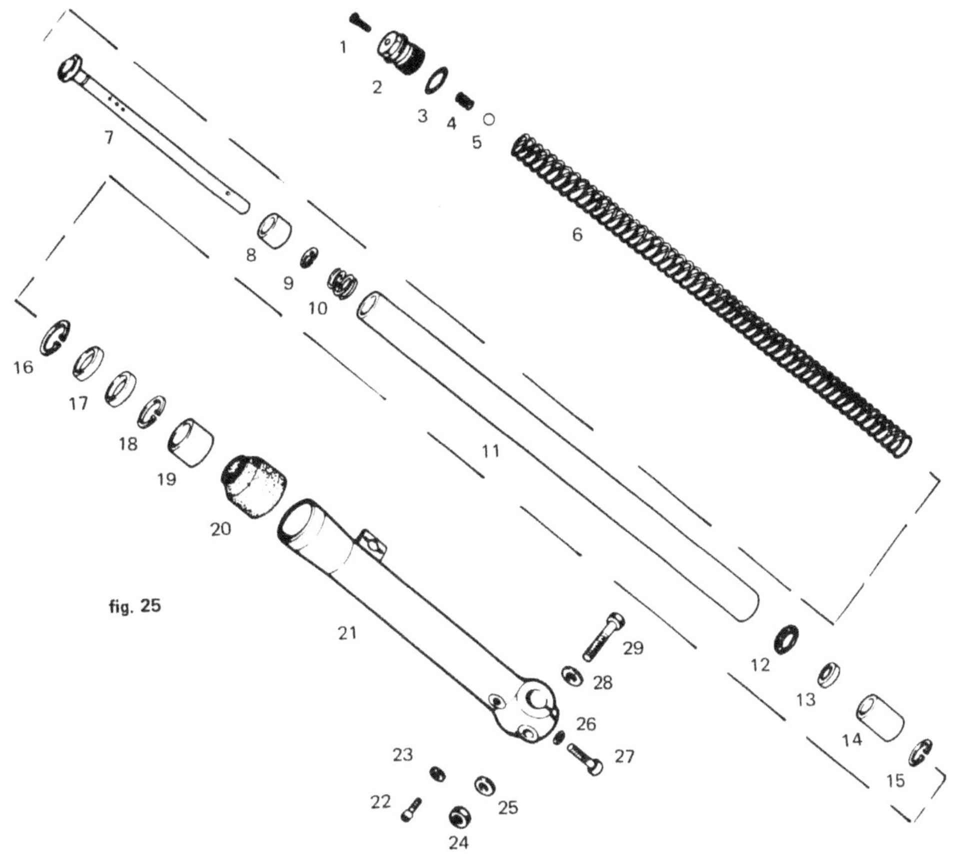

1	Screw
2	Fork tube nut
3	"O" Ring
4	Spring
5	Ball
6	Fork spring
7	Stop valve
8	Bushing
9	Circlip
10	Return spring
11	Fork tube
12	Stop Valve
13	Valve
14	Upper bushing
15	Circlip
16	Circlip
17	Seal
18	Circlip
19	Lower bushing
20	Fork boot
21	Fork leg
22	Drain plug
23	Washer
24	Nut
25	washer
26	Washer
27	Allen head screw
28	washer
29	Hexagon head bolt

fig. 25

fig. 24

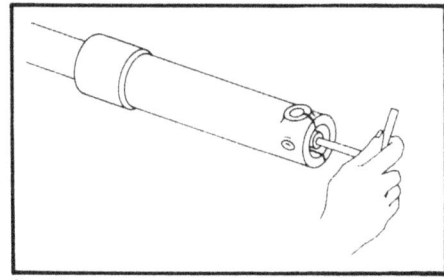

fig. 28

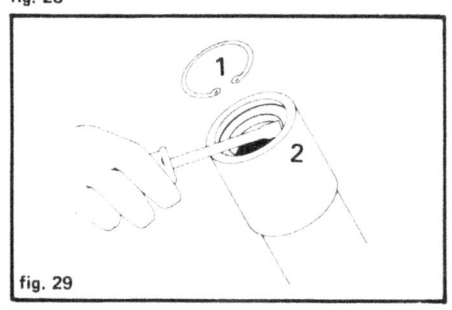

fig. 29

The forks should be maintained whenever poor fork action or excessive braking around the seals occur. The fork oil should be changed periodically and the fork legs flushed out with a solvent, if found to need it. To change the fork oil, remove oil drain plug screw fig. 24. Let all the oil drain off and spring the forks a couple of times so all oil is drained. Replace the drain screws. Remove the fork tube nuts (4, fig. 25), check and clean these out to make sure the ball check is working properly. Add 185cc of fork oil to each leg at the top fork nut opening. Remember, the lighter weight oil means a softer fork and the heavier weight oil is a stiffer fork. We have developed a new type fork fluid, Hi-Point Silicone, and have had great results with it. It does not break down no matter what the temperature - 10° or + 200° the viscosity stays constant. It also has been found not to leak around the seals. Be sure the air vent screw, spring and ball in the top fork nuts are clear of obstructions (1, 2, 3, 4, fig. 25).

Replacing Fork Seals

Remove the axle pinch bolt.

Remove the allen screw at the bottom of the fork leg (fig. 28). If the allen screw moves but cannot be unscrewed use a piece of round steel of 12 mm diameter and 600 mm length. At one end grind a triangular point and make a handle at the other. The tool is then pressed into the stop valve tube and the allen screw removed.

The forks will now separate.

The upper fork assembly may be removed but does not need to be.

With the lower fork leg in the vise remove the circlip (1, fig. 29). Snap out the 2 seals with a screwdriver by applying heat to the fork leg (2, fig. 29). Replace with new seals.

Reassemble in reverse. Be sure the allen screw at the bottom of the legs are tightly secured, or the fork may separate if the screws fall out while in operation.

OPERATION AND MAINTENANCE

Fork Crown Adjustment and Maintenance

The fork crown on the Penton should always be checked to be sure all pinch bolts and nuts are tightly secured.

Checking and Adjusting Steering Bearings

The play in the steering bearings is checked with the motorcycle blocked up so the front wheel can rotate freely. Grasp the lower part of the fork legs and try to move them forward and backward in line with the machine (fig. 30). If any play can be noticed, this must be taken up on the upper bearing nut. Follow this procedure: Loosen the pinch bolt (2, fig. 31). Loosen the top cap nut (1, fig. 31). It may also be necessary to loosen the fork leg pinch bolts for the fork plate.

With a pair of adjustable pliers tighten up the upper nut bearing as shown in (3, fig. 31) then back it off about 1/8 of a turn.

Tighten up the cap nut and pinch bolts if these have been loosened. Check that the bearings move freely and do not bind in any position.

Periodically lubricate the steering bearings with a lithium base grease and be sure the O rings are in good condition. See fig. 32 for exploded view of the fork crown.

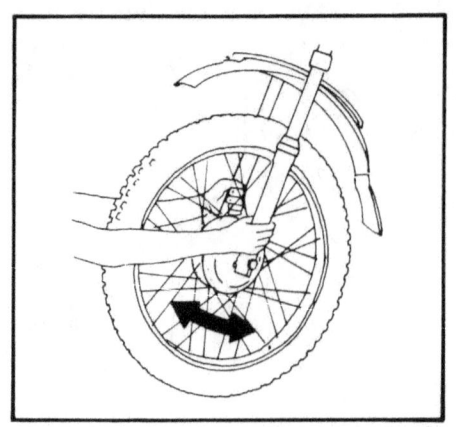

fig. 30

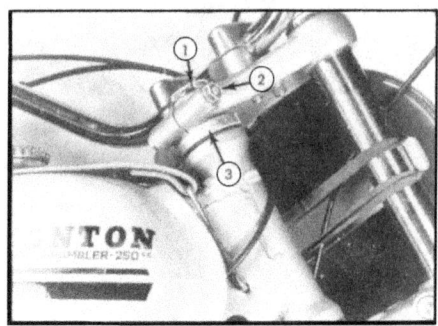

fig. 31

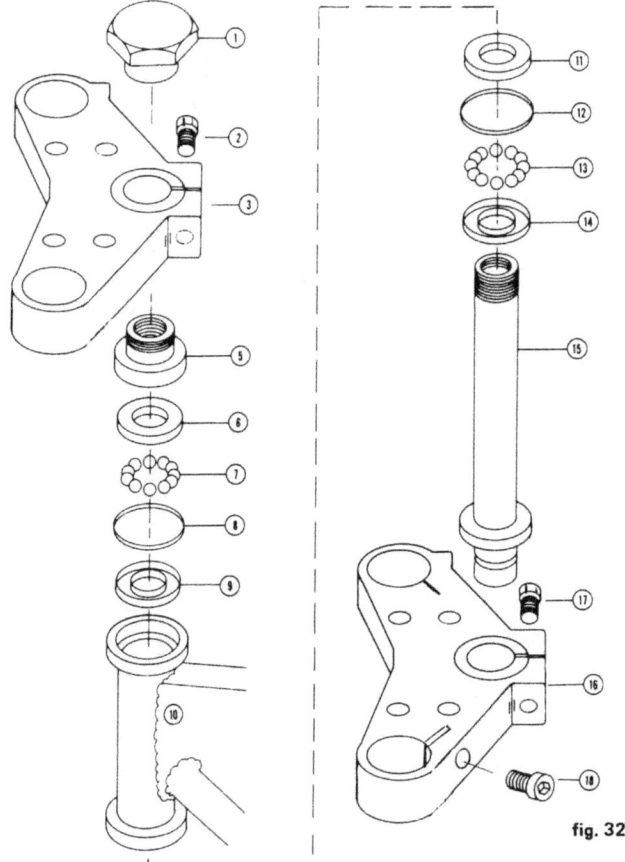

1. Cap nut
2. Pinch bolt
3. Top fork crown

5. Bearing race nut
6. Bearing race
7. Ball bearings (16)
8. O ring
9. Bearing race
10. Steering head

11. Bearing race
12. O ring
13. Ball bearings (16)
14. Bearing race
15. Fork stem
16. Fork crown, lower
17. Bolt, pinch
18. Pinch bolts

fig. 32

OPERATION AND MAINTENANCE

Rear shock absorber adjustment and maintenance

The spring rate on the shocks may be adjusted to different positions by means of the cam ring at the lower end of the shock. A hook spanner is the best tool to use for this job. Different spring rates are also available from your Penton dealer if the springs furnished do not meet a specific job requirement.

Maintenance to the shocks should be carried out periodically. Be sure the rubber bushings are all in good shape and the shock bolts tight. The shock should be straight, if not the plunger is bent and the shock should be replaced.

Suggested Shocks Spring & Positions for Pentons

Spring Lengths and Weights Available

Ceriani Gas Shock .... 13⅜" vertical and 45°
Koni 76 F 1282-SP30 .... 12⅞" vertical only
Koni 76 F 1283- .... 13⅜" vertical and 45°

Spring Weight Color Code (Hi-Point 140# Black, 125# Silver, 110# Red, 95# Blue, 80# Grey, 65# White)

Riding Condition

Heavy - Rider Weight 185# or over and/or hard riding such as moto-cross.
Medium - Rider Weight 135-185# and/or medium riding such as enduro.
Light - Rider weight 135# and under and/or light riding such as trail.

chainsag depending on shock position.

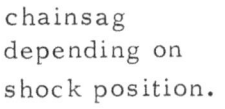

1 RWT 5" Chainsag 1.8"	2 RWT 5.2" Chainsag 2.2"
3 RWT 5.4" Chainsag 2.4"	4 RWT 5.8" Chainsag 2.4"
5 RWT 6" Chainsag 2.5"	6 RWT 7" Chainsag 3"

Rear Wheel Travel	Shock	Riding Condition	Spring Rate
45° Shock Position 7" Travel	Ceriani Gas	Heavy	140
		Medium	125
		Light	110
	Koni 76 F 1283	Heavy	140
		Medium	125
		Light	110
Vertical Position Forward hole 6" Travel	Ceriani Gas	Heavy	125
		Medium	110
		Light	95
	Koni 76 F 1282 SP 30	Heavy	110
		Medium	95
		Light	80
Vertical Position Rear hole 5" Travel	Ceriani Gas	Heavy	110
		Medium	95
		Light	80
	Koni 76 F 1282 SP 30	Heavy	95
		Medium	80
		Light	65

Do not run shocks in 45° positions without the correct spring rate as this will damage shocks.

Koni Adjusting Procedure

KONI damping may be adjusted as follows:

1. Remove spring. Extend the rod to full height and push the rubber bumper toward the shock body. If it is necessary to slide the bump rubber away from the nut, hold the top eye and twist the rubber down the rod. Be carefull not to damage the chromed rod.
2. Undo the ¾" lock-nut below the top eye.
3. Unscrew the upper eye mount and the nut and remove the bumper. Replace just top eye and lock-nut to give a hand hold.

Dampening Setting for Koni Shocks

Spring Rate	Turns Clockwise
125#	2¼
110#	1½-2
95#	1-1½
80#	½-1
65#	0

4. Fully collapse the shock absorber, at the same time turning the piston rod slowly to the left until it is felt that the teeth of the adjuster nut are engaging the recesses of the footvalve assembly.

5. Continue to turn gently to the left until the rotation stops. Do not use force or attempt to turn further to the left, once resistance has been felt. At this point you are assured that shock absorber is in the unadjusted or new position.

6. Now keeping the shock absorber collapsed, begin turning in the opposite direction, to the right. You will be able to make four half turns of 180° and a final quarter turn of approximately 90° to full hardness, each one of which is an adjustment compensating for approximately 20,000 miles of riding, depending upon the usage. You will know when you have reached the maximum adjusting position because you will encounter another stop. Do not force.

7. Pull the shock absorber apart vertically, without turning for about ½" to allow the teeth of the adjuster nut to disengage. The piston rod can now be turned freely. Reassemble in reverse order. Be sure to install the rubber bumper and *do not shorten it*. The shock absorber will be permanently damaged if the rod is depressed too far when ridden.

OPERATION AND MAINTENANCE

Front Wheel Maintenance and Removal

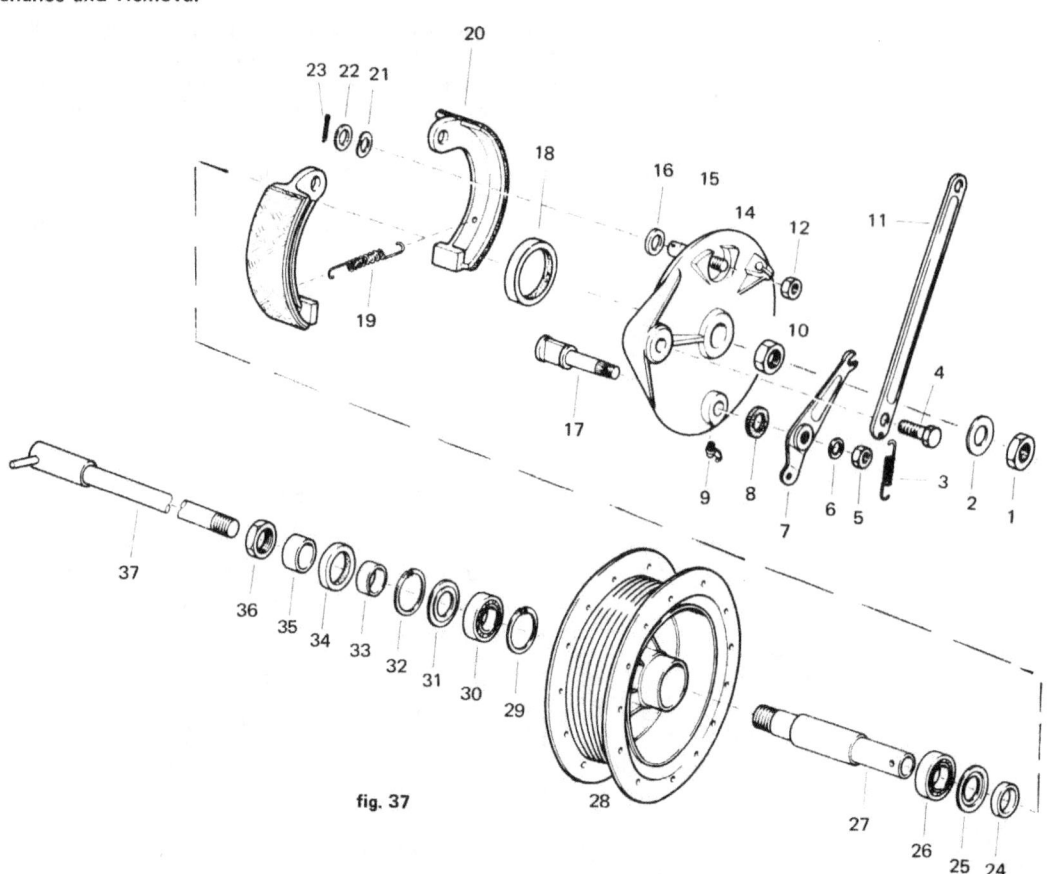

fig. 37

Removing the Front Wheel

Secure the motorcycle so the front wheel is off the ground. Remove the front brake cable (1, fig. 35). Remove the front brake anchor arm (2, fig. 35). Loosen the pinch bolts on both fork legs (3, fig. 35). Remove axle nut (4, fig. 35). From the opposite side, pull out the axle bolt completely (fig. 36). Remove the wheel, the front brake assembly will also come out with the wheel. When reassembling the wheel, lightly grease the axle before replacing.

Greasing and Changing the Wheel Bearing

The front wheel bearing should be greased regularly especially after running in water or dust. The bearings should be replaced when needed.

Removing the Wheel Bearings

All numbers refer to exploded view fig. 37.

With the wheel removed, proceed as follows:
Remove brake plate from the wheel housing (28).
Remove spacer (24) and dust shield (25). Remove axle nut (36) from the opposite side. Knock the axle out toward the brake side; the brake side bearing will come out with the axle.

Opposite the brake side, remove bushing (33) and seal (34). Remove circlip (32) and dust shield (31). Knock the bearing out from the opposite side, brake side.

Replace bearings and seals if in poor condition. Regrease and assemble in reverse. Be sure all bearings are fully seated on both sides. Tighten axle nuts finger tight.

Before replacing the brake plate, check the wear on the brake shoes. Replace if necessary.

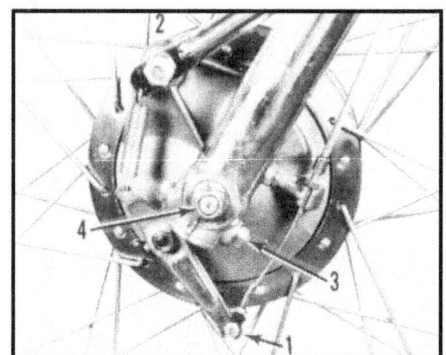

fig. 35

fig. 36

OPERATION AND MAINTENANCE

Rear Wheel Removal and Maintenance

fig. 38

fig. 39

Removing the Rear Wheel

Secure the motorcycle so the rear wheel is off the ground. Remove the brake anchor nut (2, fig. 38). Remove the brake rod (1, fig. 38). Remove the axle nut (3, fig. 38) and pull out the axle from the opposite side. Remove the rear wheel. The chain need not be taken apart as you can easily slip it off with the axle out.

Removing Rear Wheel Bearings   All numbers refer to fig. 40.

With the wheel removed from the cycle, remove the brake plate. From the brake side remove the snap ring holding the bearing, (1). With a press, press the bearing on the opposite side (3) down toward the brake side until the brake bearing (2) comes out. (Do not press bearing any farther than you have to.) Remove the inner spacer bushing (5). From the brake side press out the remaining bearing (1).

To replace the bearings make sure the inner snap ring (4) is secure and press in bearing (2) to its stop, replace snap ring (1). Place the inner spacer bushing (5) and press in bearing (3) until it comes up against the inner spacer bushing.

The rear wheel bearings are prelubricated and sealed. When bad simply replace. There is no repacking of the bearings.

Replacing Spokes on Brake Side Rear Wheel

Remove the rear wheel and the braking plate. Around the inner hub is a snap ring that holds in a sheet metal plate. Remove the snap ring and metal plate and you can replace the spokes. Be sure to replace the metal plate as it keeps spokes that may break off from falling into the brake drum.

NOTE:

When the rear wheel or sprocket housing has been removed the chain tension and wheel alignment should be checked. The chain adjusters (3, fig. 39) are for this purpose. See Checking the chain and sprockets for more information.

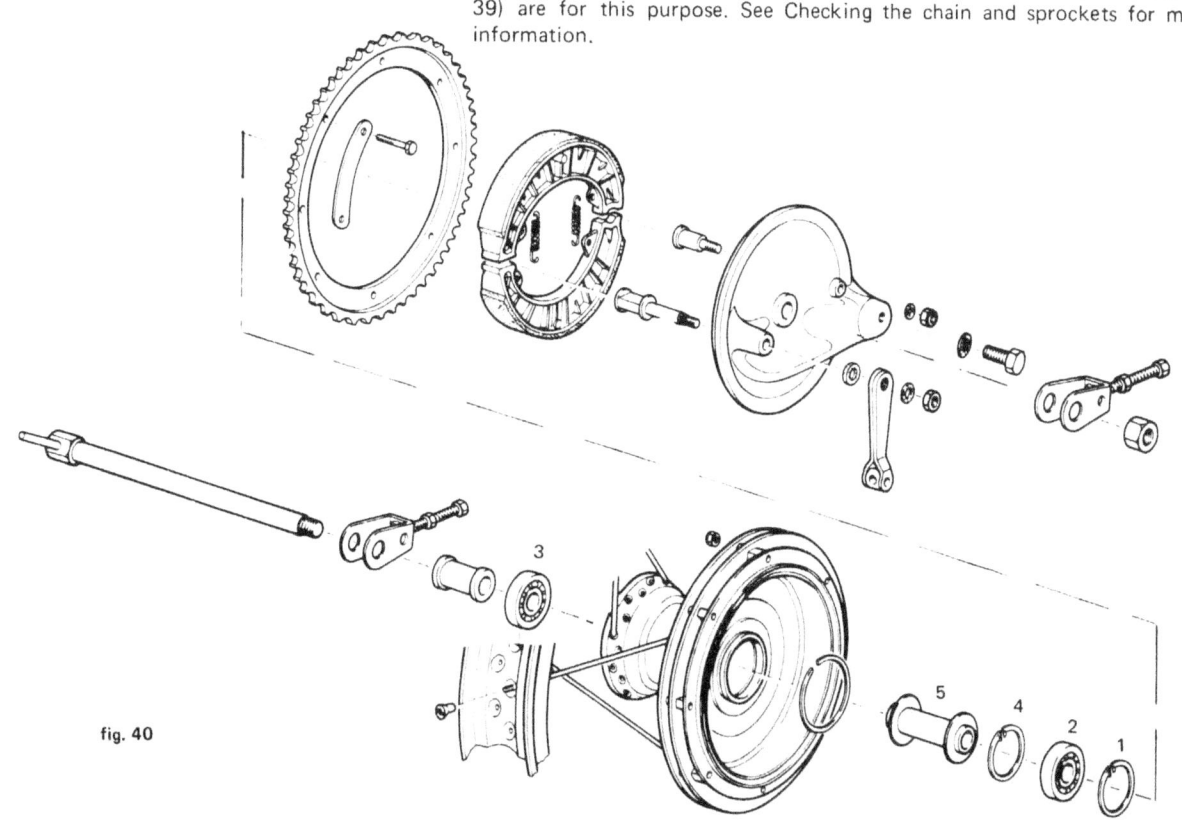
fig. 40

OPERATION AND MAINTENANCE

Swingarm Bearings

Please take note of the attached drawing, that the new Penton rear swingarm is fitted and supported on needle bearings. This type of needle bearing is a new application for our models and we would ask you to study the drawing closely and read the description below, so there can be no mistakes in the assembly, disassembly and service of the swingarm.

Description

A double-row-needle cage N is pressed into each side of the swingarm pipe. These needle cages are to be put into the swingarm pipe in a way that the punched letters show to the outside. This side is hardened and has the advantage that it can be used as a thrust surface for the adjustment nut N.

The bearing sleeve L is put into the swingarm pipe so that the lock-tightened nut on the sleeve will end up on the right hand side of the motorcycle. But, first you must slide the two "O" rings on the fixed adjustment nut. On the second adjustment nut E the remaining two "O" rings O are slid on, and there the adjustment nut is screwed on the end of the thread which is projecting out on the left of the swingarm pipe. Then you must tighten with care until the bearing sleeve L has no side play in the swingarm pipe S. Now, the left adjustment nut has to be released again for approximately a quarter turn, so we get side play of approximately 0.4mm. Please pay attention that the "O" rings O aren't damaged when putting together. This you can prevent, if the "O" rings O are oiled properly before inserting the adjustment nut into the swingarm pipe. Then the swingarm is assembled to the frame. After putting in the swingarm, the swingarm bolt B is inserted from the right hand side through the bearing sleeve L. The swingarm bolt B may be turned only when the hexagon of the right hand side adjustment nut of the swingarm pipe S is held in position by a narrow ground open end 24mm wrench.

Very Important

When tightening the swingarm bolt B, the right hand side adjustment nut E must be kept from turning; otherwise, the bearing sleeve L will be turned and the side play will get out of adjustment. When the swingarm bolt is tightened, it must be filled with gear oil, transmission lub or high viscosity engine oil. Both filler plugs must be opened when filling with oil, so that it can be completely filled with oil and no vacuum is created. Check this often to see it is always filled with oil and check for leaks.

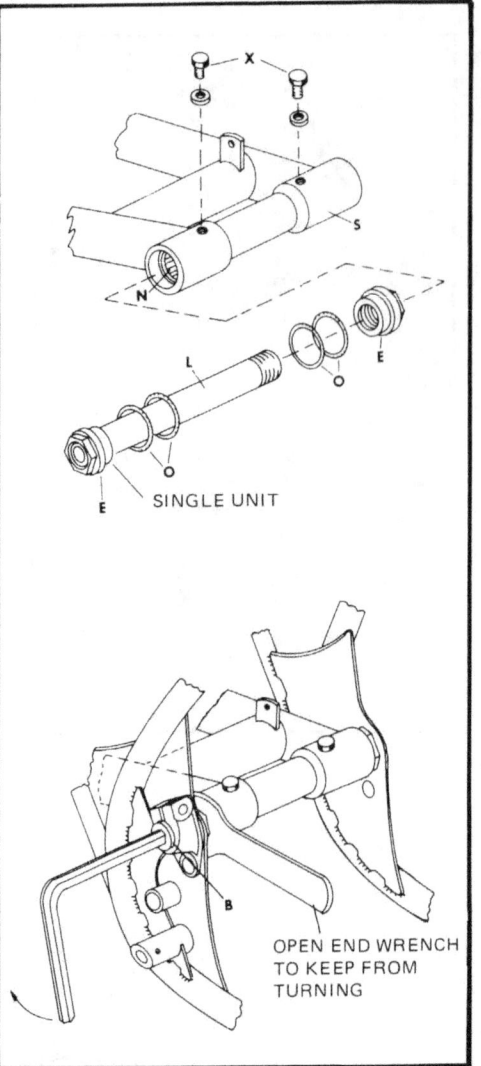

SINGLE UNIT

OPEN END WRENCH TO KEEP FROM TURNING

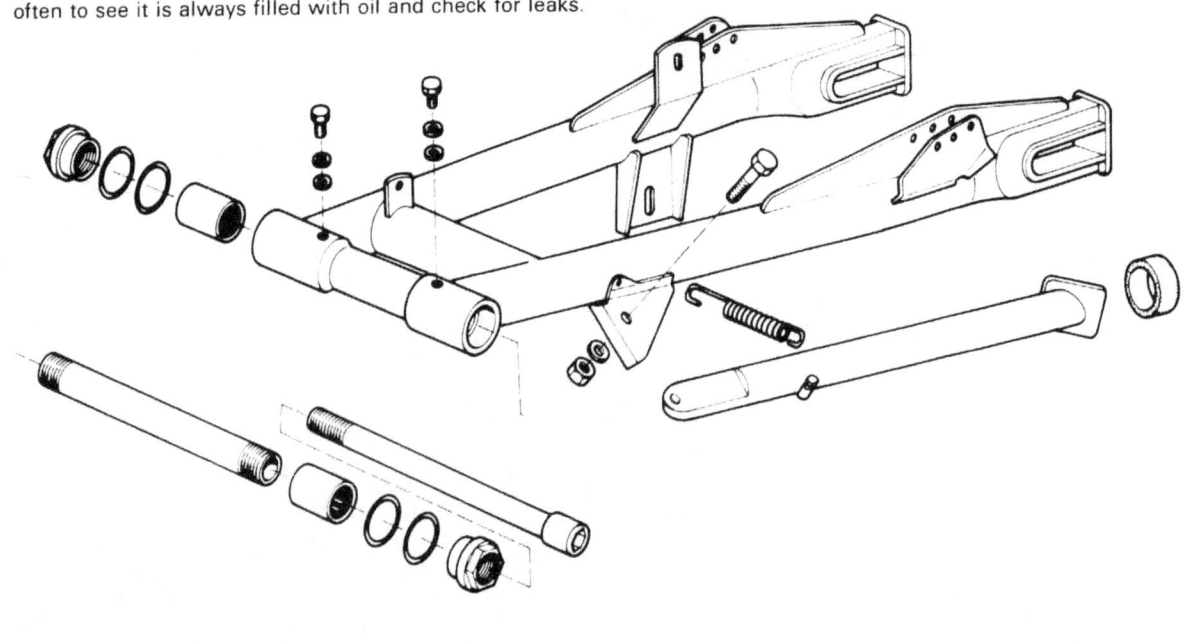

16

OPERATION AND MAINTENANCE

Decarbonizing the Engine

In any 2-cycle engine a small amount of lubricating oil is burnt and forms carbon deposits in the engine. Decarbonizing is usually needed after 2000 miles/50 hours or when the engine performance drops or four-stroking occurs in spite of proper engine tune.

Decarbonizing properly is a major job and care and thinking must be upper most in your mind when carrying out this job. It is handled easiest with the engine out of the frame, but this is not necessary.

Follow This Procedure for the Proper Job

The engine must be super clean before starting. Remove the exhaust pipe, carburetor and left-hand engine brace. Remove cylinder head, cylinder and piston (see Dismantling the Engine). With the engine still in the frame, lay the machine on its side before removing cylinder so any dirt or water will not fall into crankcase. Stuff a clean rag into the crankcase opening to keep out dirt.

Remove the spark plug from the head and clean the carbon from the head, being careful not to scratch or nick the metal surface. Clean the exhaust ports and exhaust header. Carefully remove the rings from the piston and clean the ring lands and crown of the piston, being careful not to scratch the metal. New rings should always be fitted at this time.

Check the wear of the cylinder by placing the new ring at the piston turning point in the cylinder bore. If the distance exceeds .07 mm or 1/32" it is recommended that the cylinder be rebored and a new piston fitted. Note also that there may be wear on the piston too.

With all the parts thoroughly clean from carbon and dirt you can start reassembling. See **Rebuilding the Engine** for refitting the piston, cylinder and head. All new gaskets should be used. With the piston, cylinder and head all carefully assembled replace the exhaust pipe and all other parts that were removed.

It is important that you keep a record of all the work done to the engine for future reference. Use the forms included in this manual.

Rims and Spokes Maintenance

Before every event the wheels should be checked to see that the spokes are all tightened, and the inner tube stem straight and capped. Check to see the rims are not damaged and the tires displaced on the rims.

The tire pressure is optional to conditions and rider, pressures from 12 to 25 lbs. psi are recommended. Remember rocks can cause bad rim damage and the tire pressures should be higher than say for riding in mud or sand.

Always replace broken spokes and damaged rims. Tires should be in good shape and tubes should not be over-patched but replaced.

Always check the alignment of the wheels and that all wheel nuts are tight.

OPERATION AND MAINTENANCE

Motoplat (CD Ignition System)

We have found in our Test Department that by employing this pointless type ignition, it has increased the power on our 100cc and 125cc engines by better that 1 h.p. Further, these units deliver a stronger spark with increased rpm's and will not start breaking up. Tests show these units to perform perfectly to 20,000 rpm's which is far in excess of anything we need in a motorcycle. As pointed out previously, these units are service free and used properly are a lifetime unit.

Replacement and Checking Ignition Timing

The Motoplat ignition on the engine should never need adjustment as it is set at the factory and should never change. It is good to once in a while pull the mag cover off and let the unit air dry. Also pull the flywheel off and clean the inside as it may build up corrosion.

To remove the unit follow this procedure: Remove mag cover. With magneto holding tool remove M 12 nut (left-hand thread) **(fig. 42)**. Place magneto puller on flywheel and remove flywheel; do not lose key **(fig. 43)**. Remove three screws in center of stator (1, fig.**45**) and remove stator. Screws (2, fig.**46**) remove the stator base plate (this need not be removed).

To Replace and Time Unit:

Place baseplate on engine, turned all the way counterclockwise in slots. (Fig. 46, 1) Tighten screws. Install stator, leaving screws loose enough to allow stator to turn freely in its slots. (Fig. 45, 1) Place the flywheel with key on crankpin. Insert timing pin through flywheel, and turn until it drops into the hole in stator. (Fig. 45, 2) Move flywheel/stator to the proper timing setting (see chart), using a gauge or metric rule inserted through the sparkplug hole. If stator will not move far enough in its screw slots, readjustment of baseplate will be necessary.

Carefully remove pin and flywheel. Tighten stator screws. Replace flywheel and tighten to 40 ft./lb. Recheck timing. If it is off, the timing procedure must be repeated.

Make absolutely positive that you have a good ground to the frame. Make sure all wire connections are perfect and constantly clean the terminals at the coil as they will tend to build up corrosion. Do not use silicone sealer or any other type of sealer on the coil terminal connections.

When not employing lights or a battery in your motorcycle, tape up those leads, but DO NOT GROUND THEM. See the wiring diagram for proper connections.

ELECTRICAL	175cc JACKPINER	250cc HARE SCRAMBLER	400cc MINT
Type	Motoplat, transistor, solid state, magneto ignition with 35 watt main lighting coil		
†Timing	2.7mm btdc	2.55mm btdc	2.4mm btdc
Spark plug	Bosch W-280-MI	Bosch W-290-T16	Bosch W-290-T16

When laying the cycle up till the following week we find it a good practice to remove the ignition cover and let the ignition dry out as it will corrode if not dried out.

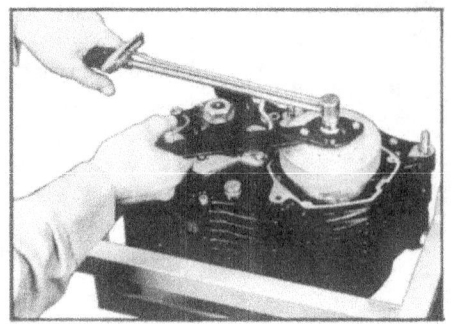
fig. 42

fig. 43

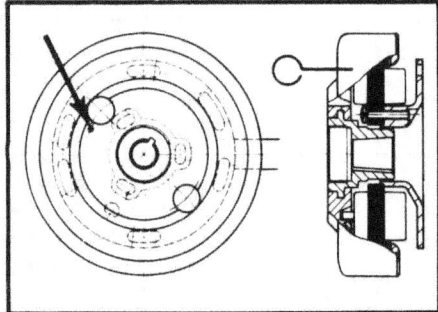
fig. 44

fig. 45

fig. 46

OPERATION AND MAINTENANCE

Wiring and Diagrams

The Penton motorcycle is pre-wired, but all wiring should be checked to see that connections are tight, no rubbing of wires or contact with the hot cylinder or head take place. All wiring should be wrapped in electrical tape and secured to the frame to keep from being snagged. All wires that come together should be soldered and taped up.

On the Penton Moto-Cross models no lights are fitted and the wiring is quite simple (fig. 45). Be sure the ground on the coil is tight and contact with bare metal made.

On the Enduro model the wiring is more complicated by the introduction of lights. (fig. 46) is the correct wiring for the Enduro model.

The leads coming from the magneto should be sealed to keep water and dirt from the magneto. Covers are also fitted to the ignition coil and should keep water tight and clean.

The wiring terminal is located under the gas tank (fig. 47). Be sure all the screws are tight and contact is being made.

fig. 47

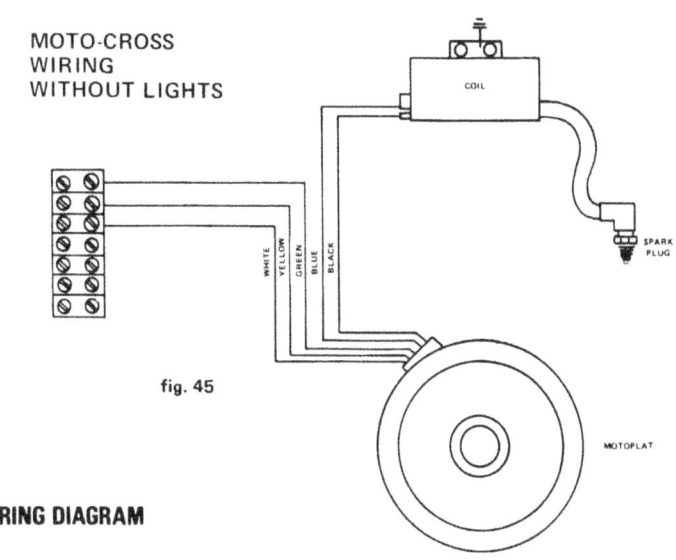

MOTO-CROSS WIRING WITHOUT LIGHTS

fig. 45

WIRES FROM MOTOPLAT
BLUE & BLACK – COIL
YELLOW – HEADLIGHT 6V/35W
GREEN – STOPLIGHT 6V/18W
WHITE – TAILLIGHT 6V/4W

ENDURO WIRING DIAGRAM

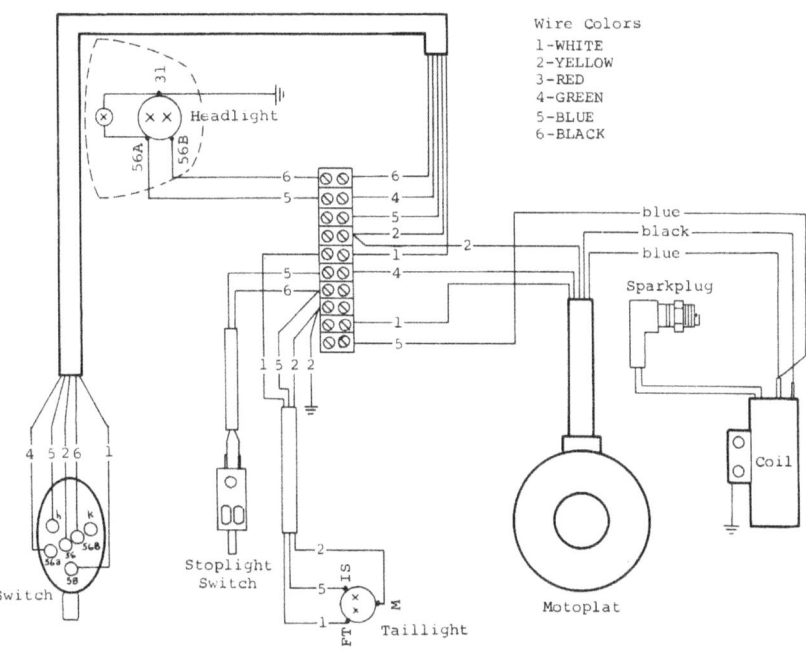

Wire Colors
1-WHITE
2-YELLOW
3-RED
4-GREEN
5-BLUE
6-BLACK

OPERATION AND MAINTENANCE

Spark Plug Maintenance

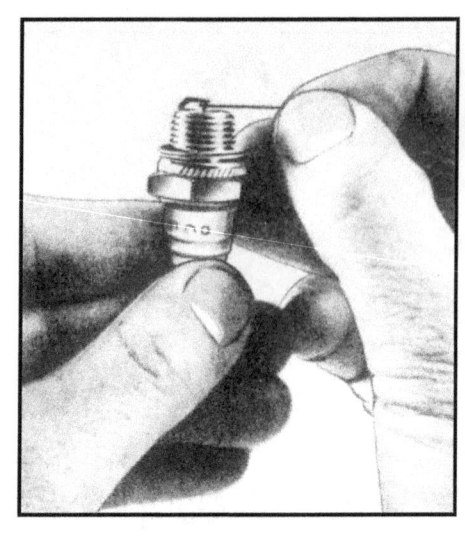

Note the plug for the Penton is a short reach plug; never use a long reach plug as engine damage will result to the piston immediately.

The spark plug gap of the electrode should be .020 - .024 in. Use only a wire gauge when checking. Adjustment should be done on the side electrode by bending in or away from the central electrode. The spark plug should be cleaned and gapped before every event and replaced if in doubtful condition.

The heat rating indicates the degree of heat load which a spark plug can withstand. A plug with a high heat range can withstand a higher heat load than one with a lower heat rating. The higher the heat rating, the greater the resistance to glow ignition and the less to carbonizing and oiling up.

A plug with too high a heat rating and which glows, usually causes overheating and piston seizure. In doubtful cases it is better to fit a plug with a cold rating than one with too hot a rating. The engine will not start so easy and will not run as well at low loading in the lower speed range, it will also never be damaged in the way it could be using a plug with too hot a rating.

Appearance of the Sparking Plug

Correct Appearance:

Medium-brown insulator base, dark grey socket with grey carbon deposit. No excessive burning of the electrodes.

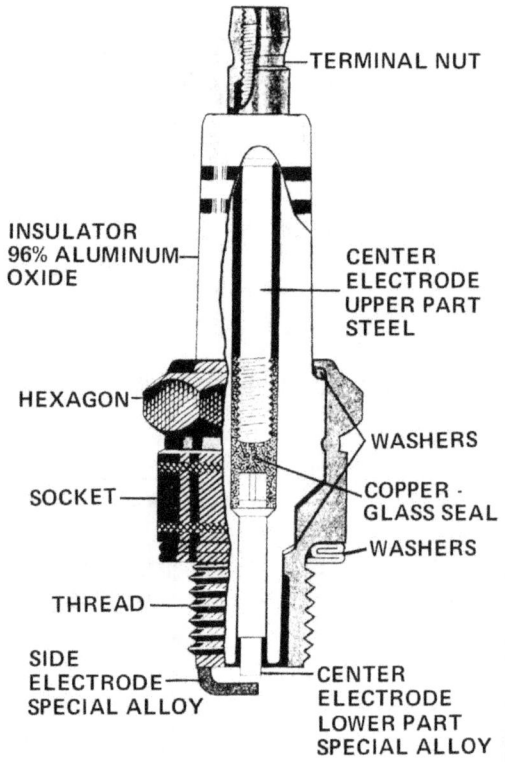

Incorrect Appearance:	Possible Faults:
Beads on insulator base, which is burnt white. Electrodes "blued".	Heat rating too low. Fuel/air mixture too lean. Ignition too early. Sparking plug insufficiently tightened.
Insulator base, socket and electrodes coated with oil and carbon deposits.	Heat rating too high. Too much oil in the gas.
Insulator base, socket and electrodes coated with dry, black soot.	Heat rating too high. Fuel/air mixture too rich. Air cleaner blocked.
Dry, powder-like coating on socket and part of the insulator base. Insulator base point burnt clean.	Correct heat rating. High lead content in gasoline.
Lead compounds on insulator base. Electrodes heavily corroded.	Heat rating too low and too high a lead content in the gasoline.

Plug recommendations

	Bosch	Champion
175cc	W-280-M1	L-77-J-MC L-3G-MC, gold
250cc	W-290-T16	L-57-R L-3G-MC, gold
400cc	W-290-T16	L-57-R L-3G-MC, gold

OPERATION AND MAINTENANCE

Air Cleaner Maintenance

The Penton is fitted with a specially designed still air box matched to give the engine its most power.

The air filter is one of the most important maintenance items on your motorcycle and should be constantly maintained before and after every ride. In long enduros and cross country runs, where dirt and water are heavy, it is advisable to change the filter at the halfway point. Having more than one filter handy at one time is a wise thing to do. A good working filter will double the life of your engine and keep your spark plug from whiskering plugs.

The Pentons come with either a paper filter or the foam filter element. You should be aware of the drawbacks and good points of each type and then use your common knowledge as to the one most suitable to you and what type to use on each run.

The Twin Air foam element is very useful in dusty and sandy conditions. It traps most small airborne particles and is popular in desert and dusty motocross racing. The filtron element has no basic fault. If splashed or becomes wet with water, it will pass the water and mud right through. Needless to say, you can imagine what will happen.

The paper is a dual purpose filter. It will work good in dusty conditions, but will sometimes overload with dust and dirt and pass a little. However, it will not pass water and mud unless completely submerged and only cause the filter to become wet making the machine run ragged, but at least not ruin your engine. We recommend the paper filter on enduros where water and mud will be an unknown factor.

The general maintenance of the air box should be to check and clean it meticulously after every race and check for leaks in the air box and connecting hose.

Also check for cracks in the air box itself. A little trick we use is to coat the inside of the air box with a coating of white grease to pick up any dirt that may escape through the filter.

In running where it is muddy and wet, we advise you to purchase the Penton carburetor apron that protects the carb from mud and water.

Remember the air box is probably the most important maintenance item on your bike to insure long engine life.

VERY IMPORTANT!!!! Silicone between boot and air box. Also, tape over top of frame (Fig. 49, 1-2)

fig. 48

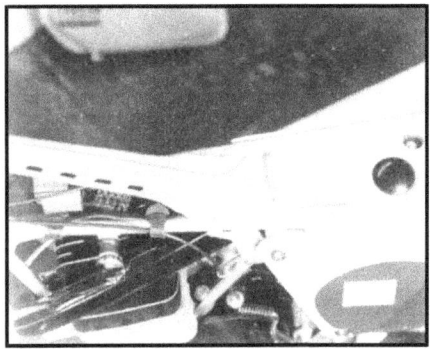
Fig. 49

WASHING your filter.	**OILING** your filter before installation.	
1. Remove element from screen.	1. Remove element from screen.	4. Replace element on screen. Be sure inside sealing edge of foam overlaps screen.
2. Wash with gas, kerosene or soap and water.	2. Saturate with motor oil. Use petroleum oil only.	
3. Squeeze out excess. Let dry. Re-oil per instructions.	3. Squeeze out excess oil.	5. Install assembly in air cleaner.

Expansion Chamber/Muffler

The Penton is fitted with a combination expansion chamber/muffler. Fig. **50** shows the muffler in position. This should always be used when riding in enduros and cross country events where the general population may be annoyed by unmuffled motorcycles. It is a courtesy that assures you of being able to ride there again.

The muffler is tuned to perform on the cycle and should not be removed. Occasionally you should remove the end and clean out the baffles of oil and grime.

(fig. 50)

(fig. 51)

OPERATION AND MAINTENANCE

Washing the Cycle

After using the cycle thoroughly wash it down. Best results are obtained by using hot water and detergent after spraying with water. Before spraying, remove the air filter and block the air filter passage with a rag. Do not spray directly into the brake drums.

Take off the rubber protecting covers on the front forks and clean underneath them.

After having wiped the motorcycle dry with a cloth, it is advisable to start the engine. Run the cycle and apply both front and rear brakes lightly so any moisture is dryed-up. Run the engine at a moderately high speed and pump a little oil into the carb at the side of the throttle. This deposits a film of oil on the engine parts and counteracts any rust that may form from condensation.

Remove the magneto casing to enable moisture to evaporate.

In order to prevent unslightly rust marks on the footrests and other parts that the paint is normally rubbed off, it is advisable to lightly wipe with a rag soaked in oil.

Lubricate the drive chain, control cables and associated joints.

Keeping the Penton in Tip-Top Shape

Service and maintenance to your Penton cycle is the most important thing in any competition motorcycle. You should make out a routine service schedule and follow it before and after every outing. You should keep a notebook with all the information you have acquired in servicing and running your Penton.

If parts look like they are in doubtful shape, they should be replaced immediately so they in turn do not effect another good part.

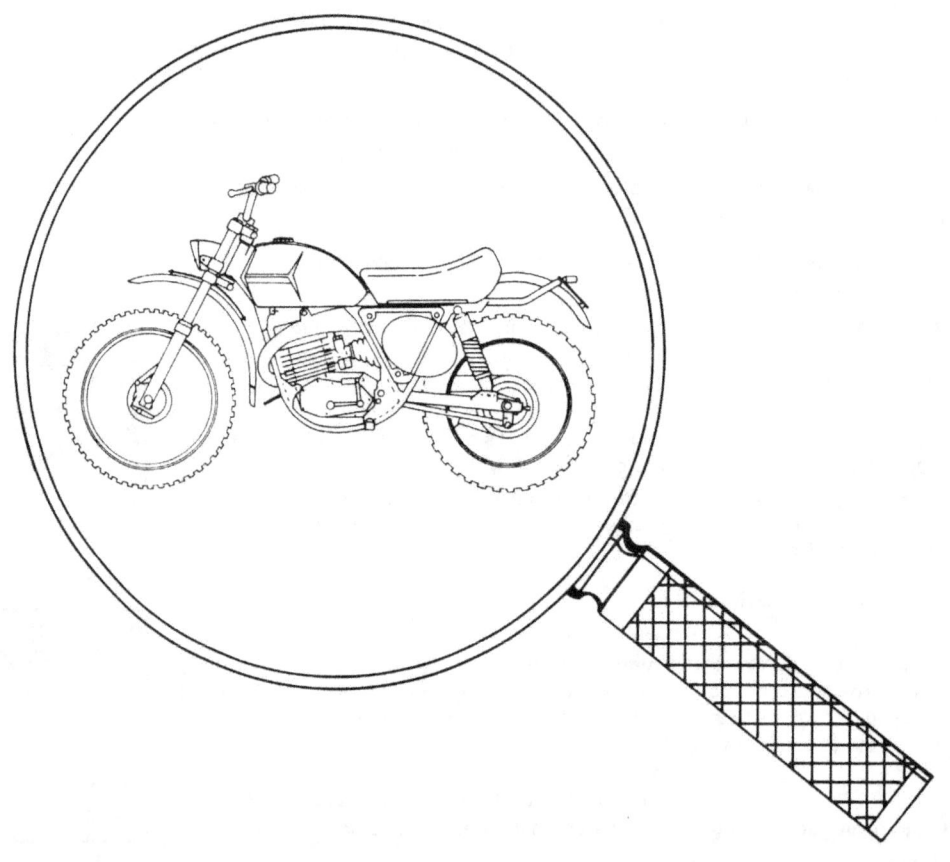

OPERATION AND MAINTENANCE

NOTES ON YOUR PENTON

Whenever work or tuning is performed on your Penton, keep the changes noted here for future reference and forseeing maintenance requirements.

DATE BIKE PURCHASED: _____

DATE OF CHANGE
OR REPAIR

ENGINE
Piston _____
Rings _____
Cylinder _____
Clutch _____
Bearings _____
Con Rod _____
Gears _____
Ignition _____
Overhaul _____
Decarbonized _____
Spark plug _____
Oil changed _____

CARBURETOR
Jets _____
Needle Position _____
Rebuild _____

WHEELS
Front Brake Lining _____
Rear Brake Lining _____
Front Bearings _____
Rear Bearings _____
Sprockets, Engine and Rear _____
Chain _____
Greasing _____

FORKS
Seals _____
Steering Crown _____
Oil _____

REAR SHOCKS
Spring Position _____
Spring Rate _____
Greasing _____
Replacement _____

CONTROLS
Throttle Cable _____
Front Brake Cable _____
Clutch Cable _____
Choke Cable _____

DISMANTLING THE ENGINE

Before dismantling the engine read over this chapter thoroughly to see what you are getting into. Many special tools and a good knowledge of mechanics are required to do the job properly. If you are unsure, it is best left to your dealer who has the proper tools and knowledge.

Repair Tools

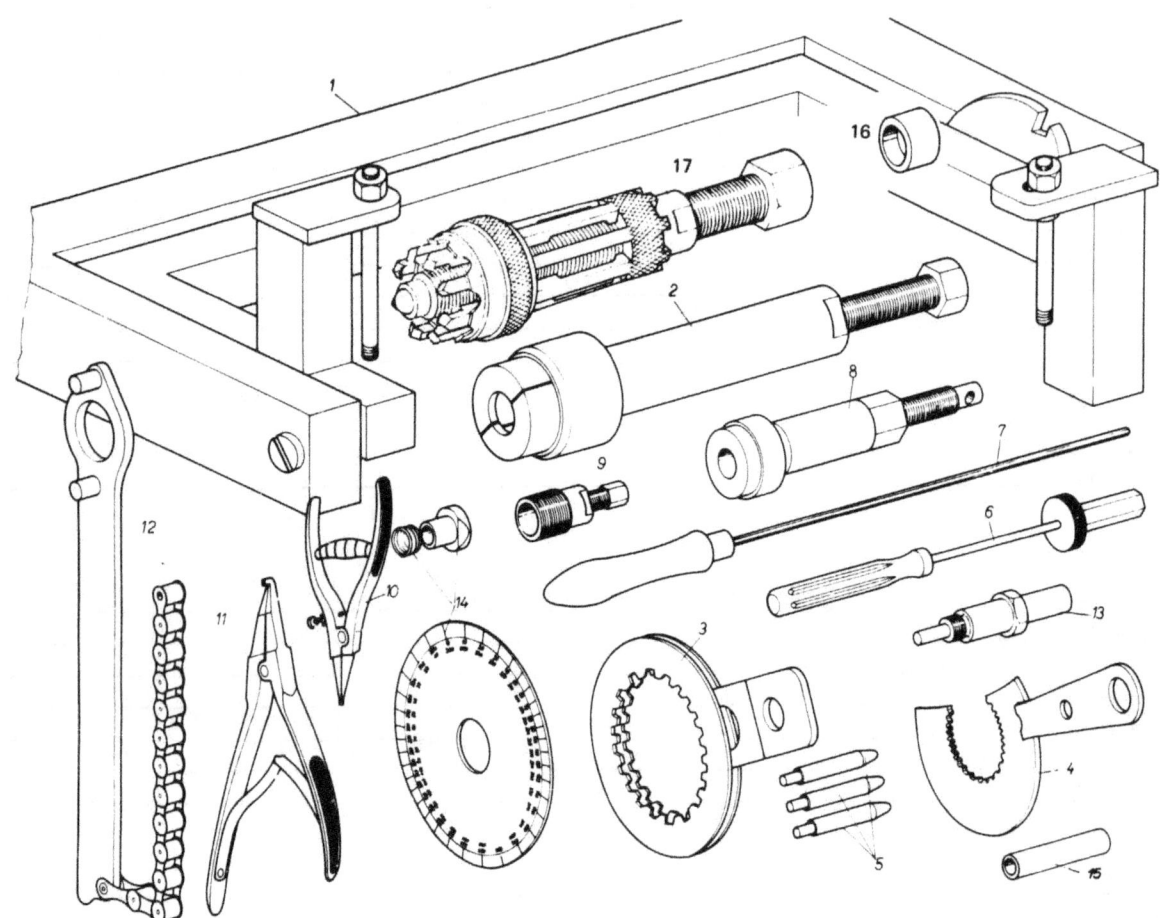

1. Repair stand
2. Extractor for inner races of main bearings M 20
3. Holding plate for clutch hub
4. Holding plate for driving pinion
5. Selector rod guide pins
6. Special screwdriver for clutch screws
7. Special hexagon screwdriver
8. Bearing inserting tool
9. Puller for magneto flywheel
10. Needle nose pliers
11. Special circlip pliers
12. Spanner for sprocket and flywheel
13. Adjusting gauge for ignition advance
14. Timing degree disc
15. Wrist pin extractor guide
16. Protective cap for flywheel puller.
17. Bearing extractor

DISMANTLING THE ENGINE

fig. 53

Draining the Gearbox Oil
fig. 53

Remove the magneto side and remove drain plug (1). Tilt machine to drain off all the oil. (Do not remove plug at the bottom of the engine as this is the kick starter stop bolt.)

fig. 54

Removing the Engine From the Frame
fig. 54

Remove engine braces, exhaust pipe, chain, cables and engine mount bolts, etc. and remove engine from frame.

Place in repair stand.

Remove the cylinder head. The 175 has four nuts and one bolt. The 250 and the 400 have four nuts and four allen head bolts.

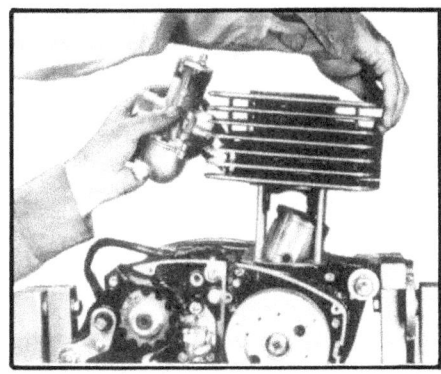
fig. 55

Cylinder and Piston
fig. 55

Remove cylinder, carburetor and manifold as an assembly. Remove base gaskets. Place rag in crankcase opening. With a sharp tool such as an awl, snap out the wrist pin clip in the piston.

Push out wrist pin using the wrist pin extractor guide. Do not beat the wrist pin out. If tight, use wrist pin extractor. Remove wrist pin, piston and needle bearing cage.

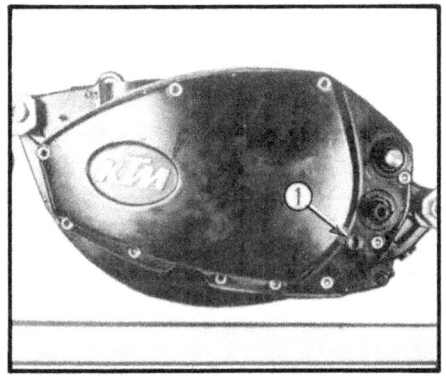
fig. 56

Removing Clutch
fig. 56

Remove kick starter and gear change pedal. Below the kick starter shaft is the oil level check plug; this need not be removed (1).

Remove the 2 bushings from the cover.

Remove clutch cover.

DISMANTLING THE ENGINE

NOTE: The clutch need not be removed to split crankcases. To change rod, crankshaft, shift shafts, transmission gears and seals, clutch can be left on.

Removing Clutch Plates

fig. 57 58

Before removing clutch stud nuts count the number of threads showing so you can reassemble the same way.

Remove cotter keys in nuts, salvage if possible.

Using special tool as shown, hold screwdriver firmly and turn socket to remove nuts. Alternate across from each other when removing so clutch does not bind on studs. Remove pressure plate and clutch plates. Remove clutch push rods (two push rods with a ball bearing between them).

fig. 57

fig. 59

If you cannot undo a spring nut with the special screwdriver 51.12.006.000, e.g. if the slot for the screwdriver on the spring bolt is badly damaged, follow this way:

Assemble push rods, ball and clutch disengager. Screw back on as many spring nuts as necessary to disengage clutch with clutch disengager. Unscrew plug M 8 on right-hand side above the disengaging lever and turn engine horizontal. Insert special hexagon screwdriver 51.12.007.000 through plug hole, after 6 in. screwdriver hits the left-hand sidewall of the engine housing. About 1/2 in. lower than on the right sidewall you will find a hole (1/4 in. dia.) on the left sidewall. Insert the screwdriver through this hole as well and keep on pushing it slightly while turning the clutch hub until screwdriver finds the corresponding hole there too. Disengage the clutch now and turn the pressure plate with the inner hub until the screwdriver hits the hex. head of the damaged bolt. Insert screwdriver into hex. head and hold it tight at the handle. Engage clutch again. Place special screwdriver 51.12.006.000 on spring nut and loosen it.

fig. 58

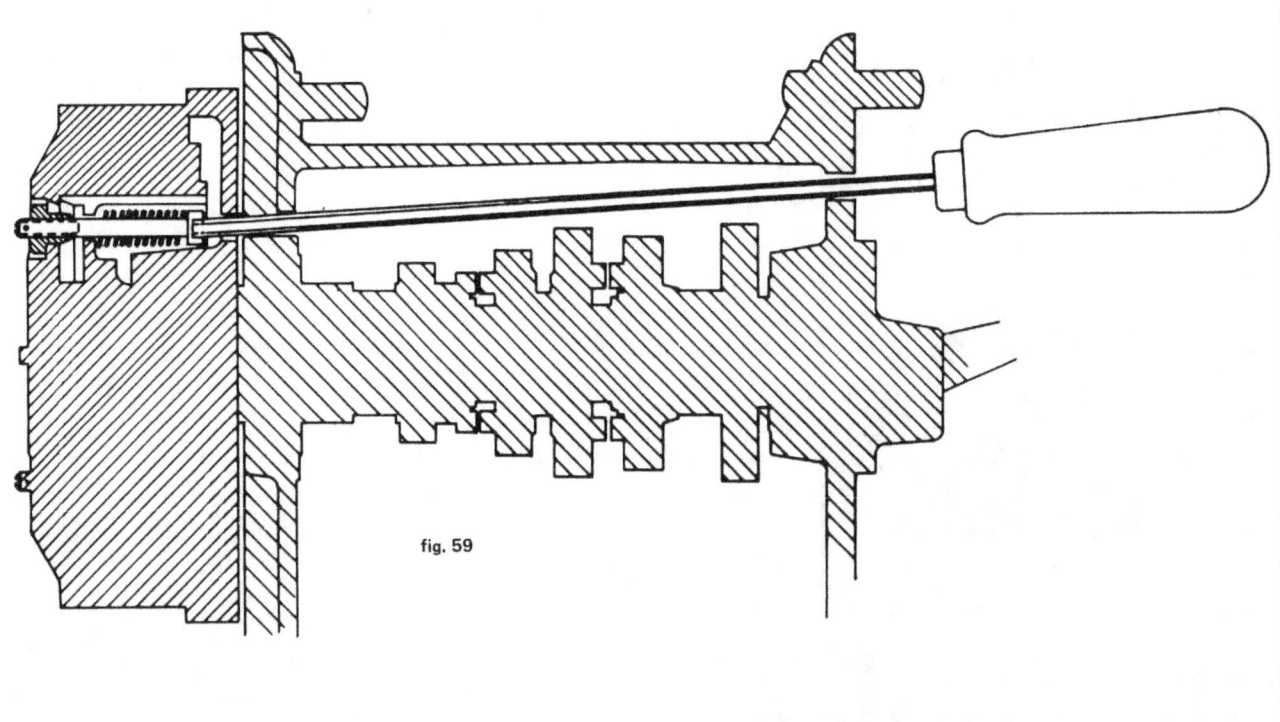
fig. 59

DISMANTLING THE ENGINE

fig. 60

Removing Clutch Hub
fig. 60

After removing the clutch plates put all the pressure spring nuts back on the studs. This will keep the inner clutch hub from popping off when the clutch nut is released.

Place special holding plate for clutch hub in place. Unlock locking washer tab and remove 32mm nut. Remove hub.

fig. 61

Driving Pinion
fig. 61

Place special driving pinion holding plate in place. Unlock lock washer tab and 14mm nut.

Remove pinion gear with a puller, remove woodruff key and spacer washer beneath.

Remove outer clutch hub and spacer washer beneath hub.

fig. 62

fig. 62

Remove shifting drum sleeve.

All necessary parts are now removed from this side and we will now start on the magneto side.

fig. 63

Removing Flywheel
fig. 63

With flywheel holder tool remove flywheel nut 12mm (left-hand threads).

DISMANTLING THE ENGINE

fig. 64

Fit protective cap over crankshaft end. Screw in flywheel puller securely and pull off flywheel. Remove protective cap, flywheel and woodruff key.

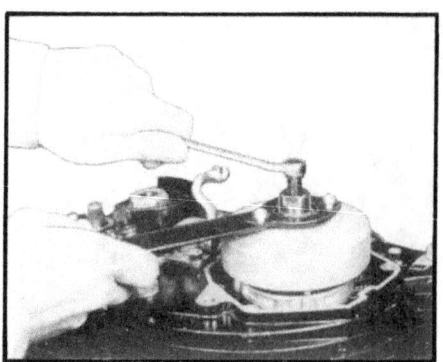

fig. 64

Motoplat Stator and Base Plate

fig. 65

You need not remove the stator or base plate unless you are going to change it. If you do remove it, follow instructions in section (Operation and Maintenance) for this procedure.

fig. 65

Case Protector

fig. 66

Remove case protector.

fig. 66

Clutch Activator Bearing Cover

fig. 67

Remove clutch activator bearing cover and gasket.

If clutch has not been removed push down on arm to lift cover from engine.

fig. 67

DISMANTLING THE ENGINE

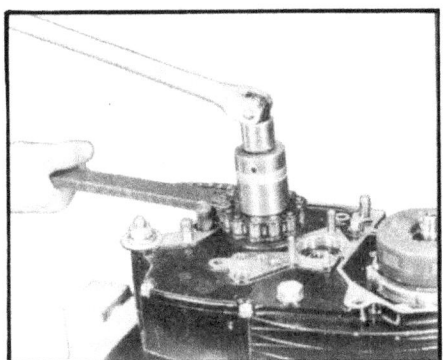
fig. 68

Removing Sprocket
fig. 68

Place sprocket holding tool on sprocket. Unlock lock washer tab and unscrew 20mm nut (right-hand thread). Remove sprocket, sleeve beneath sprocket and rubber "O" ring beneath sleeve.

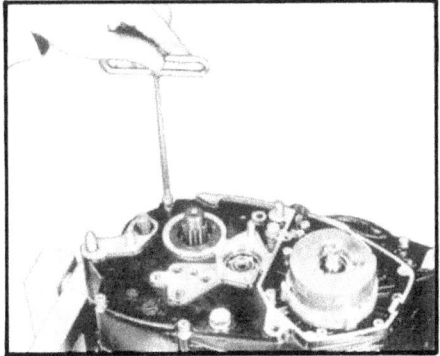
fig. 69

Splitting Cases
fig. 69

Remove crankcase Allen screws (four long and six short).

fig. 70

fig. 70

Release the two crankcase halves by tapping with a plastic hammer upon the mag side crankcase half, on inside of cylinder stud (close to case so as not to bend stud). Top down on countershaft. Fig. 70.

Remove the gasket.

fig. 71

Removing Gears
fig. 71

Remove shifter shaft quadrant(1).

Remove shifting drum(2).

Remove transmission gears as a unit with shifting forks attached. The back shifting fork will stay in the case when gears are removed. Remove remaining shifting fork and gear left in bottom. (Try to keep gears together in a cluster.)

If clutch is left on engine, it is necessary to remove 6th and 4th gears from mainshaft, and remove the circlip holding 3rd/5th gear so that when the countershaft is removed, 3rd/5th will slide out.

DISMANTLING THE ENGINE

Removing Kick Starter Assembly

fig. 72 fig. 73

Do not remove kick starter assembly if repairs to it need not be made.

To remove unit, remove kick start stop bolt in rear bottom of engine case.

Unlock lock washer tab and remove sleeved nut.

Pull kick starter shaft out (fig. 73)

Compress spring and lift out kick starter gear.

Remove locating lever by removing spring from cotter key.

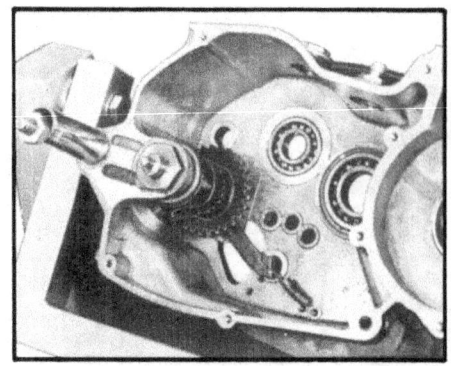

fig. 72

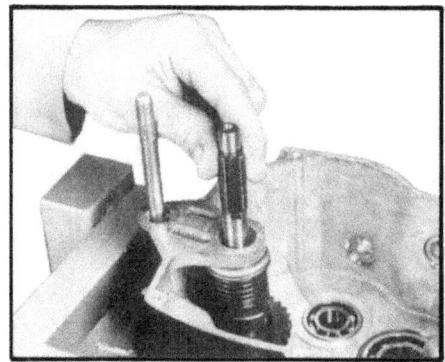

fig. 73

Removing Crankshaft

fig. 74

If you are removing the crank a special tool must be used to press the crank out, as the bearing is a press fit. Place the tool on and press the crank out.

fig. 74

Removing Crankshaft Clutch Side Bearing

fig. 75

You now must remove the bearing by heating the cases and lightly tapping out the bearing with a brass drift. Tap from inside cases to outside.

The engine is now completely disassembled.

Clean all components, check them for wear and replace them if necessary.

It is advisable to replace all gaskets and seals when the engine is being given a complete overhaul.

Note: The engine has a chamfered thrust washer that will fall out when the bearing is removed. The chamfered side goes toward the engine. The 175 does not have this washer.

fig. 75

DISMANTLING THE ENGINE

ENGINE NOTES:

WORK ON INDIVIDUAL PARTS

Removing and Replacing Engine Bearings

Clutch Side Bearings

fig. 76

Heat clutch side case to 158-176°F on a hot plate and remove mainshaft (1) and countershaft (2) bearings by lightly tapping the case with a plastic hammer. The bearings remove from the outside to the inside of the case.

fig. 78

If you are replacing the crankshaft bearing race proceed as follows: With the case still warm press out the spacer in the case from the outside to the inside with a drift that fits the outside edges of spacer as close as possible. The bearing race and seal will both come out with the spacer. Remove the seal from the spacer and replace with a new seal with the sealing lips pointing out from the spacer. With the case still warm press in the spacer with the "O"-ring in place and press down to its stop. Press in the outer race bearing down to its stop. Do not hammer in bearings or seals.

Replace the mainshaft bearing, being sure the circlip is firmly on the bearing and press in from the inside of the case down to its stop while the case is warm. The deepest part of the bearing from the circlip goes into the case.

Press in the countershaft bearing from inside case to outside down to its stop; circlip in the case is used for the stop.

NOTE: You need not reshim the crankshaft if replacing main bearings.

Mag Side Bearings

fig. 77

Heat mag side case to 158-176°F on a hot plate and remove mainshaft (1) and countershaft (2) bearings by lightly tapping the case with a plastic hammer. The bearings remove from the outside of the case to the inside.

fig. 78

If replacing crankshaft main bearing and seal proceed as follows: Remove the seal retaining plate on the outside of the case. The seal is in the plate. Remove and replace the seal with a new seal with the sealing lips pointing to the inside.

When assembling the seal, pay attention, that it is pressed far enough to the inside, that the seal lip runs for sure on the cylindrical part of the mag pin.

Reassemble the seal plate on the case. Press in the race from the inside down to its stop, which is the seal plate, while case is still warm.

Replace the mainshaft bearing down to its stop in the case. A circlip in the case is the stop; be sure it is seated properly.

Replace the countershaft bearing down to its stop in the case, which is also a circlip. A seal is on the outside of the countershaft bearing and should be replaced if old and leaking.

NOTE: After cases have cooled be sure all bearings are seated properly.

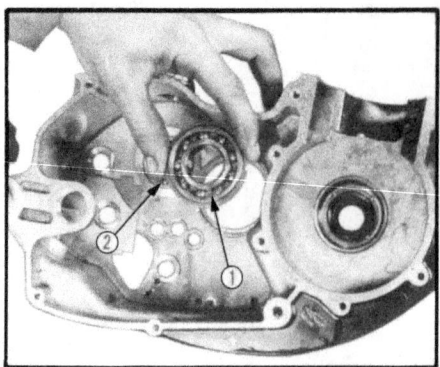

fig. 76

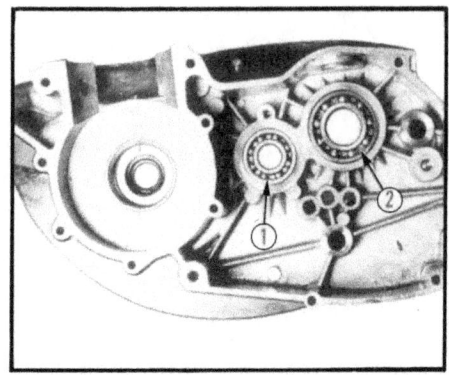

fig. 77

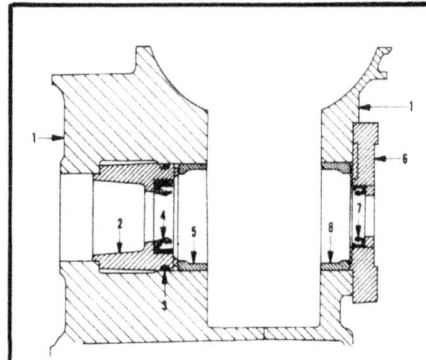

1. Crankcases
2. Spacer
3. Rubber "O" ring
4. Seal
5. Bearing race (clutch side)
6. Seal retainer plate
7. Seal
8. Bearing race (mag side)

fig. 78

WORK ON INDIVIDUAL PARTS

fig. 79

Pre-assembly of the Crankshaft

fig. 79

If crank assembly is taken apart do not mix up races and shims. Tag them or put in a special place marked in order.

If a new rod assembly is needed, contact your dealer for this procedure and work to be done. This is a critical procedure requiring special tools and skills.

Press the ball cages (5) off the inside races (3).

Fit protective caps (2 & 6) over the threaded pins of the crankshaft and pull the inner races off with a puller (7).

Heat the inside races (3) before pressing them on.

NOTE:

Do not interchange the outer and inner races of the magneto bearing.

A spacer plate (1) must in every case be placed between the two crankwebs when pressing on the inner races. This plate must be large enough to be supported on both sides so that the crankshaft rests freely.

Never grip the crankshaft ends or crank webs in a vise, and never try to fit the inner races by tapping them on.

Such treatment would squeeze the crank webs together and damage the big end bearing, thereby ruining the crankshaft.

fig. 80

Measuring the Axial Play of the Crankshaft

Permissible axial play 0.005 ... 0.010 in.

If installing new cases or if the crank main bearings or outer races have been disassembled, follow this procedure:

Place the inner bearing rings into the outer bearing rings.

Example: **fig. 80 fig. 81**

Place the inner bearing rings into the outer bearing rings.

Example:

Crankshaft, clutch side: Distance from sealing surface (with gasket) to inner race of bearing .... 1.106"

Crankcase half, magneto side: Distance from sealing surface (without gasket) to inner race of bearing .... +1.096"

Internal width of crankcase .... 2.202"

Dimension of crankshaft (measured over both webs) .... −2.135"

Existing axial play ....068"

Shim .030 on each side of crankshaft (4, fig.79). Shims are always placed directly under the inner bearing races on both sides of the crankshaft −.060"

Permissible axial play ....008"

Note:

If the difference cannot be taken up equally with the shimming washers on hand, the larger amount is to be fitted on the clutch side.

fig. 81

WORK ON INDIVIDUAL PARTS

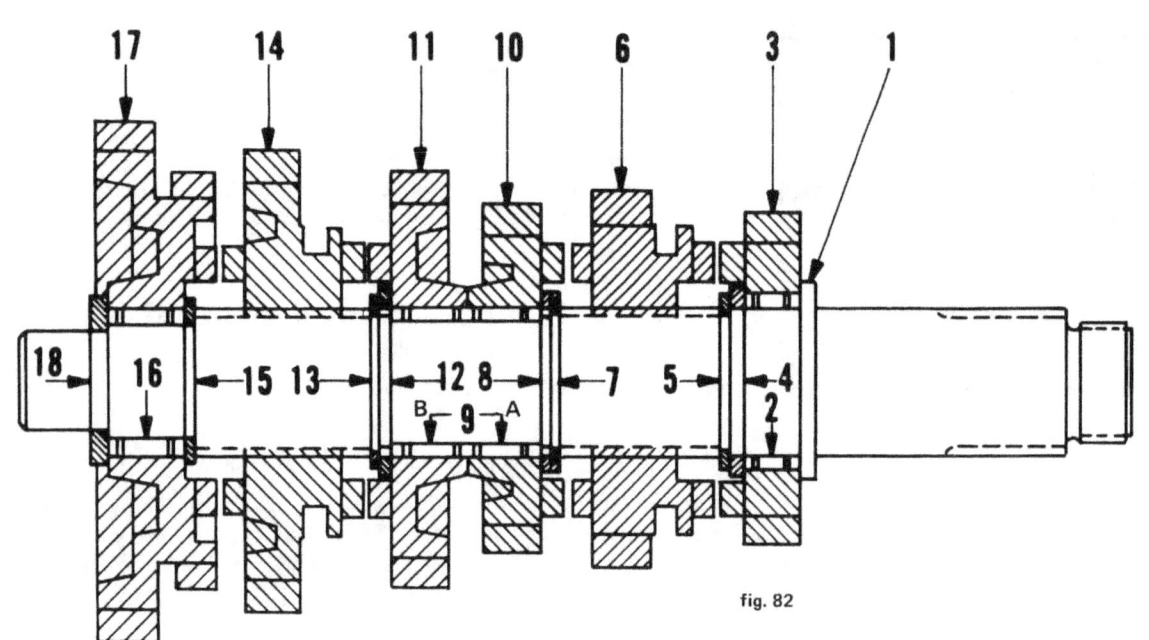

fig. 82

Work on Countershaft

Reassembly of Countershaft

If gears are replaced or shaft is disassembled, assemble the countershaft as follows:

Place needle cage bearing (2) on countershaft down to shoulder (1).

Place 6th gear (3) over bearings so shifting dogs are away from shoulder.

Place supporting disc (4) against 6th gear.

Fit snap ring (5) onto snap ring groove at 6th gear.

Place 4th gear (6) on shaft so shifting fork groove is towards 6th gear.

Place snap ring (7), smallest and thinnest, at front of splined shaft in snap ring groove.

Next place recessed part in thrust washer with splines (8) over snap ring (7). Recess in thrust washer should cover snap ring.

Place the split needle cage bearings (9a) on shaft and place 5th gear (10) over bearings with shifting dogs facing 4th gear.

Place split needle cage bearings (9b) beside 5th gear and place 3rd gear (11) with shifting dogs facing away from 5th gear.

Place splined thrust washer (12) on shaft against 3rd gear and put snap ring (13) in snap ring groove.

Place 2nd gear (14) with shifting fork groove towards 3rd gear and place on shaft.

Place supporting washer (15) on shaft down to splined shoulder.

Place on needle cage bearing (16).

Place 1st gear (17) with kick starter gear, smallest, towards 2nd gear.

Place on thrust washer (18) to complete countershaft assembly.

WORK ON INDIVIDUAL PARTS

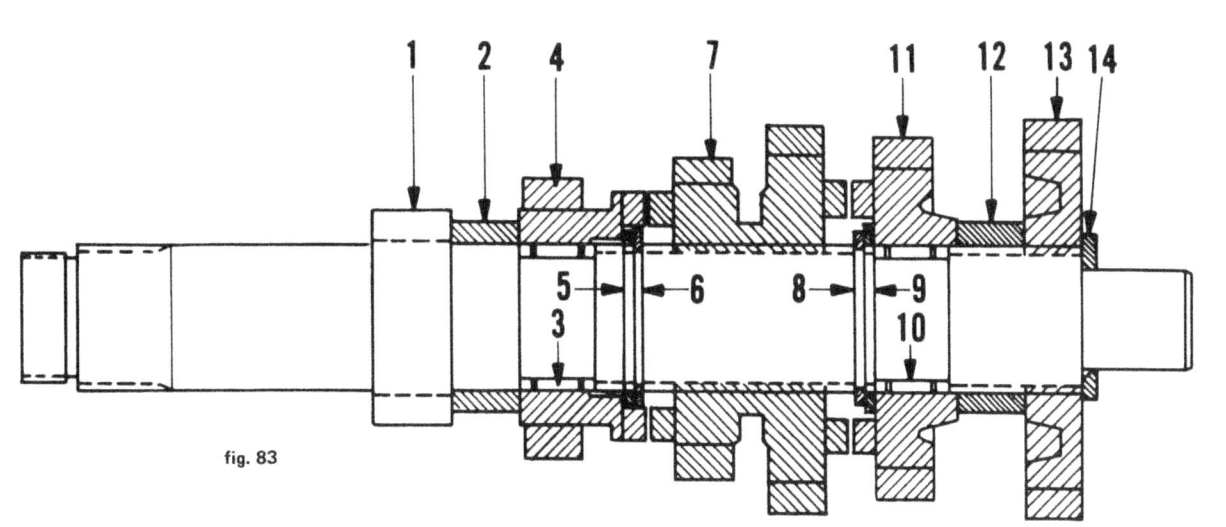

fig. 83

Reassembly of Mainshaft

If gears are replaced or shaft is disassembled, assemble the mainshaft as follows:

First place on aluminum spacer (2) down to 1st gear (1) machined on mainshaft.

Place on split needle cage bearings (3) and place 2nd gear (4) on shaft over bearing with shifting dogs facing away from 1st gear.

Place splined thrust washer (5), smallest of two against 2nd gear. Place smallest of two snap rings (6) in snap ring groove against 2nd gear thrust washer.

Place 3rd and 5th gear cluster (7) on shaft with 3rd (smallest gear) facing toward 2nd gear.

Place largest snap ring (8) in snap ring groove at top of spline.

Place the largest splined thrust washer (9) against the snap ring (8).

Place split needle cage bearings (10) in place and fit 4th gear (11) on shaft over bearings with shifting dogs facing towards 5th gear.

Place steel spacer (12) against 4th gear and place on 6th gear (13).

Fit thrust washer on top of 6th gear to complete assembly (14).

fig. 84

WORK ON INDIVIDUAL PARTS

If you keep all parts in order when disassembling the engine as shown above, reassembly will be 100% easier with less chance of leaving out or putting in the wrong part. Always work methodically on a section at a time and don't rush or jam parts to try to make them fit.

REBUILDING THE ENGINE

fig. 87

fig. 88

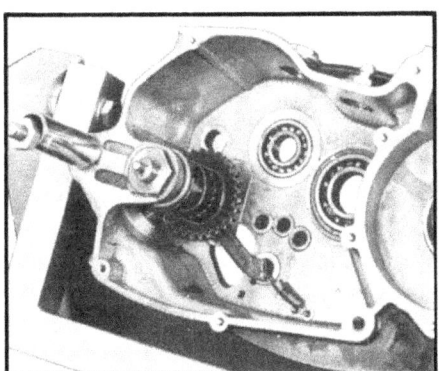

fig. 89

Rebuilding the Engine

Place clutch side crankcase in engine jig.

fig. 87 88 89 90

NOTE:

The kickstart assembly in the 175 differs from that in the 250/400, the latter machines having larger kickstart shafts. Assembly is basically the same.

Place locating lever over kick starter shaft opening.

Place kick starter gear with ratchets pointing up over locating lever.

Place thrust washer on top of gear. The 250/400 large shaft assembly does not have this washer.

Assemble kick starter ratchet, kick starter spring and spring clip in an assembly and compress spring and place on top of kick starter gear. Place kick starter spring so it contacts the stop on top of the case.

The 175 small shaft assembly has two holes in the kickstarter ratchet for spring tension adjustment. Place spring in the hole which will give ½ turn preload. (180° away from kickstarter stop screw). The 250/400 large shaft assembly does not have an adjustment.

Place kick starter on provisionally and wind kick starter spring approximately one turn so kick starter stop screw will turn in freely. Tighten kickstarter stop screw. Check assembly operation for proper spring tension and that the kick starter ratchet disengages completely from the kick starter gear when its cam is backed fully against the kick starter stop screw.

Hook locating lever spring to cotter key located on bottom of case.

Note: The late 250 engine carries a large diameter shaft and does not have the thrust washer (4 fig. 90). Assembly is the same.

1. Kick starter shaft
2. Locating lever
3. Kick starter gear
4. Thrust washer
5. Kick starter ratchet
6. Spring
7. Spring clip
8. Lock washer
9. Screw bushing
10. Kick starter stop screw

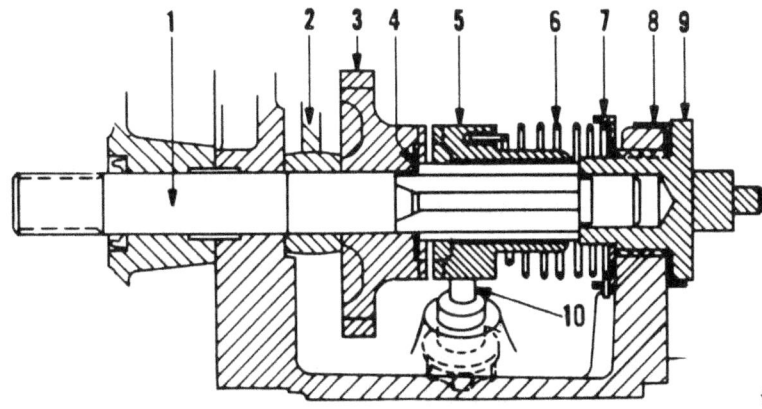

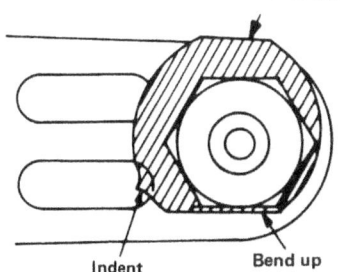

fig. 90

REBUILDING THE ENGINE

Gearbox

fig. 91

Place thrust washer, first gear, needle cage and support washer in case over countershaft hole and line up

fig. 91

fig. 92

Match the two gear assemblies, countershaft and mainshaft, with shifting forks in place. The first shifting fork, fork in lowest position on shaft, fits on 2nd gear countershaft; the second shifting fork, fork in center of shaft, fits on 3rd and 5th gear cluster of mainshaft. The last shifting fork, fork in highest position on shaft, fits on 4th gear of countershaft.

(See "Work on Individual Parts" for complete gear cluster assemblies.)

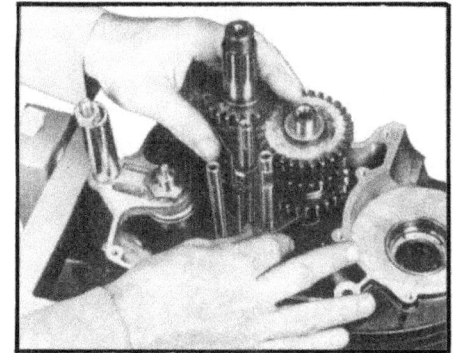

fig. 92

fig. 93

Place the entire assembly together and drop in place in the correct positions. Be sure all holes are lined up carefully and all shifting forks are in their proper positions.

If clutch was left installed, 3rd/5th mainshaft will have to be slid down while installing the countershaft assembly.

fig. 93

fig. 94

Place shifter drum in position being sure locating lever at bottom of case is pulled back so drum will seat properly and locating lever will be in position on indexes of shifting drum.

Work the gears and shifting forks back and forth to locate the shifting forks on the shifting drum.

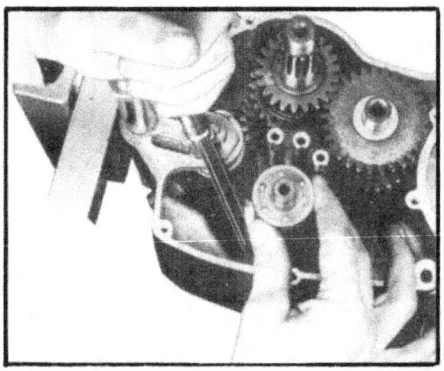

fig. 94

REBUILDING THE ENGINE

fig. 95

Replace bushing for shifting drum and tighten down.

fig. 96

Place shifter quadrant into place, making sure return spring is located over the kick starter screw bushing stud.

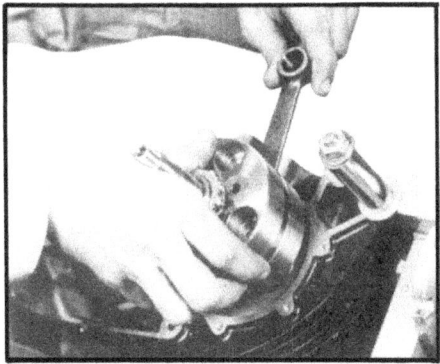

fig. 97

Place assembled crank into clutch side half.

fig. 98

The transmission is now fully assembled.

Engine is now ready for mag side case half.

REBUILDING THE ENGINE

fig. 99

When replacing any gaskets in the engine, do not use gasket cement. Use a light film of grease on the case halves. Also soaking the gasket in water will make the gaskets easier to handle and put in place.

Place crankcase gasket on clutch side of case and line up all holes. Place the three bullet shaped special tools in Penton dealers tool kit on shifter fork shafts. These are guides when lining up cases for reassembly.

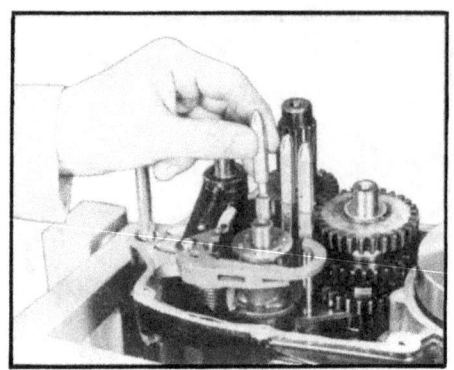
fig. 99

fig. 100   fig. 101

Replace mag side case half. Do not beat on cases to assemble. Cases should push together by hand. Remove the three bullet shaped guides. Replace case screws. Do Not use loctite on any nuts or bolts on this engine. Tighten Allen head screws from five to six ft. lbs. (Do not over tighten screws or they may break.)

Note: Before tightening screws down securely check that the transmission shifts properly.

NOTE: Difficulty in getting the cases to go together may arise from the shift shaft not locating in the blind hold in the mag case. Play with the shift to get it to line up.

fig. 100

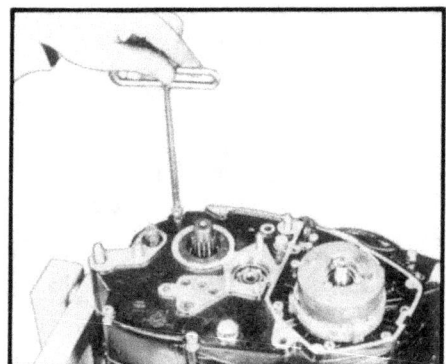
fig. 101

Replacing Clutch Side Crankshaft Bearing
fig. 102

With the special bearing inserting tool (51-12-008-000) press the clutch side crankshaft bearing down even with the case. Be sure the tool is used properly; the bolt screws onto the crankshaft end and the outside of the inserting tool is turned (not the bolt) to press the bearing on. When the pinion gear is torqued down the bearing will seat itself properly.

This bearing must fit tightly on both the crankshaft and case.

Note: place the chamfered thrust washer, with the chamfer toward the engine, on the crankshaft end before installing the bearing. No washer on the 175 engine.

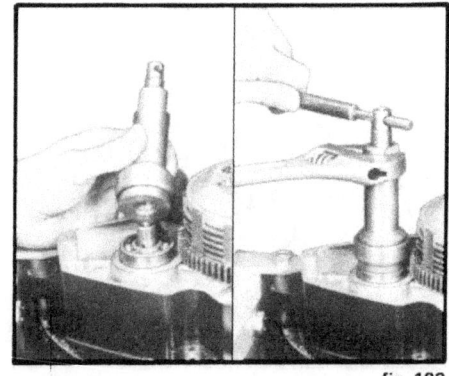
fig. 102

REBUILDING THE ENGINE

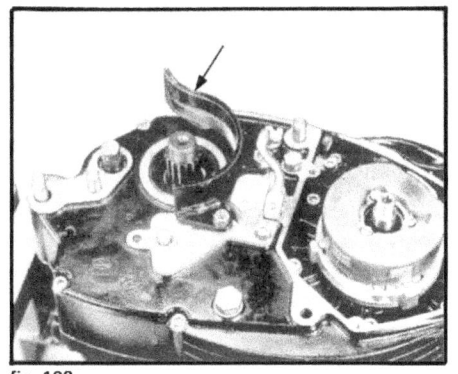

fig. 103

Rebuilding Mag Side of Engine

fig. 103

Place gasket for bearing cover/clutch activator and crankcase protector and tighten down.

If clutch is already installed, don't forget pushrods and ball bearing fig. 106.

fig. 104

fig. 104

Place rubber "O" ring that goes over sprocket shaft and place on spacer over shaft so cambered side is towards the "O" ring.

Place sprocket on shaft with shoulder towards the engine case.

Place locking tab and nut on countershaft and torque to 45-50 ft. lbs. using special holding tool. Bend locking tab over nut.

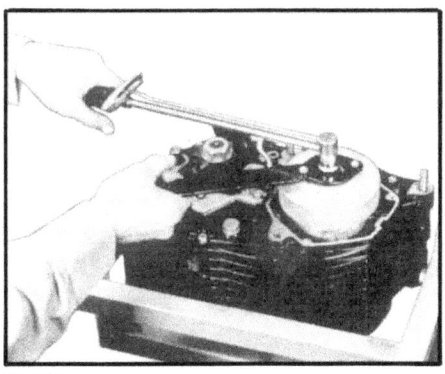

fig. 105

Installing Flywheel

fig. 105

Place flywheel on crankshaft being sure key is in place. (If you did not remove the stator or base plate, no timing need be done. If not, see section on timing in Operation and Maintenance. Torque left-hand threads to 40 ft. lbs. Use special holding tool.

This completes mag side of engine.

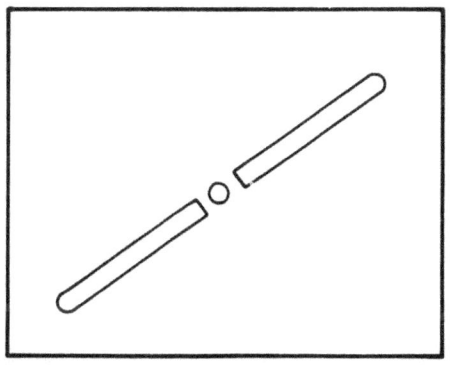

fig. 106

Reassembling Clutch Side

fig. 106

Position engine to work on clutch side.

Drop one clutch push rod down center of mainshaft with rounded end facing down. Drop in ball bearing. Drop in other clutch push rod with rounded end facing out.

REBUILDING THE ENGINE

fig. 107

Place small spacer washer over crankshaft end. Place woodruff key and pinion gear on shaft. Place locking washer and nut and torque to 40-45 ft. lbs. using special holding tool. Lock tab washer on nut.

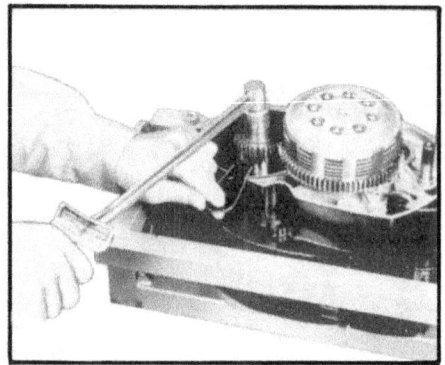

fig. 107

fig. 108

Place all clutch studs with springs into clutch hub as shown and tighten down all nuts until about four threads show.

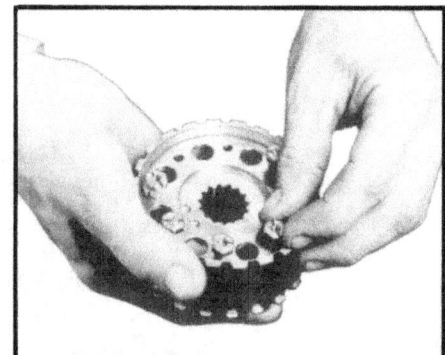

fig. 108

fig. 109

Place spacer washer over mainshaft. Place outer clutch hub on mainshaft and place inner clutch hub on mainshaft. Put on locking washer and nut, with chamfer pointing up and tighten nut to 50 ft. lbs. using special holding tool. Lock washer to nut.

Now remove the clutch stud nuts from clutch hub using special tool.

fig. 109

fig. 110

Reassemble clutch plates as removed. Various clutch changes have taken place so no one way is correct. On all late model clutches the order of sequence is fiber steel, etc. ending with steel. The 175 has 5 fiber and 5 steel discs. The 250 and 400 have 7 fiber and 7 steel discs. On early model clutches a steel ring without spines was first placed in followed by a splined steel disc.

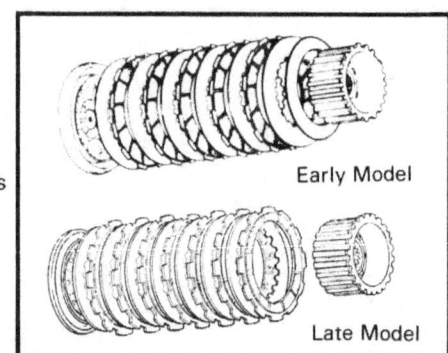

fig. 110

REBUILDING THE ENGINE

fig. 111

Place the clutch pressure place on clutch. Note: The center bolt and nut on the pressure plate are not for adjustment and should be kept tight. Do not try to make adjustments here. Put on clutch nuts with special tool till the correct number of threads show as when taken apart, usually 3-4 threads.

After adjusting nuts to proper depth, replace cotter keys in holes or use .040 in. wire to hold the nuts.

fig. 111

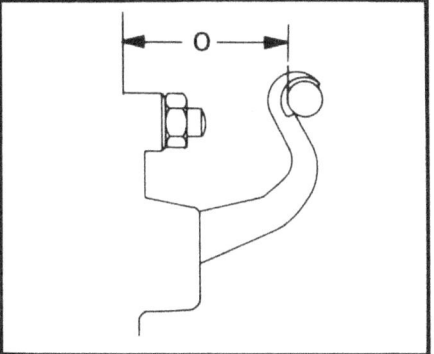

fig. 112

Clutch Dimensions

	175cc	250cc 400cc
Thickness of clutch plates	3.5mm	2.5mm
Thickness of steel plates	1.4-1.5mm	
Length of springs (new)	40.5mm	38.5mm
Distance of clutch lever at 0 clearance	42.5-43.5mm	

wire diameter springs 175/250 1.6   400 1.7

fig. 112

fig. 113

The clutch side of the engine is now complete.

fig. 113

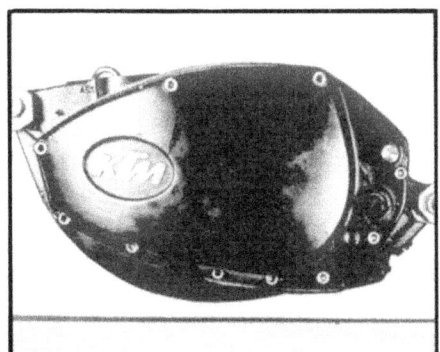

fig. 114

Replace gasket using a thin grease coating and replace clutch cover. Tighten Allen head screws to 5-6 ft. lbs. Do not over tighten.

fig. 114

REBUILDING THE ENGINE

IMPORTANT NOTE: This page for setting up the 175cc engine only.

Fitting New Pistons

When fitting new pistons where reboring or horning is to take place, have your dealer do this job for you. If he cannot, he can forward it to us to have the work done. More damage is done by poor boring jobs than any one other item, so be sure the place that does your cylinder work is known for doing good work.

When fitting new pistons, the clearance should be .003 in.-.0035 in.

The proper ring gap should be from .011-.018 in.

Replace piston on connecting rod. Heat piston to 158-176°F. before inserting wrist pin. Be sure needle cage bearing is in place and the piston is facing the proper direction, the intake hold in the piston faces toward the back of the engine.

Secure wrist pin with circlips being sure they are in their grooves firmly.

Measuring the Cylinder and Piston
fig. 115

Place the cylinder with gasket and bolt down with two studs. Move the piston to top dead center. Measure from the top edge of the L-ring to the cylinder top. This measurement must be 0.7mm (.028-.030 in.). Note: The measurement for this is stamped on the top cylinder fin and in almost all cases is 0.7mm.

If the measurement is not correct, use various size base gaskets to achieve the measurement as near perfect as possible.

Drilling Lubricating Hole and Timing Intake Port in New Pistons
NOTE: For 175cc piston only.

With the correct measurement at the top of the piston and the cylinder on with two studs holding it down, follow this procedure.

1. Set piston in a way that the piston rings become visible on the upper edge of exhaust port.

2. With a scriber make a very fine scratch on the left and right side of the exhaust rib **fig. 116**

3. Place a timing degree wheel on the crankshaft mag side and put the piston in position 80°-81° before top dead center.

4. Make a scratch with a scriber at the bottom edge of the intake port (fig. **117**. Check if this mark comes to the same position after again turning 161°-162° over top dead center.

5. Take off cylinder and piston.

6. On the intake side of the piston file the piston to the scratch and break the corners slightly.

7. Drill a 0.040 in. hole vertically through the piston wall exactly in the center of both scratches, approximately 0.315 in. underneath the lower edge of the rectangular ring on the front of the piston. Break the edges slightly **fig. 118**.

Reassemble piston to connecting rod and replace cylinder. Be sure piston is warm before inserting wrist pin.

Place cylinder head gasket and cylinder head on when engine is back in the frame for ease of assembly.

```
Torques:   Cylinder studs  . . . . . . . . . . . . . . . . . .  7 ft. lbs.
           Cylinder head nuts  . . . . . . . . . . . . . . . .20 ft. lbs.
           Cylinder head bolts . . . . . . . . . . . . . . . .  7 ft. lbs.
```

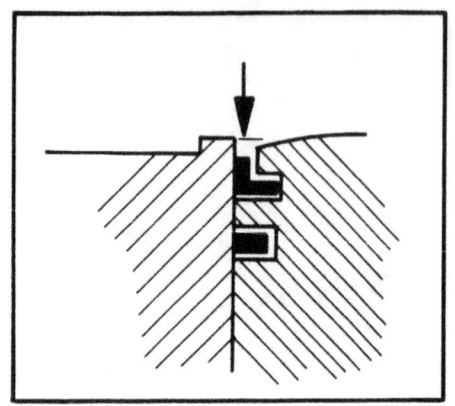

fig. 115

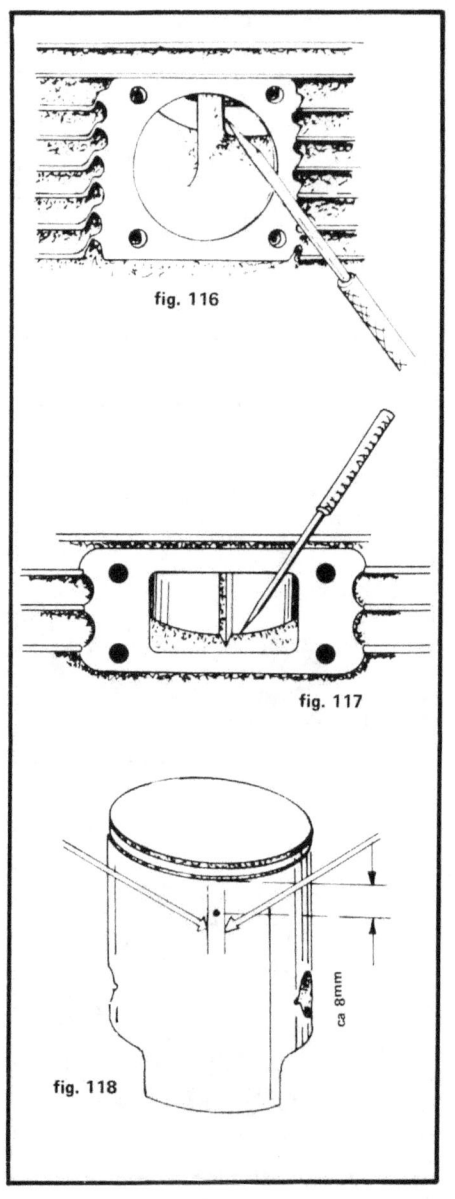

fig. 116

fig. 117

fig. 118

REBUILDING THE ENGINE

IMPORTANT NOTE: This page for setting up 250 & 400cc only.

Fitting New Pistons

When fitting new pistons where reboring or horning is to take place, have your dealer do this job for you. If he cannot, he can forward it to us to have the work done. More damage is done by poor boring jobs than any one other item, so be sure the place that does your cylinder work is known for doing good work.

When fitting new pistons, the clearance should be .002 in.-.0025 in.

The proper ring gap should be from .011-.018 in.

Replace piston on connecting rod. Heat piston to 158-176°F. before inserting wrist pin. Be sure needle cage bearing is in place and the piston is facing the proper direction, the intake hold in the piston faces toward the back of the engine.

Secure wrist pin with circlips being sure they are in their grooves firmly.

Measuring the Cylinder and Piston
fig. 119

Place the cylinder with gasket and bolt down with two studs. Move the piston to top dead center. Measure from the top edge of the L-ring to the cylinder top.

If the measurement is not correct, use various size base gaskets to achieve the measurement as near perfect as possible.

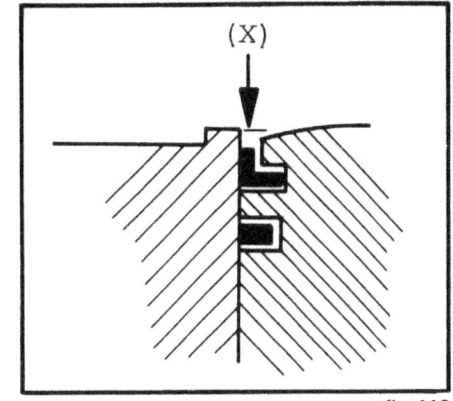

fig. 119

Measurement X
250cc... Piston 1274, (.040")
             Piston 1274a, (.047")
400cc... (.051")

Drilling Lubricating Hole in New Pistons

With the correct measurement at the top of the piston and the cylinder on with two studs holding it down, follow this procedure.

1. Set piston in a way that the piston rings become visible on the upper edge of exhaust port.

2. With a scriber make a very fine scratch on the left and right side of the exhaust rib **fig. 120**

3. Drill a 0.040 in. hole vertically through the piston wall exactly in the center of both scratches, approximately 0.472 in. underneath the lower edge of the rectangular ring on the front of the piston. Break the edges slightly **fig. 121**.

Reassemble piston to connecting rod and replace cylinder. Be sure piston is warm before inserting wrist pin.

Place cylinder head gasket and cylinder head on when engine is back in the frame for ease of assembly.

Torques: Cylinder studs . . . . .12 ft. lbs.
          Cylinder head nuts . . . . .20 ft. lbs.
          Cylinder head bolts .20 ft. lbs.

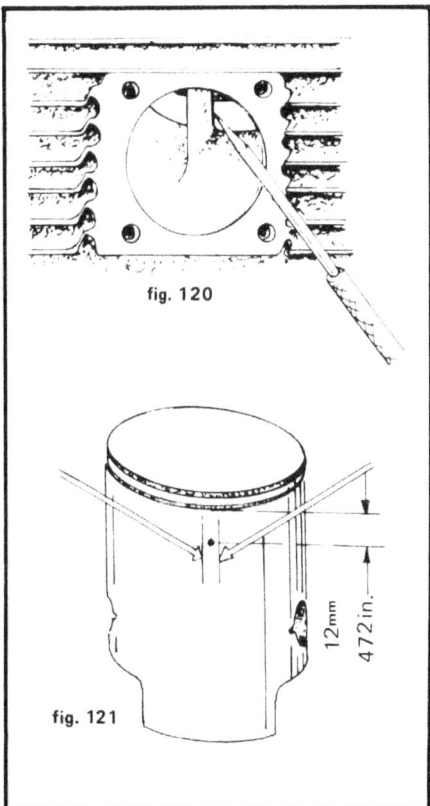

fig. 120

fig. 121

Displacement of Engine after boring for oversize pistons.

175cc

Bore	Stroke	Displacement
63.5	54mm	171.01
63.75		172.36
64.0		173.72
64.25		175.08
64.5		176.44
64.75		177.79
65.0		179.19
65.25		180.57
65.5		181.96

250cc

Bore	Stroke	Displacement
71.0	62mm	245.47
71.25		247.20
71.5		248.94
71.75		250.68
72.0		252.43
72.25		254.19
72.5		255.96
72.75		257.72
73.0		259.49

400cc

Bore	Stroke	Displacement
80.0	69mm	346.83
80.25		349.00
80.5		351.18
80.75		353.37
81.0		355.56
81.25		357.76
81.5		359.96
81.75		362.17
82.0		364.39
82.25		366.62
82.5		368.84
82.75		371.09
83.0		373.33

PENTON-KTM
Frame & Chassis Parts Manual
1972 to 1975
PENTON Jackpiner - Hare & Mint
KTM MC & GS Models
(Motocross & Gelande Sport)

INDEX

Group		Page No.
01	Front Fork	48
02	Handlebar - Controls	52
03	Frame - Footrests - Rear Brake	55
03A	Swingarm - Side Stand	58
04	Shock Absorbers	60
05	Exhaust System	62
06	Airfilter Box	65
07	Gas Tank - Seat - Chain Guide	67
08	Fenders	70
09	Front Wheel	72
10	Rear Wheel	75
11	Electrical - Speedometer	78
12	Accessories - Tools	81
12A	Repair Tools and Jig for 175cc Engine	83

A Floyd Clymer Publication - 2025 VelocePress.com

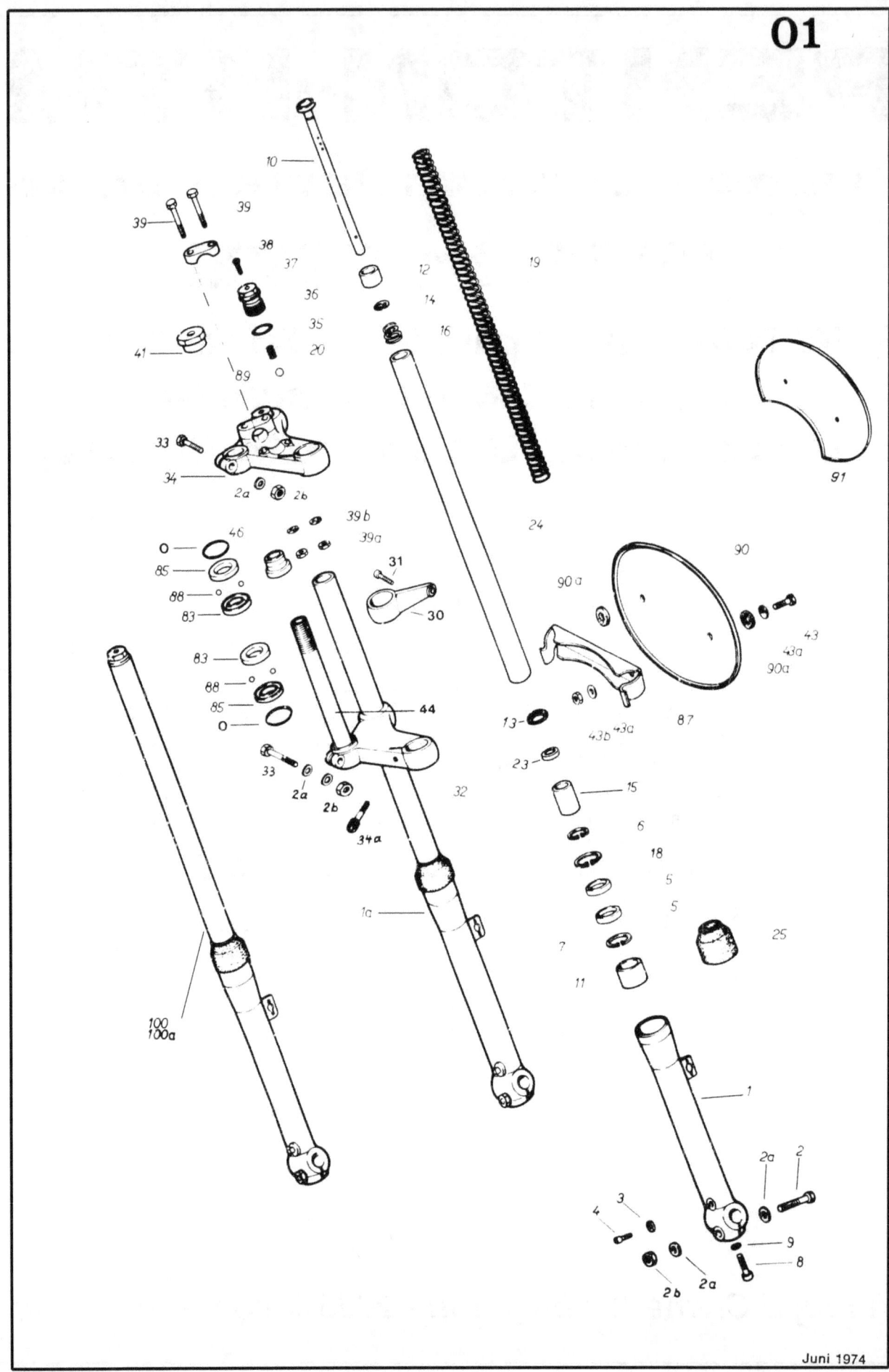

Gruppe 01: Telegabel, Steuersatz
Group 01: Telescopic front fork
Gruppo 01: Forcella anteriore

Bild Picture Foto	Teil-Nr. Part-No. Parte No	Benennung Description Descrizione	Stk./Fzg. Pos./Machine Pezzi/Macch.		
			175	250	400
—	ES 1.672	**Teleskopgabel** kpl. Front fork compl. Forcella anetriore cpl.	1	1	1
0	2.52.000	Parker O-Ring Parker O-ring Anello O Parker	2	2	2
1	1.672.07	Gleitrohr rechts Fork slider tube R/S Assieme scorrevole destro	1	1	1
1a	1.672.08	Gleitrohr links Fork slider tube L/S Assieme scorrevole sinistro	1	1	1
2	1.209.032	Sechskantschraube DIN 831 Hexagon head bolt DIN 831 Vite serra morsetto supporto perno ruota	2	2	2
2a	1.69.024	Scheibe 8,4 DIN 125 Flat washer 8,4 DIN 125 Rondella per vite 8,4 DIN 125	8	8	8
2b	1.42.05.01.07	Sechskantmutter M 8 DIN 934 Hexagon nut M 8 DIN 934 Dado M 8 DIN 934	2	2	2
3	1.88.0512	Dichtring für Ablaßschraube Washer – drain plug Guarnizione per vite scarico olio	2	2	2
4	1.88.0511	Zylinderschraube M 6x8 DIN 84 Drain plug M 6x8 Vite scarico olio M 6x8	2	2	2
5	1.265.0514	Simmering Seal Guarnizione tenuta olio asta di forza	4	4	4
6	1.209.0613	Seegerring Circlip Seeger ritegno corpo valvola	2	2	2
7	1.110.064	Seeger-Sprengring Snap ring Anello seeger	2	2	2
8	1.4.06.01.06	Innensechskantschraube Allen head screw Vite bloccagio variatore allo scorrevole	2	2	2
9	1.88.049	Kupferdichtring Washer Guarnizione per vite	2	2	2
10	1.672.061	Kolbenstange Stop valve Assieme variatore	2	2	2
11	1.622.073	Führungsbüchse Lower bushing Bussola di guida per scorrevole	2	2	2
12	1.209.067	Kolben Bushing Pistone	2	2	2
13	1.209.0610	Einstellfeder kpl. Stop valve Ghiera limitatrice	2	2	2
14	1.209.068	Seegerring Circlip Seeger ritegno pistone	2	2	2
15	1.622.0612	Ventilkörper Upper bushing Corpo valvola semplice	2	2	2
16	1.622.069	Ventilrückholfeder Valve return spring Moletta richiamo valvola	2	2	2

Gruppe 01: Telegabel, Steuersatz
Group 01: Telescopic front fork
Gruppo 01: Forcella anteriore

Bild Picture Foto	Teil-Nr. Part-No. Parte No	Benennung Description Descrizione	Stk./Fzg. Pos./Machine Pezzi/Macch. 175	250	400
18	1.209.092	Seegerring / Circlip / Seeger ritegno guarnizione	2	2	2
19	1.672.10	Druckfeder / Fork spring / Molla	2	2	2
20	1.240.023	Ventilfeder / Valve spring / Molla springi valvola	2	2	2
23	1.622.0611	Ventil / Valve / Valvola	2	2	2
24	1.672.05	Gabelholm lose / Fork tube – loose / Asta di forza	2	2	2
25	1.637.09	Gummimanschette / Fork boot / Manicotto in gomma	1	1	1
30	1.31.000	Scheinwerferhalter / Headlight bracket / Aletta porta faro	2	2	2
31	1.343.09	Schraube für Scheinwerferhalter / Bolt for headlight bracket / Vite per aletta porta faro	2	2	2
32	1.672.031	Gabelbrücke unten / Bottom fork plate / Base sterzo semplice	1	1	1
33	1.211.042	Sechskantschraube / Hexagon head bolt / Vite serra morsetto testa perno sterzo	2	2	2
34	1.622.011	Gabelbrücke oben / Top fork plate / Testa di sterzo	1	1	1
34a	1.209.035	Innensechskantschraube / Allen head screw / Vite serra morsetto testa asta di forza	2	2	2
35	1.209.022	Dichtring für Verschlußschraube / Seal / Anello di tenuta per tappo	2	2	2
36	1.622.021	Holmverschlußschraube / Nut – fork tube / Tappo bloccaggio asta di forza semplice	2	2	2
37	1.240.022	Linsensenkschraube / Tapered head screw / Vite per tappo bloccaggio	2	2	2
38	1.627.012	Lenkerklemmbrücke / Handlebar clamp / Morsetto serraggio manubrio	2	2	2
39	1.207.TL.014	Sechskantschraube M 6 / Hexagon head bolt M 6 / Vite per morsetto M 6	4	4	4
39a	1.55/1.01.023	Sechskantmutter M 6 / Hexagon nut M 6 / Dado M 6	4	4	4
39b	1.55/1.01.022	Federring B 6 DIN 127 / Spring washer B 6 DIN 127 / Rondella grower B 6 DIN 127	4	4	4
41	1.623.032	Abschlußmutter für Gabelschaftrohr / Nut – top fork plate / Dado per perno sterzo	1	1	1
43	2.79.00	Sechskantschraube M 6x20 / Hexagon heat bolt M 6x20 / Vite per morsetto M 6x20	2	2	2

Gruppe 01: Telegabel, Steuersatz
Group 01: Telescopic front fork
Gruppo 01: Forcella anteriore

Bild Picture Foto	Teil-Nr. Part-No. Parte No	Benennung Description Descrizione	Stk./Fzg. Pos./Machine Pezzi/Macch.		
			175	250	400
43a	DIN 125/6.4	Beilagscheibe 6,4 DIN 125 Flat washer 6,4 DIN 125 Rondella 6,4 DIN 125	4	4	4
43b	261.000	SS-Mutter M 6 DIN 934 Self-locking nut M 6 DIN 934 Dado M 6 DIN 934	2	2	2
44	1.623.036	Gabelschaftrohr Fork stem Perno sterzo	1	1	1
46	1.623.042	Einstellmutter Threaded bushing Ghiera regolazione calotte	1	1	1
83	51.01.083.000	Steuerschale innen Bearing race — inner Calotta telaio — interiore	2	2	2
85	51.01.085.000	Steuerschale außen Bearing race — outer Calotta telaio — exteriore	2	2	2
87	51.01.087.000	Nummerntafelhalterung Bracket for number plate Calotta per portanumero ant.	1	1	1
88	251.000	Stahlkugeln ¼" DIN 5401 (6,35 mm) Steel balls ¼" DIN 5401 (6,35 mm) Sfera ¼" DIN 5401 (6,35 mm)	32	32	32
89	1.88.043	Kugelventil (Kugel 4 mm ⌀) Steel ball (ball 4 mm ⌀) Valvola sfera (sfera 4 mm ⌀)	2	2	2
90	51.01.090.000	Startnummerntafel vorne Front number plate Portanumero anteriore	1	1	1
90a	5.10.000	Gummibeilage Rubber washer Rondella in gomma	2	2	2
91	51.01.091.000	Startnummerntafel mit Ausschnitt Cut-out front number plate Portanumero anteriore	1	1	1
100	1.672.08.01	Gabelbein links kpl. Fork leg compl. L/S Gamba sinistra compl.	1	1	1
100a	1.672.07.01	Gabelbein rechts kpl. Fork leg compl. R/S Gamba destra compl.	1	1	1
—	1.672.12	Dichtungssatz kompl. Gasket set compl. Serie compl. di guarnizione	1	1	1
—	1.672.11	Schraubensatz kpl. Bolt set compl. Serie compl. di bulloni	1	1	1
—	1.656.09	Gummimanschette mit Öse für Seilführung Fork boot with eye for cable guide Manicotto in gomma per guida cavo	1	1	1

02

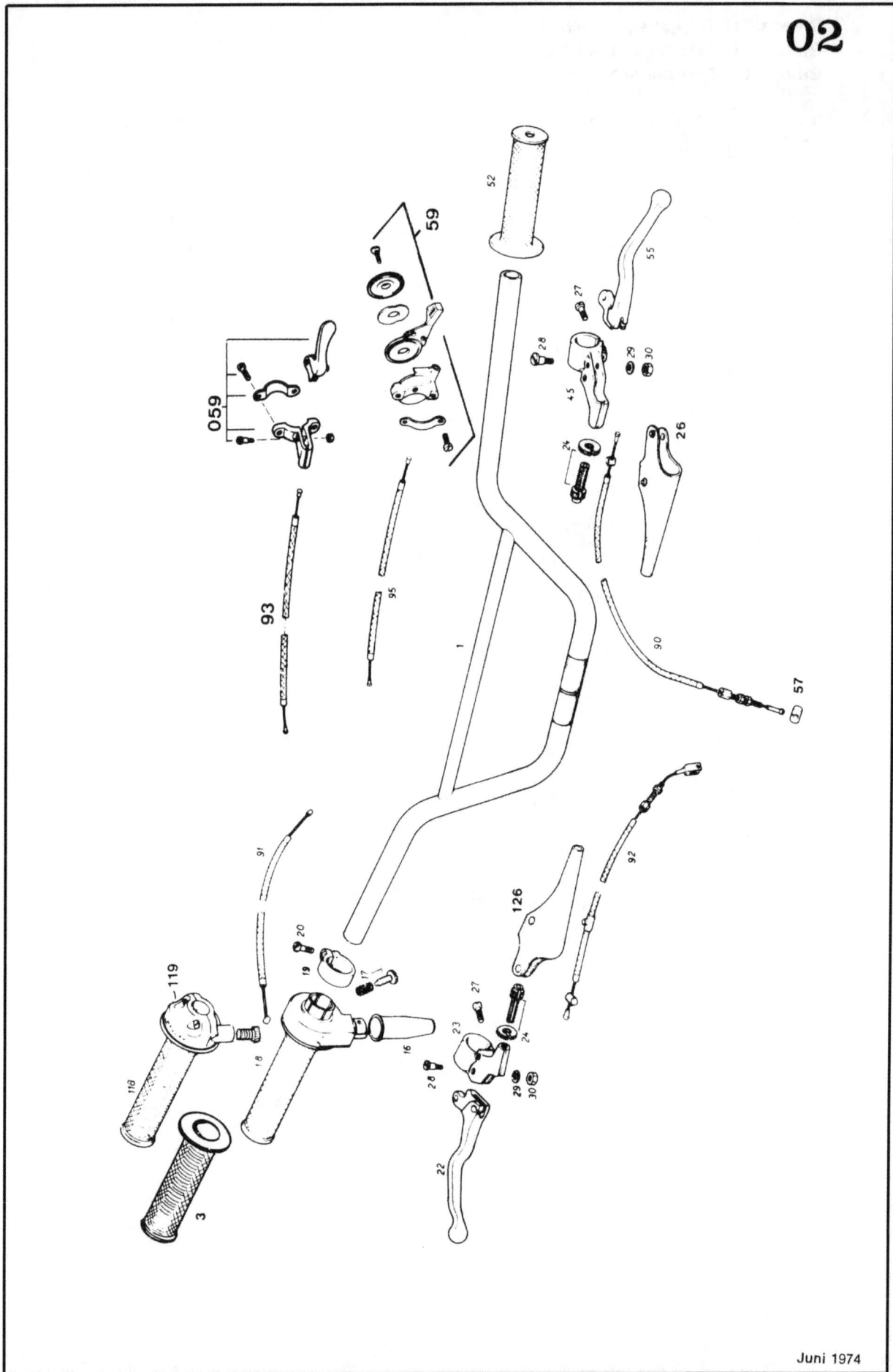

Juni 1974

Gruppe 02: Lenker — Lenkerarmaturen
Group 02: Handlebar — controls
Gruppo 02: Manubrio — leve

Bild Picture Foto	Teil-Nr. Part-No. Parte-No.	Benennung Description Descrizione	Stk./Fzg. Pos./Machine Pezzi/Macch.		
			175	250	400
1	51.02.001.400	**Lenker** Handlebar Manubrio	1	1	1
—	51.02.010.000	**Gasdrehgriff** kpl. Twist grip assy. Comando gas compl.	1	1	1
3	54.02.015.000	Drehgriffüberzug Twist grip cover Coperchio comando gas	1	1	1
16	54.02.016.000	Schutzkappe Rubber twist grip Cuffia comando	1	1	1
17	51.02.021.000	Druckfeder mit Rändelschraube Pressure spring with screw for throttle tension Mola fermo con vite fermo acceleratore	1	1	1
18	54.02.018.000	Griffrohr Twist grip tube Manopola destra	1	1	1
118	54.02.118.000	**Gasdrehgriff — Kunststoff,** kpl. Twist grip — plastic, compl. Comando gas — plastica, compl.	1	1	1
19	51.02.019.000	Klemmschelle Drum — twist grip	1	1	1
119	54.02.019.000	**Drum — plastic**	**1**	**1**	1
20	51.02.020.000	Klemmschraube Screw Vite fermo comando	1	1	1
22	54.02.022.000	Handhebel Front brake lever — loose Leva freno	1	1	1
23	51.02.023.000	Gelenkstück Lever holder R/S Corpo comando freno	1	1	1
24	51.02.025.000	Rändelmutter, geschlitzt, mit Seilzug-Verstellschraube Split lock nut with cable adjuster Fermo registro con vite	2	2	2
26	51.02.026.000	Schutzkappe — Kunststoff, links Plastic cocer L/S Coprileva sinistra	1	1	1
27	51.02.027.000	Linsenschraube M 6x15 Flat head bolt M 6x15 Vite M 6x15	2	2	2
28	51.02.028.000	Hebelschraube Pivot pin Vite leva	2	2	2
29	265.000	Zahnscheibe J 6,4 DIN 6797 Lock washer J 6,4 DIN 6797 Rondella J 6,4 DIN 6797	2	2	2
30	M6	Sechskantmutter M 6 DIN 934 Hexagon nut M 6 DIN 934 Dado M 6 DIN 934	2	2	2
—	54.02.031.000	**Handbremshebel** kpl. Brake lever assy. R/S Comando compl., destro	1	1	1
—	54.02.040.000	**Kupplungshebel** kpl. Clutch lever assy. L/S Comando compl. sinistro	1	1	1
45	51.02.045.000	Gelenkstück Lever holder L/S Corpo comando frizione	1	1	1
52	51.02.052.000	Festgriff Rubber grip L/S Manopola sinistra	1	1	1
55	54.02.055.000	Kupplungshebel Clutch lever — loose Leva frizione	1	1	1

Gruppe 02: Lenker — Lenkerarmaturen
Group   02: Handlebar — controls
Gruppo 02: Manubrio — leve

Bild Picture Foto	Teil-Nr. Part-No. Parte-No.	Benennung Description Descrizione	Stk./Fzg. Pos./Machine Pezzi/Macch.		
			175	250	400
57	327.000	Lötnippelaufnahme Grease fitting Punto di attacco per saldataure	1	1	1
59	52.02.059.000	Luftregulierhebel kpl. Lever assy. — choke n Leva starter compl.	1	1	1
059	51.02.059.000	Dekompressorhebel kpl. Lever assy. — Decompressor Leva starter compl.	—	1	1
90	52.02.090.000	Kupplungsseilzug (Teflon) Clutch cable Cavo frizzione	1	1	1
91	54.02.091.000	Gasseilzug Throttle cable Cavo acceleratore	—	1	1
—	54.02.091.100	Gasseilzug für Kunststoffdrehgriff Throttle cable for plastic twist grip Cavo acceleratore per comando gas in plastica	—	1	1
—	52.02.091.000	Gasseilzug Throttle cable Cavo acceleratore	1	—	—
—	52.02.091.100	Gasseilzug für Kunststoffdrehgriff Throttle cable for plastic twist grip Cavo acceleratore per comando gas in plastica	1	—	—
92	52.02.092.000	Handbremsseilzug Front brake cable Cavo freno anteriore	1	1	1
—	52.02.092.100	Handbremsseilzug mit 8 mm Einstellschraube und mit Dichtmanschetten front brake cable with 8 mm adjusting screw and seal boots Cavo freno anteriore con 8 mm vite e con manicotto guarnizione	1	1	1
93	55.02.093.000	Deko-Seilzug Decompressor cable Cavo starter	—	1	1
95	54.02.095.000	Luftregulierseilzug Choke cable Cavo starter	—	1	1
—	52.02.095.000	Luftregulierseilzug Choke cable Amal Cavo starter	1	—	—
—	52.02.095.100	Choke cable Bing	1	—	—

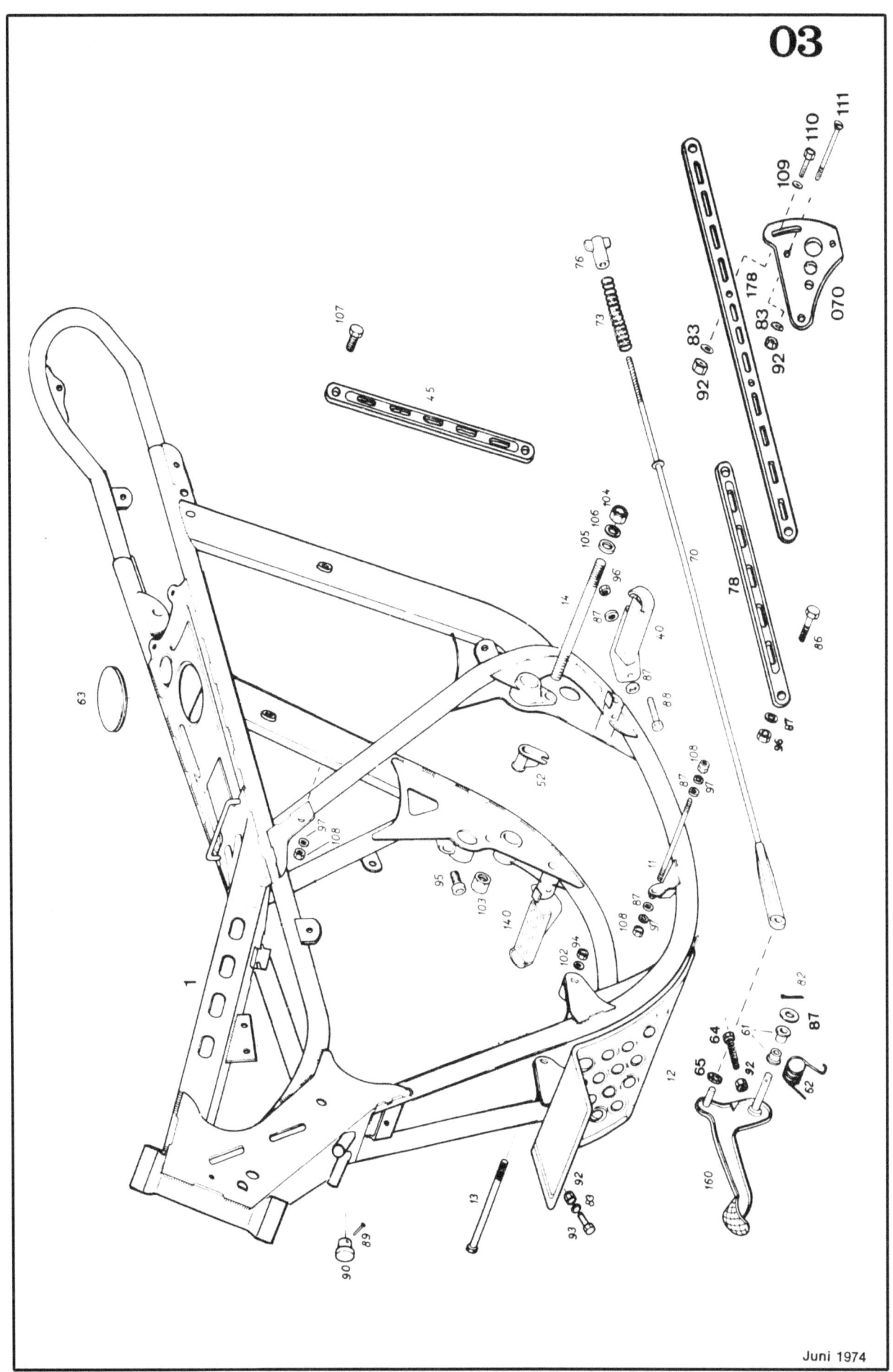

Gruppe 03: Rahmen, Fußrasten, Fußbremse
Group 03: Frame – footrests – rear brake
Gruppo 03: Telaio – pedane –freno posteriore

Bild / Picture / Foto	Teil-Nr. / Part-No. / Parte-No	Benennung / Description / Descrizione	Stk./Fzg. Pos./Machine Pezzi/Macch. 175	250	400
1	54.03.001.400	**Hauptrahmen** / Frame / Telaio	1	1	1
11	51.03.011.000	Gewindebolzen / Engine mount bolt – front / Peano motore anteriore	1	1	1
12	51.03.012.000	Steinschutzblech / Skid plate / Protezione motore	1	1	1
13	HH 10x160	Sechskantschraube M 10x160 DIN 931 / Hexagon head bolt M 10x160 DIN 931 / Vite M 10x160 DIN 931	1	1	1
14	51.03.014.000	Gewindebolzen / Engine mount bolt – rear / Peano motore posteriore	1	1	1
40	51.03.040.000	Fußraste links / Foot peg L/S / Pedana sinistra	1	1	1
140	51.03.140.000	Fußraste rechts / Foot peg R/S / Pedana destra	1	1	1
45	54.03.045.100	Motorstrebe (links und rechts) / Reinforcing bracket (R/S + L/S) / Sostegno	2	2	2
52	52.03.052.200	Distanzstück / Spacer / Distanziale	1	1	1
160	54.03.160.100	Bremspedal / Brake pedal / Pedana freno	1	1	1
61	31.03.061.000	Lagerbüchse / Nylon bushing / Boccola naylon	2	2	2
62	54.03.062.000	Drehfeder / Spring for brake pedal / Molla pedale freno	1	1	1
63	54.03.063.000	Verschlußkappe PVC / Plastic cap / Coperchio plastica	1	1	1
64	54.03.064.000	Bremshebelanschlag / Brake pedal stop bolt / Vite	1	1	1
65	54.03.065.000	Gummischeibe / Rubber washer / Rondella gomma	1	1	1
070	54.07.070.000	Kettenführungsstückhalterung / Plate / Sostegno	1	1	1
–	1.54.03.070.000	**Bremsstange** kpl. / Brake rod compl. / Asta freno compl.	1	1	1
70	54.03.070.000	Bremsstange lose / Brake rod – loose / Asta freno	1	1	1
73	51.03.073.000	Druckfeder / Pressure spring / Molla asta freno	1	1	1
76	51.03.076.000	Einstellmutter / Wing nut / Registro freno	1	1	1
78	54.03.078.400	GS-Zuganker hinten / Rear brake anchor rod – GS / Asta ferma mozzo – GS	1	1	1
178	54.03.178.400	MC-Zuganker hinten / Rear brake anchor rod – MC / Asta ferma mozzo – MC	1	1	1
82	PIN 1,5x12	Splint 1,5x12 DIN 94 / Pin 1,5x12 / Cupiglia 1,5x12	1	1	1

Gruppe 03: Rahmen, Fußrasten, Fußbremse
Group 03: Frame — footrests — rear brake
Gruppo 03: Telaio — pedane — freno posteriore

Bild / Picture / Foto	Teil-Nr. / Part-No. / Parte-No	Benennung / Description / Descrizione	175	250	400
83	265.000	Zahnscheibe J 6,4 / Lock washer J 6,4 / Rondella J 6,4	8	8	8
86	264.000	Sechskantschraube M 8x20 / Hexagon head bolt M 8x20 / Vite M 8x20	1	1	1
87	DIN 125/8.4	Scheibe 8,4 DIN 125 / Flat washer 8,4 DIN 125 / Rondella 8,4 DIN 125	7	7	7
88	HH 8x40	Sechskantschraube M 8x40 / Hexagon head bolt M 8x40 / Vite M 8x40	2	2	2
89	51.03.089.000	Stahlnagel 2x16 / Steel nail 2x16 / Spina 2x16	2	2	2
90	51.03.090.000	PVC-Gabelanschlag / Fork stop bumper / Fermasterzo gomma	2	2	2
92	M6	Sechskantmutter M 6 DIN 934 / Hexagon nut M 6 DIN 934 / Dado M 6 DIN 934	9	9	9
93	HH 6x10	Sechskantschraube M 6x10 DIN 933 / Hexagon head bolt M 6x10 DIN 933 / Vite M 6x10 DIN 933	4	4	4
94	M10	Sechskantmutter M 10 DIN 934 / Hexagon nut M 10 DIN 934 / Dado M 10 DIN 934	1	1	1
95	246.000	Innensechskantschraube M 10x30 DIN 912 / Allen head screw M 10x30 DIN 912 / Vite fermo forcellone M 10x30 DIN 912	1	1	1
96	259.000	SS-Mutter M 8 DIN 985-53 / self-locking nut M 8 DIN 985-53 / Dado M 8 DIN 985-53	3	3	3
97	275.000	Zahnscheibe J 8,4 DIN 6797 / Lock washer J 8,4 DIN 6797 / Rondella J 8,4 DIN 6797	4	4	4
102	LW 10,5	Zahnscheibe J 10,5 DIN 6797 / Lock washer J 10,5 DIN 6797 / Rondella J 10,5 DIN 6797	1	1	1
103	M12	Sechskantmutter M 12 DIN 934 / Hexagon nut M 12 DIN 934 / Dado M 12 DIN 934	1	1	1
104	637.000	SS-Mutter M 12 DIN 985 / Self-locking nut M 12 DIN 985 / Dado M 12 DIN 985	2	2	2
105	FW 12,5	Scheibe 12,5 DIN 125 / Flat washer 12,5 DIN 125 / Rondella 12,5 DIN 125	2	2	2
106	LW 12,5	Zahnscheibe J 12,5 / Lock washer J 12,5 / Rondella J 12,5	2	2	2
107	HH 8x15	Sechskantschraube M 8x15 DIN 933 / Hexagon head bolt M 8x15 DIN 933 / Vite M 8x15 DIN 933	3	3	3
108	M8	Sechskantmutter M 8 DIN 934 / Hexaggon nut M 8 DIN 934 / Dado M 8 DIN 934	1	1	1
109	DIN 125/6.4	Scheibe 6,4 DIN 125 / Flat washer 6,4 DIN 125 / Rondella 6,4	1	1	1
110	279.000	Sechskantschraube M 6x20 DIN 933 / Hexagon head bolt 6x20 DIN 933 / Vite M 6x20 DIN 933	1	1	1
111	260.000	Senkkopfschraube M 6x50 DIN 604 / Flat head bolt 6x50 DIN 604 / Vite M 6x50 DIN 604	2	2	2

03a

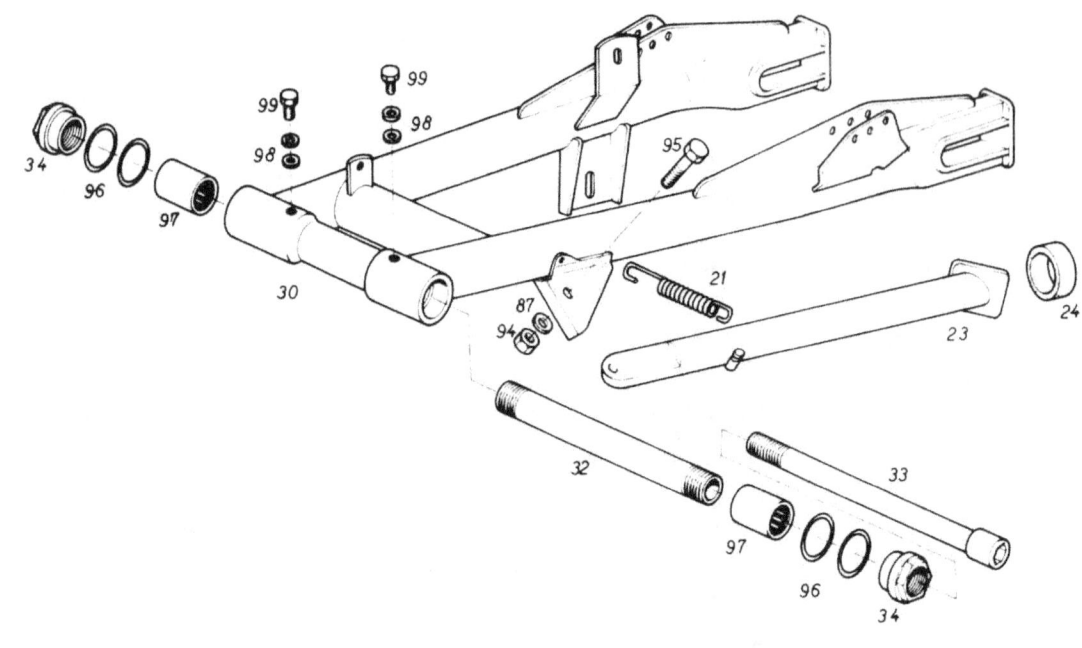

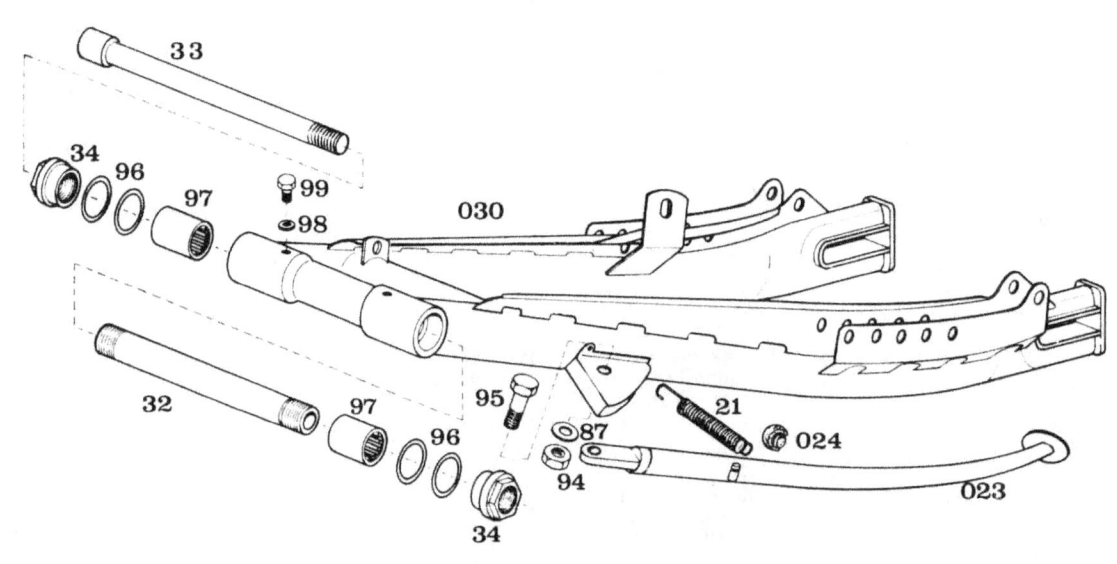

Juni 1974

Gruppe 03a: Schwingarm — Seitenständer
Group 03a: Swingarm — side stand
Gruppo 03a: Forcellone — cavaletto laterale

Bild / Picture / Foto	Teil-Nr. / Part-No. / Parte-No.	Benennung / Description / Descrizione	Stk./Fzg. Pos./Machine Pezzi/Macch. 175	250	400
21	31.03.021.000	Ständerfeder / Side stand spring / Molla cavalletto	1	1	1
23	51.03.023.300	**Seitenständer** kpl. / Side stand compl. / Cavalletto laterale compl.	1	1	–
24	51.03.024.300	Anschlaggummi / Rubber stop / Gomma	1	1	–
–	1.54.03.030.000	**Schwingarm kpl. montiert** / Swingarm compl. mounted / Forcellone compl.	1	1	–
30	54.03.030.000	Schwingarm lose / Swingarm – loose / Forcellone	1	1	–
32	54.03.032.000	Lagerhülse / Bearing sleeve / Copricuscinetto	1	1	1
33	51.03.033.000	Schwingarmbolzen / Swingarm bolt / Perno forcellone	1	1	1
34	54.03.034.000	Einstellmutter / Adjustment nut / Dado di regolazione	2	2	2
87	DIN 125/8.4	Scheibe 8,4 / Flat washer 8,4 / Rondella 8,4	1	1	1
96	Parker 2-214	O-Ring / O-ring / Anello O	4	4	4
97	HK 2030	Nadelhülse / Needle cage / Copriago	2	2	2
98	54.03.098.000	Alu-Dichtring / Aluminium seal ring / Guarnizione aluminium	2	2	2
99	HH 6x8	Sechskantschraube M 6x8 / Hexaggon head bolt M 6x8 / Vite M 6x8	2	2	2
--	1.54.03.030.300	**Schwingarm kpl. montiert** (Neue Ausführung) / Swingarm compl. monted (new execution) / Forcellone compl. (nuovo)	1	1	1
030	54.03.030.300	Schwingarm lose (neue Ausführung) / Swingarm – loose (new execution) / Forcellone (nuovo tipo)	1	1	1
023	54.03.023.000	**Seitenständer** (neue Ausführung) / Side stand (new execution) / Cavalletto laterale (nuovo tipo)	1	1	1
024	51.03.024.500	Anschlaggummi (neue Ausführung) / Rubber stop (new execution) / Gomma	1	1	1
94	259.000	SS-Mutter M 8 / Self-locking nut M 8 / Dado M 8 SS	1	1	1
95	HH 8x25	Sechskantschraube M 8x25/10 / Hexagon head bolt M 8x25/10 / Vite M 8x25/10	1	1	1

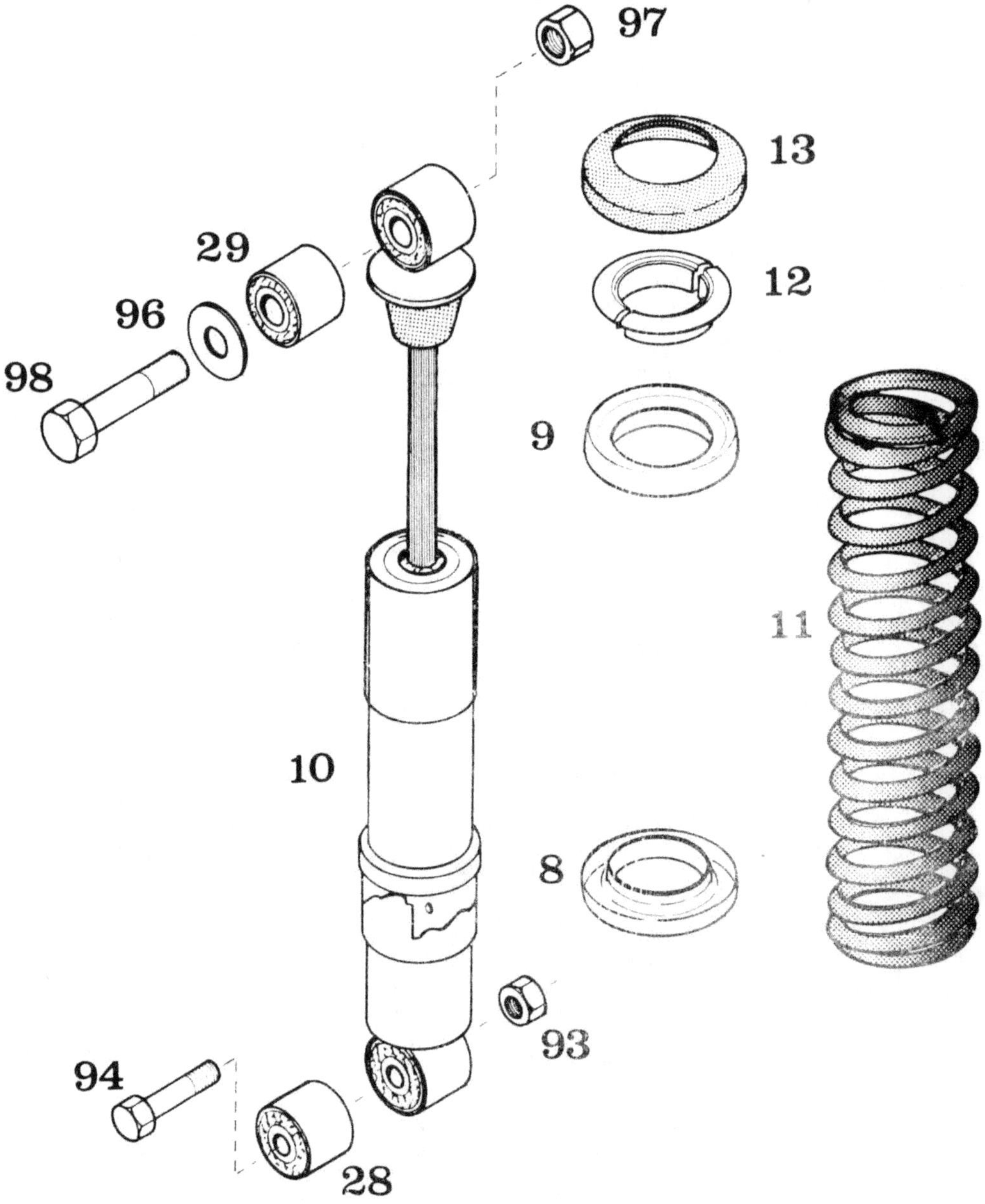

04

Gruppe 04: Federbeine
Group 04: Shock absorbers
Gruppo 04: Amortizzatori

Bild / Picture / Foto	Teil-Nr. / Part-No. / Parte No	Benennung / Description / Descrizione	Stk./Fzg. Pos./Machine Pezzi/Macch. 175	250	400
10	54.04.010.000	**Federbein kpl.** (Ceriani-Gasdruck) Rear shock assy. Spec. 90 lb. or 120 lb. Ammortizzatore cpl.	2	2	2
11	54.04.011.100	Feder 7,2 ⌀, schwarz Spring 7,2 ⌀, black Molla 7,2 ⌀, nero	2	2	2
—	54.04.011.200	Feder 7,4 ⌀, rot Spring 7,4 ⌀, red Molla 7,4 ⌀, rosso	nach Bedarf on demand		
—	54.04.011.300	Feder 7,5 ⌀, silber Spring 7,5 ⌀, silver Molla 7,5 ⌀, argento	nach Bedarf on demand		
—	54.04.011.400	Feder 7,6 ⌀, gelb Spring 7,6 ⌀, yellow Molla 7,6 ⌀, giallo	nach Bedarf on demand		
—	54.04.011.500	Feder 7,8 ⌀, dunkelgrau Spring 7,8 ⌀, dark grey Molla 7,8 ⌀	nach Bedarf on demand		
8	54.04.008.000	Federteller unten Spring cup — lower Scodellino per molla inferiore	2	2	2
9	54.04.009.000	Federteller oben Spring cup — upper Scodellino per molla superiore	2	2	2
12	54.04.012.000	Keil Spring holder Chiavetta	4	4	4
13	54.04.013.000	Plastikschutzkappe Dirt shield Piastra di protezione in plastica	2	2	2
28	54.04.028.000	Silentblock unten Lower bushing Silenblock	2	2	2
29	54.04.029.000	Silentblock oben Upper bushing Silenblock	2	2	2
93	259.000	SS-Sechskantmutter M 8 DIN 995 Self-locking nut M 8 995 Dado M 8 DIN 995	2	2	2
94	HH 8x35	Sechskantschraube M 8x35 DIN 931 Hexaggon head bolt M 8x35 DIN 931 Vite M 8x35 DIN 931	2	2	2
96	FW 10,5	Scheibe 10,5 DIN 9021 Flat washer 10,5 DIN 9021 Rondella piama 10,5 DIN 9021	2	2	2
97	269.000	SS-Sechskantmutter M 10 DIN 934 Self-locking nut M 10 DIN 934 Dado M 10 DIN 934	2	2	2
98	HH 10x65	Sechskantschraube M 10x55 DIN 931 Hexagon head bolt M 10x55 DIN 931 Vite M 10x55 DIN 931	2	2	2

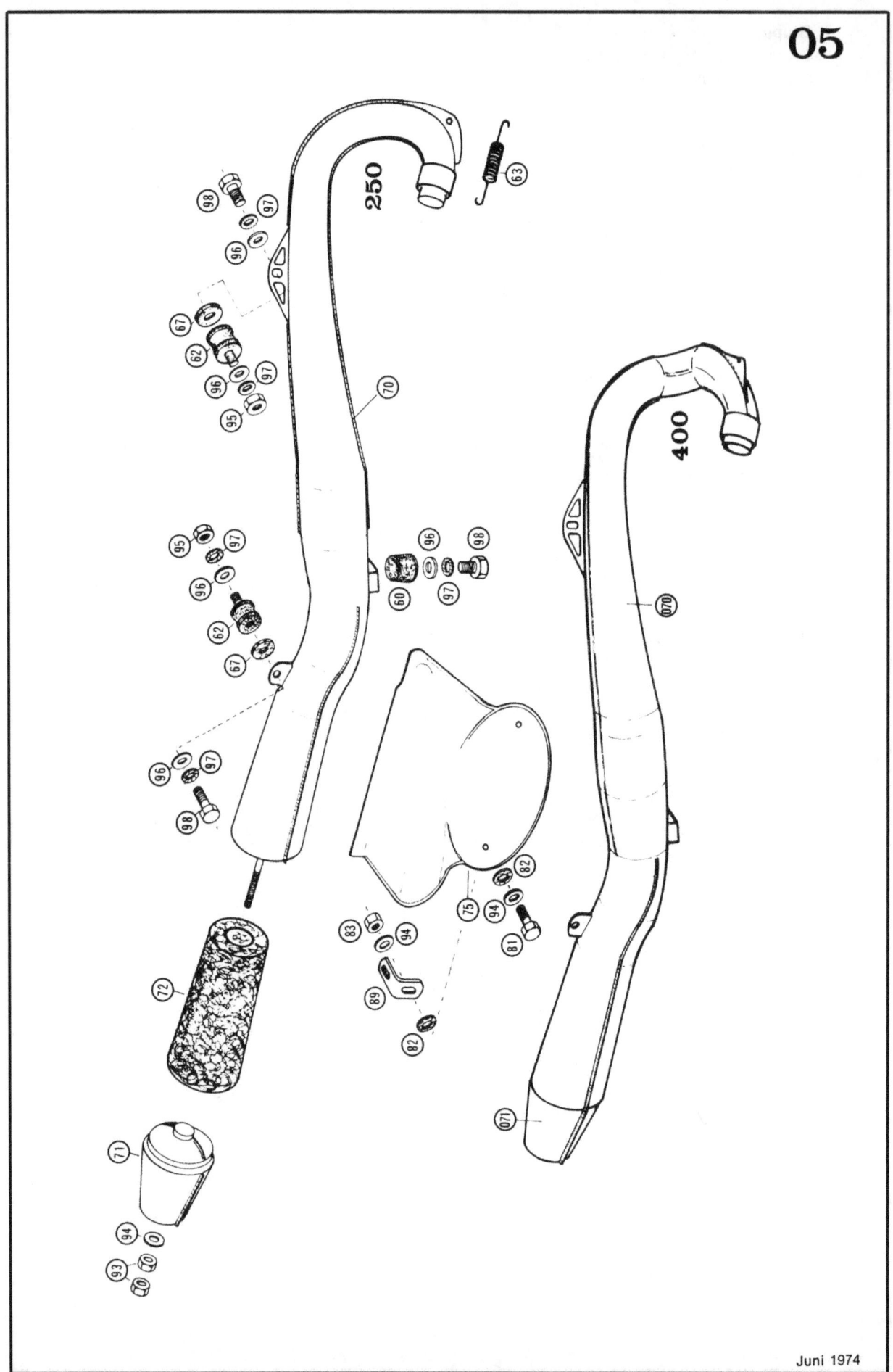

05

Juni 1974

Gruppe 05: Auspuffanlage
Group 05: Exhaust system
Gruppo 05: Tubo scarico

Bild / Picture / Foto	Teil-Nr. / Part-No. / Parte No	Benennung / Description / Descrizione	Stk./Fzg. Pos./Machine Pezzi/Macch. 175
70	52.05.070.300	Distanzbüchse GS exhaust compl. (with muffler end) GS tubo scarico compl. (con coda tubo scarico)	1
62	51.05.062.000	Gummiblock Rubber grommet Gomma marmitta	3
63	51.05.063.000	Auspuffeder Exhaust spring Molla marmitta	2
71	52.05.071.100	Auspuffendkappe Muffler end Coda turbo scarico	1
72		Glaswollfüllung Fiber glass packing Silenziatore in lana di vetro	1
73	52.05.073.000	Auspufflansch Exhaust flange Fflangia tubo scarico	1
75	51.05.075.100	△ GS Auspuffverkleidung △ GS Exhaust heat guard △ GS mascerina di protezione	1
80	260.000	Sechskantschraube M 6x50 Hexagon head bolt M 6x50 Vite M 6x50	1
81	263.000	Sechskantschraube M 6x25 Hexagon heat bolt M 6x25 Vite M 6x25	1
82	510.000	Gummischeibe Rubber washer Rondella gomma	4
83	261.000	SS-Sechskantmutter M 6 Self-locking nut M 6 Dado M 6	2
88	54.06.088.000	Distanzbüchse Spacer Distanziale	1
93	M6	Sechskantmutter M 6 DIN 985 Hexagon nut M 6 DIN 985 Dado M 6 DIN 985	3
94	DIN 125/6.4	Scheibe 6,4 DIN 125 Flat washer 6,4 DIN 125 Rondella 6,4 DIN 125	3
95	M8	Sechskantmutter M 8 Hexagon nut M 8 Dado M 8	3
96	DIN 125/8.4	Scheibe 8,4 DIN 125 Flat washer 8,4 DIN 125 Rondella 8,4 DIN 125	6
97	275.000	Zahnscheibe J 8,4 DIN 6797 Lock washer J 8,4 DIN 6797 Rondella J 8,4 DIN 6797	6
98	HH 8x10	Sechskantschraube M 8x10 Hexagon head screw M 8x10 Vite M 8x10	3

△ Bitte Farbe angeben / Please quote colour / Colore?

Gruppe 05: Auspuffanlage
Group 05: Exhaust system
Gruppo 05: Tubo scarico

Bild / Picture / Foto	Teil-Nr. / Part-No. / Parte No	Benennung / Description / Descrizione	Stk./Fzg. Pos./Machine Pezzi/Macch. 250	400
—	54.05.170.400	**MC Auspuffanlage kpl.** MC Exhaust compl. MC Tubo scarico compl.	1	—
70	54.05.070.400	**GS Auspuffanlage kpl.** (mit Endkappe) Exhaust compl. (with muffler end) GS Tubo scarico compl. (con coda tubo scarico)	1	—
—	55.05.170.400	**MC Auspuffanlage kpl.** (mit Nachschalldämpfer) MC Exhaust compl. MC Tubo scarico compl.	—	1
070	55.05.070.400	**GS Auspuffanlage kpl.** (mit Endkappe) GS Exhaust compl. (with muffler end) GS Tubo scarico compl. (con coda tubo scarico)	—	1
60	54.05.060.000	Gummiblock Rubber grommet Gomma marmitta	1	1
62	51.05.062.000	Gummiblock Rubber grommet Gomma marmitta	2	2
63	54.05.063.000	Auspuffeder Exhaust spring Molla marmitta	1	1
67	51.05.067.000	Wärmeableitscheibe Gasket washer Disco dissipazione calore	3	3
71	54.05.071.400	GS Auspuffendkappe GS Exhaust muffler end GS Coda tubo scarico	1	—
071	55.05.071.400	GS Auspuffendkappe GS Exhaust muffler end GS Coda tubo scarico	—	1
—	54.05.171.400	MC Endkappe für Nachschalldämpfer MC Exhaust muffler end MC Coda tubo scarico	1	1
75	54.05.075.400	△ GS Auspuffverkleidung △ GS Exhaust heat guard △ GS Mascerina di protezione	1	1
—	54.05.175.400	△ MC Auspuffverkleidung △ MC Exhaust heat guard △ MC Mascerina di protezione	1	1
81	263.000	Sechskantschraube M 6x25 Hexagon head bolt 6x25 Vite M 6x25	2	2
82	510.000	Gummischeibe Rubber washer Rondella gomma	4	4
83	261.000	SS-Sechskantmutter M 6 Self-locking nut M 6 Dado M 6	2	2
89	54.06.089.000	Aufhängung für Auspuffverkleidung Exhaust heat guard bracket Sospensione per rivestimento tubo di scarico	1	1
93	M6	Sechskantmutter M 6 Hexagon nut M 6 Dado M 6	3	3
94	DIN 125/6.4	Scheibe 6,4 DIN 125 Flat washer 6,4 DIN 125 Rondella 6,4 DIN 125	5	5
95	M8	Sechskantmutter M 8 Hexagon nut M 8 Dado M 8	2	2
96	DIN 125/8.4	Scheibe 8,4 Flat washer 8,4 Rondella 8,4	5	5
97	275.000	Zahnscheibe 8,4 Lock washer 8.4 Rondella 8,4	5	5
98	HH 8x10	Sechskantschraube M 8x10 Hexagon head bolt M 8x10 Vite M 8x10	3	3

△ Bitte Farbe angeben / Please quote colour / Colore?

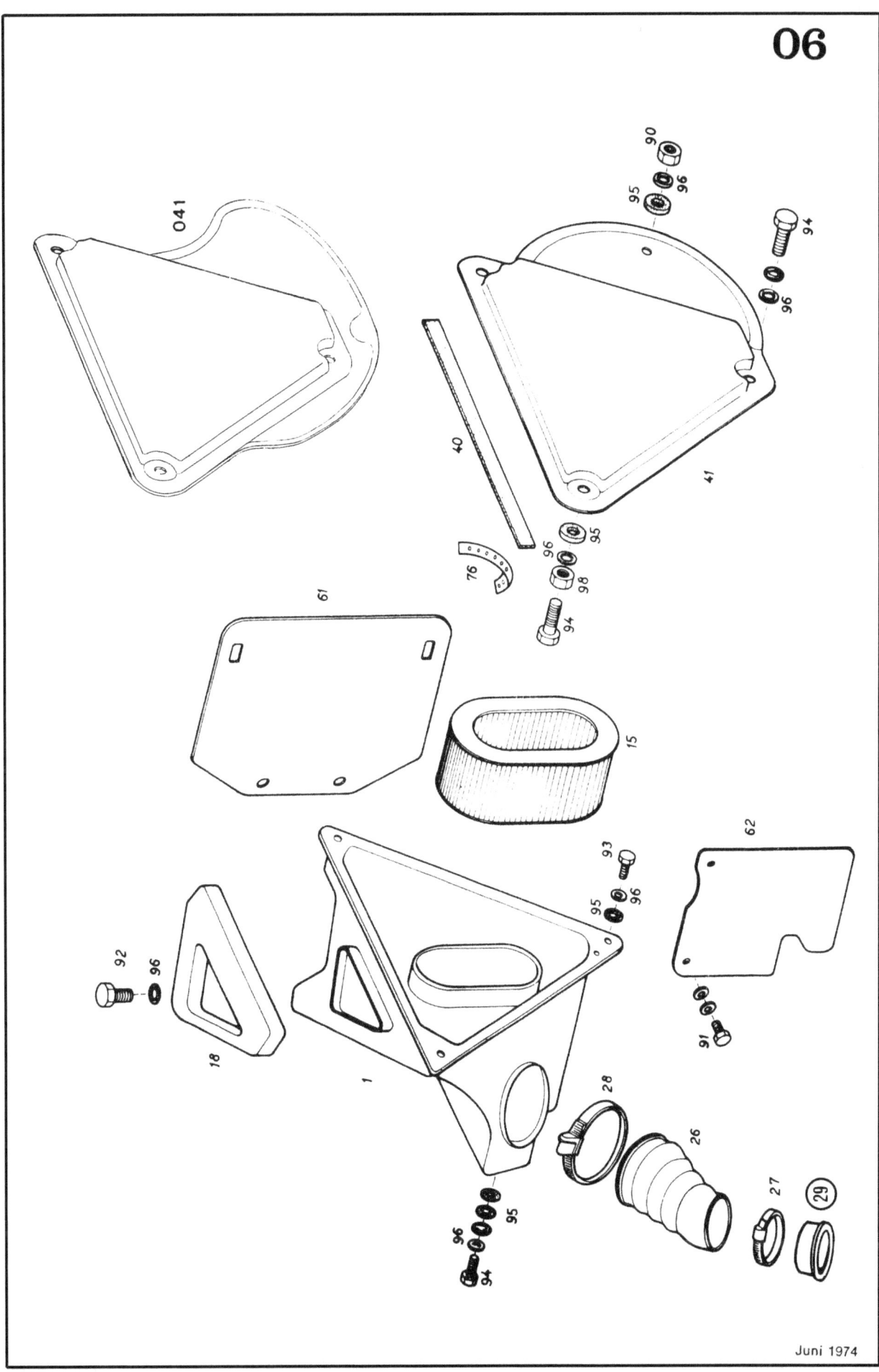

Gruppe 06: Filterkasten
Group 06: Airfilter box
Gruppo 06: Cassetta del filtro

Bild / Picture / Foto	Teil-Nr. / Part-No. / Parte No	Benennung / Description / Descrizione	Stk./Fzg. Pos./Machine Pezzi/Macch. 175	250	400
—	1.54.06.001.100	△ Filterkasten kpl. △ Airfilter box cpl. △ Cassetta del filtro compl.	1	1	1
1	54.06.001.000	△ Filterkasten lose △ Airfilter box loose △ Cassetta del filtro	1	1	1
15	54.06.015.000	**Filterpatrone** (Schaumstoff) Airfilter Filtro	1	1	1
18	54.06.018.000	Dichtung für Filterkasten Foam rubber seal Fuarnizione per cassa filtro	1	1	1
26	51.06.026.200	Luftfiltermanschette Airfilter boot Gomma carburatore filtro	1	1	1
27	51.06.027.000	Schlauchbinder A 6 Clamp A 6 Fascetta A 6	1	1	1
28	51.06.028.000	Schlauchbinder A 7 Clamp A 7 Fascetta A 7	1	1	1
29	52.06.029.000	Zwischenring für Ansaugmanschette Rubber bushing Gomma Carburatore	1	—	—
40	51.06.040.000	Filterkastendichtung Rubber gasket Guarnizione coperchio filtro	1	1	1
041	54.06.041.100	△ Filterkastendeckel f. Rahmen 54.03.001.400 △ Airfilter cover △ Coperchio filtro laterale	1	1	1
61	51.06.061.300	Spritzlappen oben Mud flap — upper Pattella gomma zup.	1	1	1
62	51.06.062.000	Spritzlappen unten Mud flap — lower Pattella gomma sot.	1	1	1
76	51.06.076.000	Kabelband mit PVC-Nagel Plastic band Fascetta in gomma	2	2	2
90	261.000	SS-Mutter M 6 DIN 985 Self-locking nut M 6 DIN 985 Dado M 6 DIN 985	2	2	2
91	HH 6x10	Sechskantschraube M 6x10 DIN 933 Hexagon head bolt M 6x10 DIN 933 Vite M 6x10 DIN 933	2	2	2
93	274.000	Sechskantschraube M 6x20 DIN 933 Hexagon head bolt M 6x20 DIN 933 Vite M 6x20 DIN 933	2	2	2
94	263.000	Sechskantschraube M 6x25 DIN 933 Hexagon head bolt M 6x25 DIN 933 Vite 6x25 DIN 933	4	4	4
95	510.000	Gummischeibe Rubber washer Rondella gomma	11	11	11
96	DIN 125/6.4	Scheibe 6,4 DIN 125 Flat washer 6,4 DIN 125 Rondella 6,4 DIN 125	12	12	12
98	M6	Sechskantmutter M 6 Hexagon nut M 6 Dado M 6	4	4	4

△ Bitte Farbe angeben / Please quote colour / Colore?

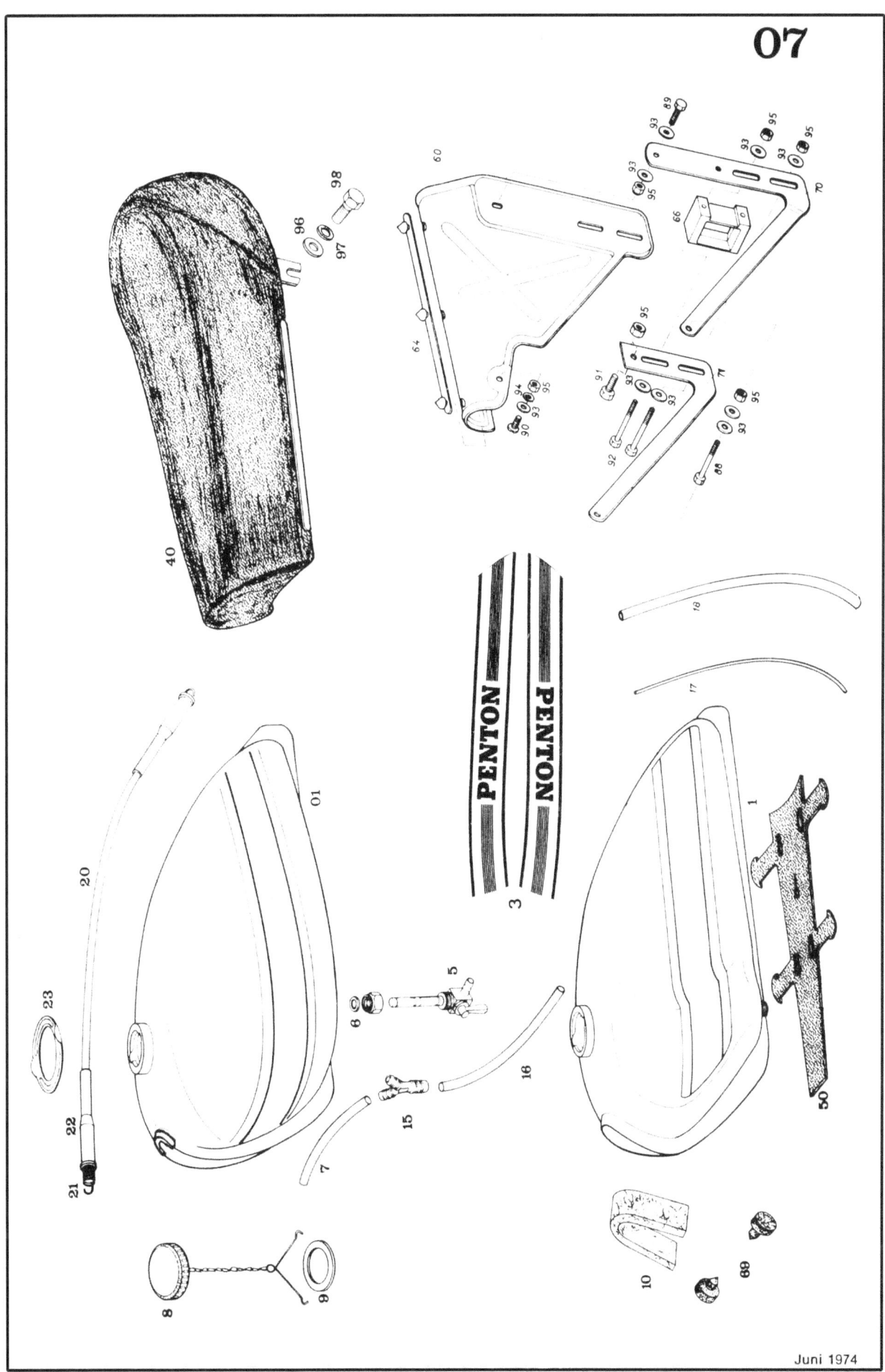

Gruppe 07: Tank, Sitzbank, Kettenschutz
Group 07: Gastank, seat, chain guard
Gruppo 07: Serbatoio, sella, carter, catena

Bild Picture Foto	Teil-Nr. Part-No. Parte No	Benennung Description Descrizione	Stk./Fzg. Pos./Mach. Pezzi/Macch. 175	250	400
01	52.07.001.400	△ Kraftstoffbehälter GS (mit Anschlag) △ Gastank GS △ Serbatoio GS	1	1	1
1	52.07.001.100	△ Kraftstoffbehälter MC (mit Anschlag) △ Gastank MC △ Serbatoio MC	1	1	1
3	54.07.003.000 54.07.003.100	Gastank decal set „PENTON" White Gastank decal set „PENTON" Black	1	1	1
103	54.07.003.200	Decal on Tank Seam	1	1	1
5	31.07.005.000	Kraftstoffhahn kpl. Gas tap cpl. Rubinetto cpl.	2	2	2
6	31.07.006.000	Dichtung für Kraftstoffhahn Washer – fiber Guarnizione rubinetto	2	2	2
7	31.07.007.000	Kraftstoffschlauch Fuel line Tubo benzina	3	3	3
8	51.07.008.000	Tankverschluß mit Kette Gas cap with chain Tappo benzina	1	1	1
9	51.07.009.000	Dichtung für Tankverschluß Gasket for gas cap Guarnizione tappo	2	2	2
10	51.07.010.000	Filzunterlage Felt pad Tampone feltro	2	2	2
15	52.07.015.300	Y-Stück 6x6x8 Y-connector Raccordo tubo benzina	1	1	1
16	52.07.016.000	Kraftstoffschlauch Fuel line Tubo benzina	1	1	1
17	52.07.017.000	Entlüftungsschlauch für Vergaser Breather hose for carburettor Tubo	1	1	1
18	52.07.018.000	Entlüftungsschlauch für Getriebe Breather hose for transmission Tubo	1	1	1
20	51.07.020.000	Tankhaltekabel Gastank retaining cable Cavo serbatoio	2	2	2
21	51.07.021.000	Zugfeder Spring Molla	4	4	4
22	51.07.022.000	Kabelmanschette Gastank cable boot Manicotto per cavo serbatoio	4	4	4
23	51.07.023.000	Kabelführung Cable guide Guidacavo	1	1	1
40	52.07.040.400	Sitzbank To use with 54.08.014.400 M-X Seat Sella To use with 54.08.013.400 Enduro	1	1	1

△ Bitte Farbe angeben / Please quote colour / Colore?

Gruppe 07: Tank, Sitzbank, Kettenschutz
Group 07: Gastank, seat, chain guard
Gruppo 07: Serbatoio, sella, carter, catena

Bild / Picture / Foto	Teil-Nr. / Part-No. / Parte No	Benennung / Description / Descrizione	Stk./Fzg. Pos./Mach. Pezzi/Macch. 175	250	400
—	52.07.040.450	Sitzbanküberzug zu 52.07.040.400 / Seat cover / Fodera sella	1	1	1
50	51.07.050.000	Spritzlappen vorne / Mudflap — front / Patella gomma	1	1	1
60	54.07.060.000	Kettenschutz / Chain guard / Carter catena	1	1	1
64	51.07.064.000	PVC-Kettenauflauf / Rubber chain guard / Gomma ripara carter	1	1	1
66	51.07.066.200	Kettenführungsstück / Chain guard / Gomma catena	1	1	1
69	51.07.069.100	Gummipuffer für Tank / Rubber bushing for gastank / Tamponi di gomma per serbatoio	2	2	2
70	51.07.070.300	Bügel für Kettenführung innen / Chain guide bracket — inside / Protezione guida catena — interna	1	1	1
71	51.07.071.400	Bügel für Kettenführung außen / Chain guide bracket — outside / Protezione guida catena — interna	1	1	1
88	260.000	Sechskantschraube M 6x50 DIN 931 / Hexagon head bolt 6x50 DIN 931 / Vite M 6x50 DIN 931	1	1	1
89	HH 6x18	Sechskantschraube M 6x18 / Hexagon head bolt M 6x18 / Vite M 6x18	1	1	1
90	FH 6x10	Linsenschraube M 6x10 / Flat head screw M 6x10 / Vite M 6x10	1	1	1
91	HH 6x12	Sechskantschraube M 6x12 / Hexagon head bold M 6x12 / Vite M 6x12	1	1	1
92	HH 6x60	Sechskantschraube M 6x60 / Hexagon head bolt M 6x60 / Vite M 6x60	2	2	2
93	DIN 125/6.4	Scheibe 6,4 DIN 125 / Flat washer 6,4 DIN 125 / Rondella 6,4 DIN 125	9	9	9
94	265.000	Zahnscheibe J 6,4 / Lock washer J 6,4 / Rondella J 6,4	6	6	6
95	M6	Sechskantmutter M 6 DIN 934 / Hexagon nut M 6 DIN 934 / Dado M 6 DIN 934	6	6	6
96	DIN 125/8.4	Scheibe 8,4 DIN 125 / Flat washer 8,4 DIN 125 / Rondella 8,4 DIN 125	4	4	4
97	275.000	Zahnscheibe J 8,4 DIN 6797 / Lock washer J 8,4 DIN 6797 / Rondella J 8,4 DIN 6797	3	3	3
98	264.000	Sechskantschraube M 8x20 / Hexagon head bolt M 8x20 / Vite M 8x20	3	3	3
—	51.07.011.000	Lederriemen für Tankbefestigung / Leather strap cpl. / Cinghia serbatoio cpl.	1	1	1

08

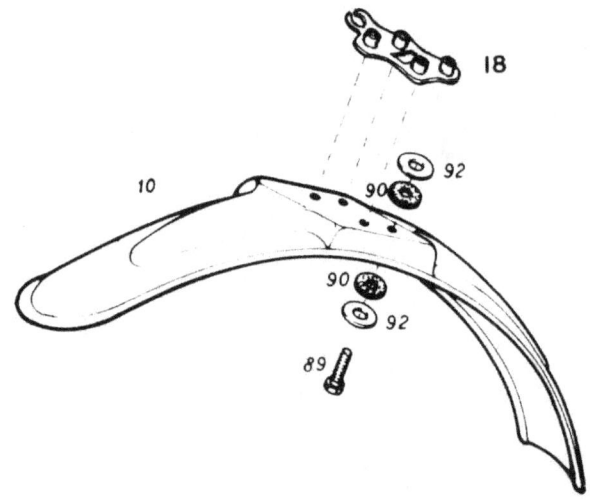

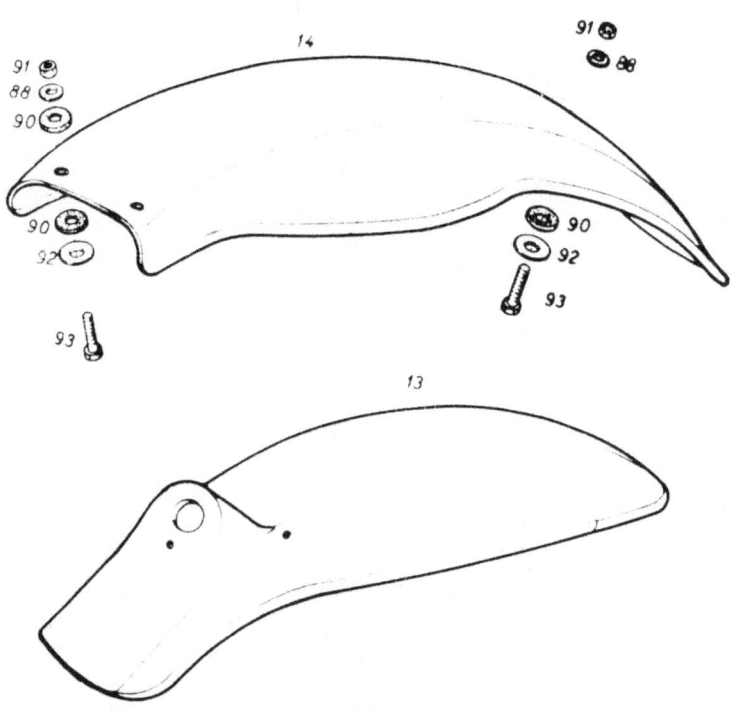

Juni 1974

Gruppe 08: Schutzbleche
Group 08: Fenders
Gruppo 08: Parafanghi

Bild Picture Foto	Teil-Nr. Part-No. Parte No	Benennung Description Descrizione	Stk./Fzg. Pos./Machine Pezzi/Macch.		
			175	250	400
10	54.08.010.000	**Vorderradschutzblech** Front fender Parafango anteriore	1	1	1
13	54.08.013.400	**GS Schutzblech hinten** GS Rear fender GS Parafango posteriore	1	1	1
14	54.08.014.400	**MC Schutzblech hinten** MC Rear fender MC Parafango posteriore	1	1	1
18	54.08.018.000	Distanzstück und Tachowellenführung Spacer for speedo shaft guide Distanziale	1	1	1
88	DIN 125/6.4	Scheibe 6,4 DIN 125 Flat washer 6,4 DIN 125 Rondella 6,4 DIN 125	4	4	4
89	HH 6x30	Sechskantschraube M 6x30 Hexagon head bolt M 6x30 Vite M 6x30	4	4	4
90	510.000	Gummibeilagscheibe Rubber washer Rondella gomma	14	14	14
91	261.000	SS-Mutter M 6 Self-locking nut M6 Dado M 6	4	4	4
92	DIN 125/6.4	Scheibe 6,4 Flat washer 6,4 Rondella 6,4	8	8	8
93	HH 6x15	Sechskantschraube M 6x15 Hexagon head bolt M 6x15 Vite M 6x15	4	4	4

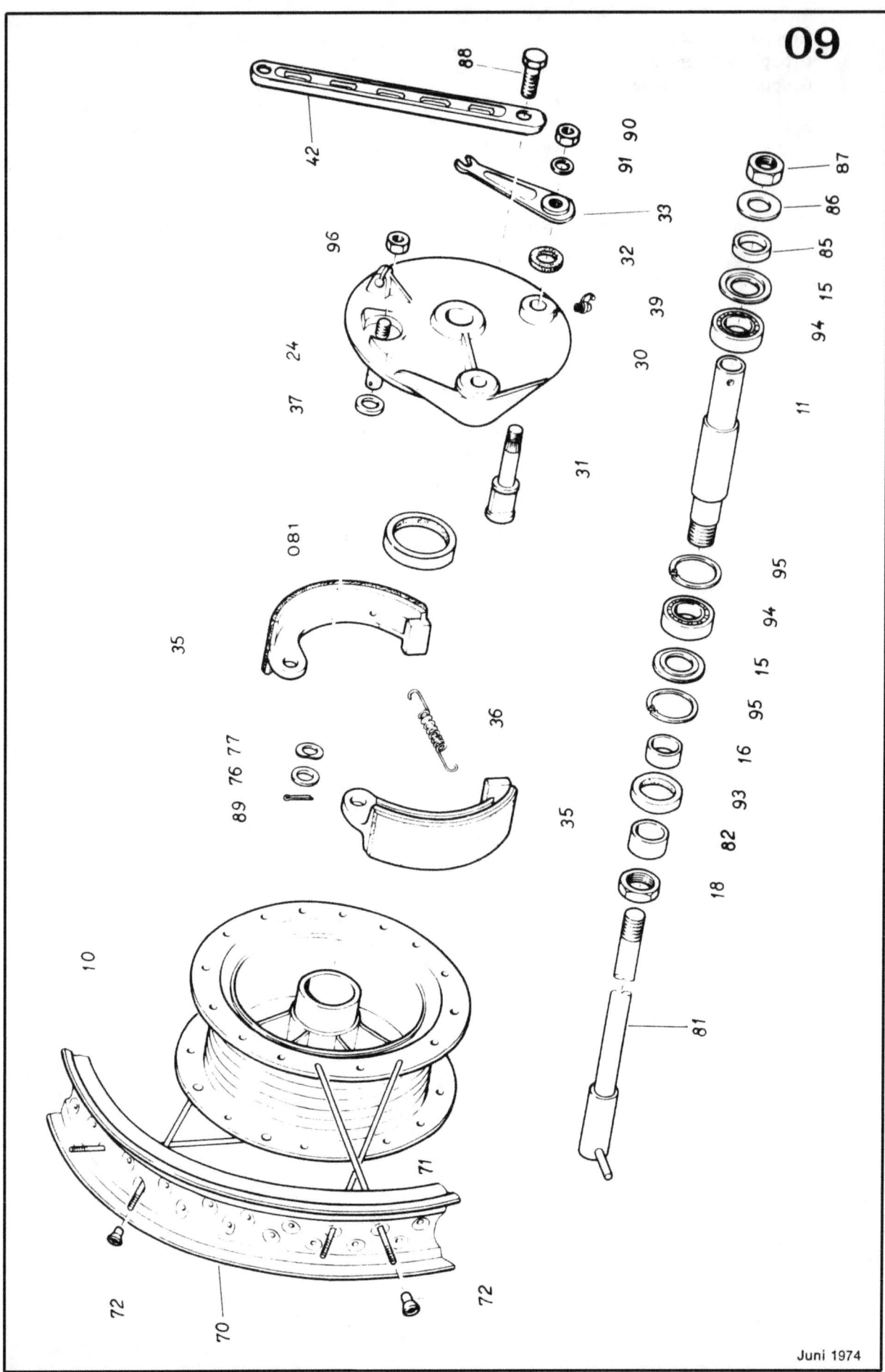

09

Juni 1974

Gruppe 09: Vorderrad
Group 09: Front wheel
Gruppo 09: Ruota anteriore

Bild / Picture / Foto	Teil-Nr. / Part-No. / Parte No	Benennung / Description / Descrizione	175	250	400
—	1.52.09.001.400	**Vorderrad kpl., ohne Bereifung** (m. Dickendspeichen u. Alu-Hochschulterfelge) Front wheel cpl., without tyre Ruota anteriore, senza gomma	1	1	1
—	1.51.09.002.400	**Vorderradnabe kpl.** Front hub compl. Mozzo anteriore compl.	1	1	1
10	51.09.010.400	Nabenkörper Front hub — loose Corpo mozzo	1	1	1
11	51.09.011.300	Hohlachse Spacer tube Distanziale cuscinetti	1	1	1
15	31.09.015.000	Nilosring 6003 AV Dust cover 6003 AV Anello gomma 6003 AV	2	2	2
16	31.09.016.000	Distanzbüchse für Simmerring Bushing forseal Distanziale paraolio	1	1	1
18	31.09.018.000	Sechskantmutter (auf einer Seite kegelförmig) Hexagon nut Dado	1	1	1
24	51.10.024.300	Ankerschraube Anchor bolt Vite	1	1	1
—	1.51.09.030.400	**Bremsankerdeckel vorne, kpl.** Bracke anchor plate front, cpl. Cartella portaceppi ant., cpl.	1	1	1
30	51.09.030.300	**Bremsankerdeckel vorne,** lose Brake anchor plate front, loose Cartella portaceppi, anteriore	1	1	1
31	31.09.031.000	Bremsnocke Cam Camme	1	1	1
32	31.09.032.000	PVC-Dichtring Plastic seal Guarnizione	1	1	1
33	51.09.033.100	Nabenbremshebel vorne Brake arm — front hub Leva freno mozzo	1	1	1
35	31.09.035.000	Bremsbacke kpl. Brake shoe compl. Ceppi freno compl.	2	2	2
36	31.09.036.100	Bremsbackenfeder (verstärkt) Return spring for brake shoes Molla	1	1	1
37	31.09.037.000	Scheibe Flat washer Rondella	1	1	1
39	31.09.039.000	Plastikschmiernippel Grease fitting Ingrassatore	1	1	1
42	54.09.042.400	Bremszuganker vorne Front rbake anchor Asta fermamozzo	1	1	1
70	54.09.070.000	Aluminium-Felge 21 " (Hochschulter) Aluminium rim 21 " Cerchio aluminium 21 "	1	1	1

Gruppe 09: Vorderrad
Group 09: Front wheel
Gruppo 09: Ruota anteriore

Bild / Picture / Foto	Teil-Nr. / Part-No. / Parte No	Benennung / Description / Descrizione	Stk./Fzg. Pos./Machine Pezzi/Macch. 175	250	400
71	51.09.071.400	Ein-Dickend-Speiche 3,5x225 mm, innen Spoke 3,5x225 mm – inner Raggio 3,5x225 mm – interiore	18	18	18
–	51.09.171.400	Ein-Dickend-Speiche 3,5x225 mm, außen Spoke 3,5x225 mm – outer Raggio 3,5x225 mm – exteriore	18	18	18
72	51.09.072.400	Nippel Nipple Niple	36	36	36
–	51.09.073.000	Felgenband Rim band Flap	1	1	1
–	51.09.074.000	Reifen 3.00x21" Tyre 3.00x21" Gomma 3.00x21"	1	1	1
–	51.09.075.000	Schlauch 3.00x21" Tube 3.00x21" Camera d'aria 3.00x21"	1	1	1
76	54.09.076.000	Scheibe 12x18x0,5 Flat washer 12x18x0,5 Rondella 12x18x0,5	1	1	1
77	54.09.077.000	Federscheibe 12 ⌀ Spring washer 12 ⌀ Rondella 12 ⌀	1	1	1
81	52.09.081.100	Steckachse vorne, kpl. Axle for front hub, cpl. Perno ruota anteriore cpl.	1	1	1
081	634.000	Simmerring 39,5/50/5 Dust seal 39,5/50/5 Paraolio 39,5/50/5	1	1	1
82	51.09.082.000	Distanzbüchse Spacer bushing Distanziale	1	1	1
85	51.09.085.000	Distanzbüchse Spacer bushing Distanziale	1	1	1
86	FW 13	Scheibe 13 DIN 125 Flat washer 13 DIN 125 Rondella 13 DIN 125	1	1	1
87	637.000	SS-Mutter M 12 DIN 985 Self-locking nut M 12 DIN 985 Dado M 12 DIN 985	1	1	1
88	HH 10x35	Sechskantschraube M 10x35 Hexagon head bolt M 10x35 Vite M 10x35	1	1	1
89	PIN 3x28	Splint 3x28 Pin 3x28 Cupiglia 3x28	1	1	1
90	HN 8x1	Sechskantmutter M 8x1 Hexagon nut M 8x1 Dado M 8x1	1	1	1
91	275.000	Zahnscheibe J 8,4 DIN 6797 Lock washer J 8,4 DIN 6797 Rondella J 8,4 DIN 6797	1	1	1
93	620.000	Simmerring 22/35/7 DIN 6504 Dust seal 22/35/7 DIN 6504 Paraolio 22/35/7 DIN 6504	1	1	1
94	672.000	Rillenkugellager 6003 DIN 625 Bearing 6003 DIN 625 Cuscinetto 6003	2	2	2
95	616.000	Seegerring 35x1,5 DIN 472 Circlip 35x1,5 DIN 472 Anello seeger 35x1,5 DIN 472	2	2	2
96	269.000	SS-Mutter M 10 DIN 985 Self-locking nut M 10 DIN 985 Dado M 10 DIN 985	1	1	1
–	51.09.100.000	Reifenhalter Tyre holder Portagomma	1	1	1

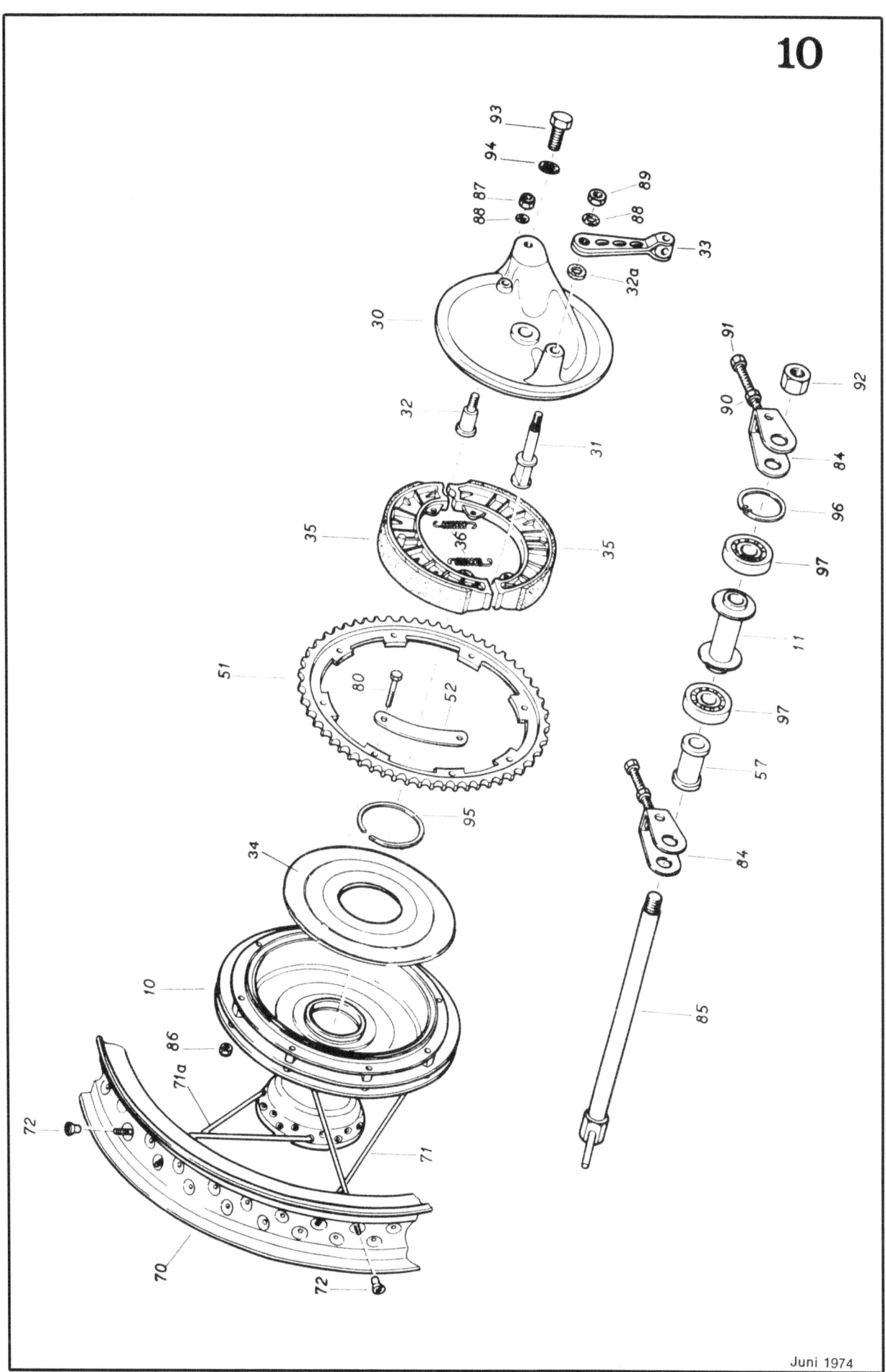

Gruppe 10: Hinterrad
Group   10: Rear wheel
Gruppo 10: Ruota posteriore

Bild Picture Foto	Teil-Nr. Part-No. Parte No	Benennung Description Descrizione	Stk./Fzg. Pos./Machine Pezzi/Macch. 175	250	400
–	1.52.10.001.000	Hinterrad kpl., ohne Bereifung Rear wheel cpl., without tyre Ruota posteriore cpl., senza gomma	1	1	1
–	1.52.10.002.000	Hinterradnabe kpl. Rear hub compl. Mozzo posteriore compl.	1	1	1
10	52.10.010.000	Hinterradnabe lose Rear hub loose Mozzo posteriore	1	1	1
11	52.10.011.000	Distanzbüchse innen Inner spacer bushing Distanziale – interiore	1	1	1
–	1.52.10.030.000	Bremsankerdeckel hinten, kpl. Brake anchor plate, rear, cpl. Cartella portaceppi, post., cpl.	1	1	1
30	52.10.030.210	Bremsankerdeckel hinten, lose Brake anchor plate, rear, loose Cartella portaceppi, posteriore	1	1	1
31	52.10.031.200	Bremsnocke Cam Camme	1	1	1
32	52.10.032.200	Bremsachse Brake bolt Asse freno	1	1	1
32a	31.09.032.000	PVC-Dichtring Plastic seal Guarnizione	1	1	1
33	52.10.033.100	Nabenbremshebel hinten, cpl. Brake arm – rear hub, cpl. Leva freno mozzo, post., cpl.	1	1	1
34	52.10.034.000	Abdeckblech Cover Lamiera di protezione			
35	52.10.035.560	Bremsbacke kpl. Brake shoe cpl. Ceppi freno cpl.	2	2	2
36	52.10.036.000	Bremsbackenfeder Return spring for brake shoes Molla freno	1	1	1
51	52.10.051.000	Kettenrad (Bitte Zähnezahl angeben!) Sprocket (Please quote size!) Corona dentata (Prego indicare il numero dei denti)	1	1	1
52	52.10.052.000	Sicherungsblech Sprocket locking plate Piastra fermo viti	4	4	4
57	52.10.057.000	Distanzbüchse außen Outer spacer bushing Distanziale exteriore	1	1	1
–	52.10.065.000	Rollenkette Chain Catena	1	1	1
–	52.10.066.000	Kettenschloß Master link Giuto catena	1	1	1
70	54.10.070.000	Alu-Felge 18 " Aluminium rim 18 " Cerchio aluminium 18 "	1	1	1
71	52.10.071.000	Speiche Spoke Raggio	20	20	20
71a	52.10.171.000	Speiche Spoke Raggio	20	20	20
72	51.09.072.400	Nippel Nipple Niple	40	40	40

Gruppe 10: Hinterrad
Group 10: Rear wheel
Gruppo 10: Ruota posteriore

Bild Picture Foto	Teil-Nr. Part-No. Parte No	Benennung **Description** Descrizione	Stk./Fzg. Pos./Machine Pezzi/Macch. 175/250/400		
—	52.10.073.000	**Felgenband 18"** Rim band 18" Flap 18"	1	1	1
—	54.10.074.000	**Reifen 4,50x18"** Tyre 4,50x18" Gomma 4,50x18"	1	1	1
—	54.10.075.000	**Schlauch 4,50x18"** Tube 4,50x18" Camer d'aria 4,50x18"	1	1	1
80	271.000	Sechskantschraube M 6x35 Hexagon head bolt M 6x35 Vite M 6x35	8	8	8
84	51.10.084.000	Kettenspanner Chain adjuster Tendicatena	2	2	2
85	52.10.085.100	Steckachse hinten Axle for rear hub Perno ruota posteriore	1	1	1
86	261.000	SS-Mutter M 6 Self-locking nut M 6 Dado M 6	8	8	8
87	259.000	SS-Mutter M 8 Self-locking nut M 8 Dado M 8	1	1	1
88	275.000	Zahnscheibe 8,4 Lock washer 8,4 Rondella 8,4	2	2	2
89	HN 8x1	Sechskantmutter M 8x1 Hexagon nut M 8x1 Dado M 8x1	1	1	1
90	M8	Sechskantmutter M 8 Hexagon nut M 8 Dado M 8	2	2	2
91	HH 8x50	**Sechskantschraube M 8x50** Hexagon head bolt M 8x50 Vite M 8x50	2	2	2
92	HN 16x1,5	Sechskantmutter M 16x1,5 Hexagon nut M 16x1,5 Dado M 16x1,5	1	1	1
93	HH 10x15	Sechskantschraube M 10x15 Hexagon head bolt M 10x15 Vite M 10x15	1	1	1
94	LW 10,5	Zahnscheibe 10,5 Lock washer 10,5 Rondella 10,5	1	1	1
95	SW 58	Seeger-Sprengring SW 58 Circlip SW 58 Anello seeger SW 58	2	2	2
96	J 47x2 Sd	Seeger-Sicherungsring Circlip Anello seeger	1	1	1
97	RB 6303 2 RS	**Rillenkugellager 6303 2 RS DIN 625** Bearing 6303 2 RS DIN 625 Cuscinetto 6303 2 RS DIN 625	2	2	2
—	51.09.100.000	Reifenhalter Tyre holder Portagomma	2	2	2

11

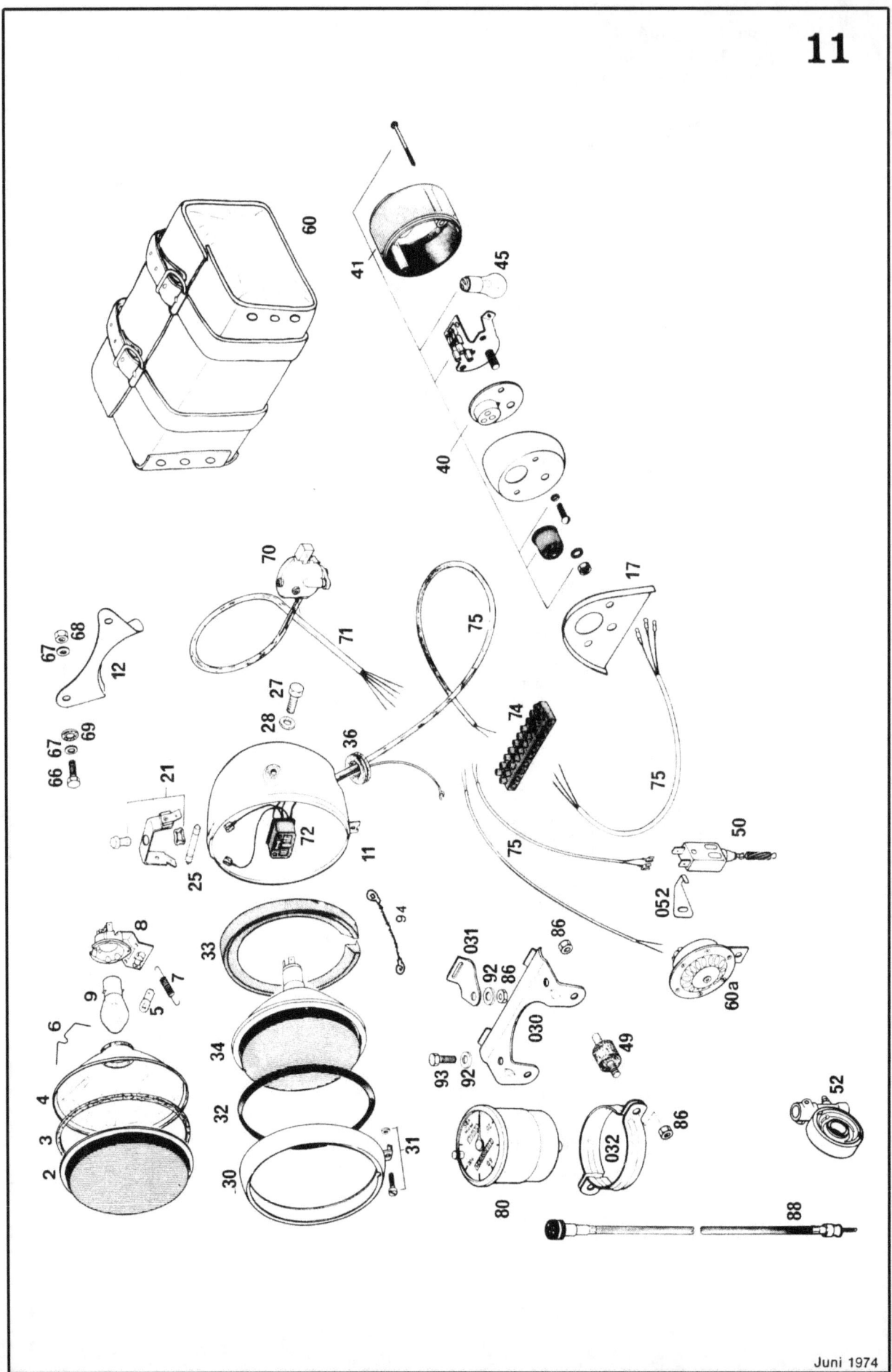

Juni 1974

Gruppe 11: Elektrische Anlage, Tachometer
Group 11: Electrical equipment, speedometer

Bild Picture	Teil-Nr. Part-No.	Benennung Description	Stk./Fzg. Pos./Macch. 175/250/400		
—	1.51.11.011.300	Scheinwerfer kpl. (Sealed Beam) / Headlight cpl. (Sealed Beam)	1	1	1
—	1.51.11.011.000	Scheinwerfer kpl. (F, A, CH, BRD, S, SF) / Headlight cpl.	1	1	1
—	1.51.11.000.300	Scheinwerfereinsatz kpl. (Sealed Beam) / Sealed beam reflector cpl.	1	1	1
—	1.51.11.002.000	Scheinwerfereinsatz kpl. / Reflector cpl.	1	1	1
2	51.11.002.000	Scheinwerferglas / Headlight glass	1	1	1
3	51.11.000.000	Dichtring / Seal ring	1	1	1
4	51.11.004.000	Reflektor / Reflector	1	1	1
5	51.11.005.000	Kugellampe 6 V, 3 W / Bulb	1	1	1
6	33.11.035.000	Spannfeder / Spring clip	6	6	6
7	33.11.007.000	Haltefeder / Socket spring	1	1	1
8	51.11.008.000	Lampenfassung / Socket	1	1	1
9	51.11.009.000	Bilux-Lampe 6 V, 25/25 W / Bilux bulb	1	1	1
11	51.11.011.300	Scheinwerfergehäuse / Headlight shell	1	1	1
12	51.11.012.000	Startnummerntafelbefestigung / Number plate bracket	1	1	1
17	54.08.017.000	Versteifungsblech für Rücklicht / Reinforcement bracket for rearlight	1	1	1
21	51.11.021.000	Fernlichtkontrolle mit Halterung / Main beam warning with socket	1	1	1
25	51.11.011.000	Fernlichtkontrolle 6 V, 1,5 W / Main beam warning bulb 6 V, 1,5 W	1	1	1
27	HH 8x25	Sechskantschraube M 8x25 DIN 933 / Hexagon head bolt M 8x33 DIN 933	2	2	2
28	25000	Zahnscheibe 8,4 DIN 679 F / Lock washer 8,4 DIN 679 F	2	2	2
—	1.51.12.030.000	Tachometerhalterung kpl. / Speedometer bracket cpl.	1	1	1
030	51.12.030.000	Halterung / Main bracket	1	1	1
30	51.11.030.300	Haltering für Scheinwerfereinsatz / Headlight ring	1	1	1
031	51.12.031.000	Bügel für Tachohalterung / Bracket for speedometer	2	2	2
31	1343.09	Linsenkopfschraube M 5x15 / Flat head screw M 5x15	1	1	1
032	51.12.032.000	Schelle für Tachohalterung / Speedometer shell	2	2	2
32	51.11.032.000	Gummidichtring / Seal ring	1	1	1
33	51.11.033.000	Gummihalterung / Rubber mounting	1	1	1
34	51.11.034.300	Scheinwerfereinsatz (Sealed Beam) / Sealed beam reflector	1	1	1
36	51.11.036.300	Kabeltülle / Rubber sleeve f. headlight shell	1	1	1
40	51.11.040.300	Rücklicht kpl. / Taillight cpl.	1	1	1
41	51.11.041.300	Rücklichtkappe / Rear lamp lens	1	1	1
45	52.11.045.000	Rücklichtbirne 6 V, 5/21 W / Taillight bulb 6 V, 5/21 W	1	1	1

Gruppe 11: Elektrische Anlage, Tachometer
Group 11: Electrical equipment, speedometer

Bild Picture	Teil-Nr. Part-No.	Benennung Description	Stk./Fzg. Pos./Macch. 175/250/400		
49	51.11.049.000	Gumliblock Rubber grommet	2	2	2
50	1.31.11.050.000	Bremslichtzugschalter Brake light switch	1	1	1
052	31.11.052.000	Einhängehaken für Bremslichtschalter Hook for brake light switch	1	1	1
52	52.09.052.000	Tachometerantrieb Speedometer drive	1	1	1
60	51.11.060.000	Werkzeugtasche Tool bag	1	1	1
60a	31.11.060.000	Schnarre Electric horn	1	1	1
66	HH 5x15	Sechskantschraube M 5x15 Hexagon head bolt	4	4	4
67	FW 5	Scheibe 5 mm Flat washer	4	4	4
68	SLN M 5	SS-Mutter M 5 Self-locking nut	8	8	8
69	510.000	Gummischeibe 5 mm ϕ Rubber washer	8	8	8
70	31.11.070.000	Abblendschalter Dimmer switch	1	1	1
71	51.11.071.000	Kabel zu Abblendschalter Cable for dimmer switch	1	1	1
72	51.11.072.000	Kabelstrang mit Stecker (f. Sealed beam-Scheinwerfer) Wiring harness with plug (for sealed beam headlight)	1	1	1
74	54.11.074.000	Klemmleiste 10teilig Junction block (10-piece)	1	1	1
—	54.11.075.000	Kabelstrang kpl. Wiring harness cpl.	1	1	1
75	54.11.075.300	Kabelstrang kpl (f. Sealed beam-Scheinwerfer) Wiring harness cpl. (for Sealed beam headlight)	1	1	1
80	51.11.000.000	Tachometer (mph-Einteilung) Speedometer (mph scale)	1	1	1
—	51.11.080.100	Tachometer (km/h-Einteilung) Speedometer (km/h scale)	1	1	1
86	261.000	SS-Mutter M 6 DIN 985 Self-locking nut M 6 DIN 985	6	6	6
88	51.11.088.000	Tachoantriebswelle Speedometer drive cable	1	1	1
92	DIN 125/6.4	Scheibe 6,4 Flat washer	4	4	4
93	HH 6x16	Sechskantschraube M 6x16 Hexagon head bolt M 6x16	2	2	2
94	54.11.073.000	Ground Wire	1	1	1

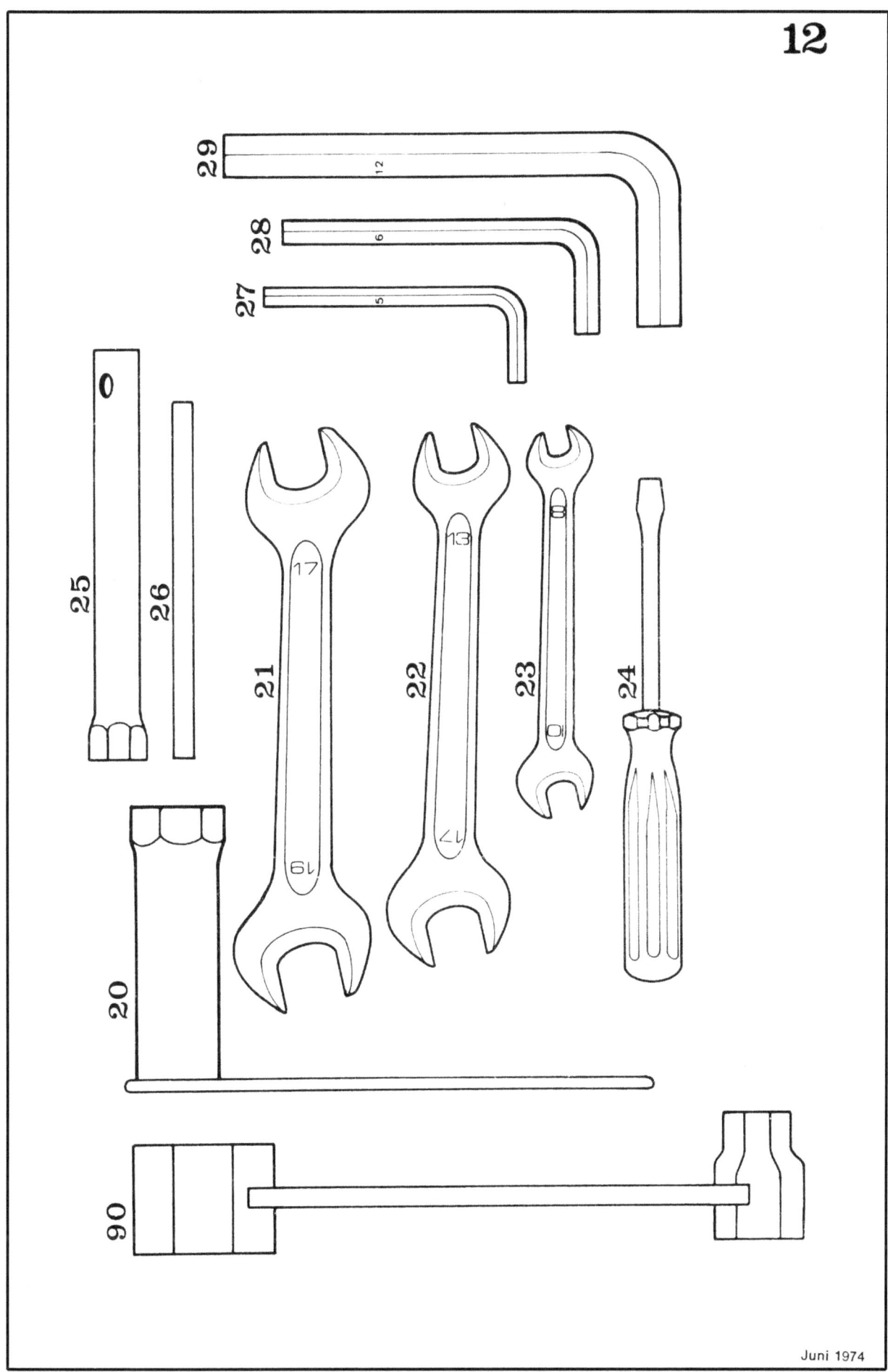

Gruppe 12: Zubehör — Werkzeuge
Group 12: Accessories — tools

Bild Picture	Teil-Nr. Part-No.	Benennung Description	Pos./Machine Stk./Fzg. 175/250/400
—	1.52.12.090.000	Bordwerkzeug kpl. / Riders tool kit cpl.	1 1 1
—	51.12.091.000	Werkzeugtasche (klein) / Toolbag (small)	1 1 1
90	51.12.090.000	Kombischlüssel 13/19/24 / Riders wrench 13/19/24	1 1 1
20	51.12.020.000	Zündkerzenschlüssel / Spark plug wrench	1 1 1
21	51.12.021.000	Gabelschlüssel 17—19 / Open end wrench	1 1 1
22	51.12.022.000	Gabelschlüssel 13—17 / Open end wrench	1 1 1
23	51.12.023.000	Gabelschlüssel 8—10 / Open end wrench	1 1 1
24	51.12.024.000	Schraubenzieher / Screw driver	1 1 1
25	51.12.025.000	Rohrsteckschlüssel 13 mm / Box wrench 13 mm	1 1 1
26	51.12.026.000	Dorn für Rohrsteckschlüssel / Rod for box wrench	1 1 1
27	51.12.027.000	Innensechskantschlüssel 5 mm / Allen key	1 1 1
28	51.12.028.000	Innnensechskantschlüssel 6 mm / Allen key	1 1 1
29	51.12.029.000	Innensechskantschlüssel 12 mm / Allen key	1 1 1

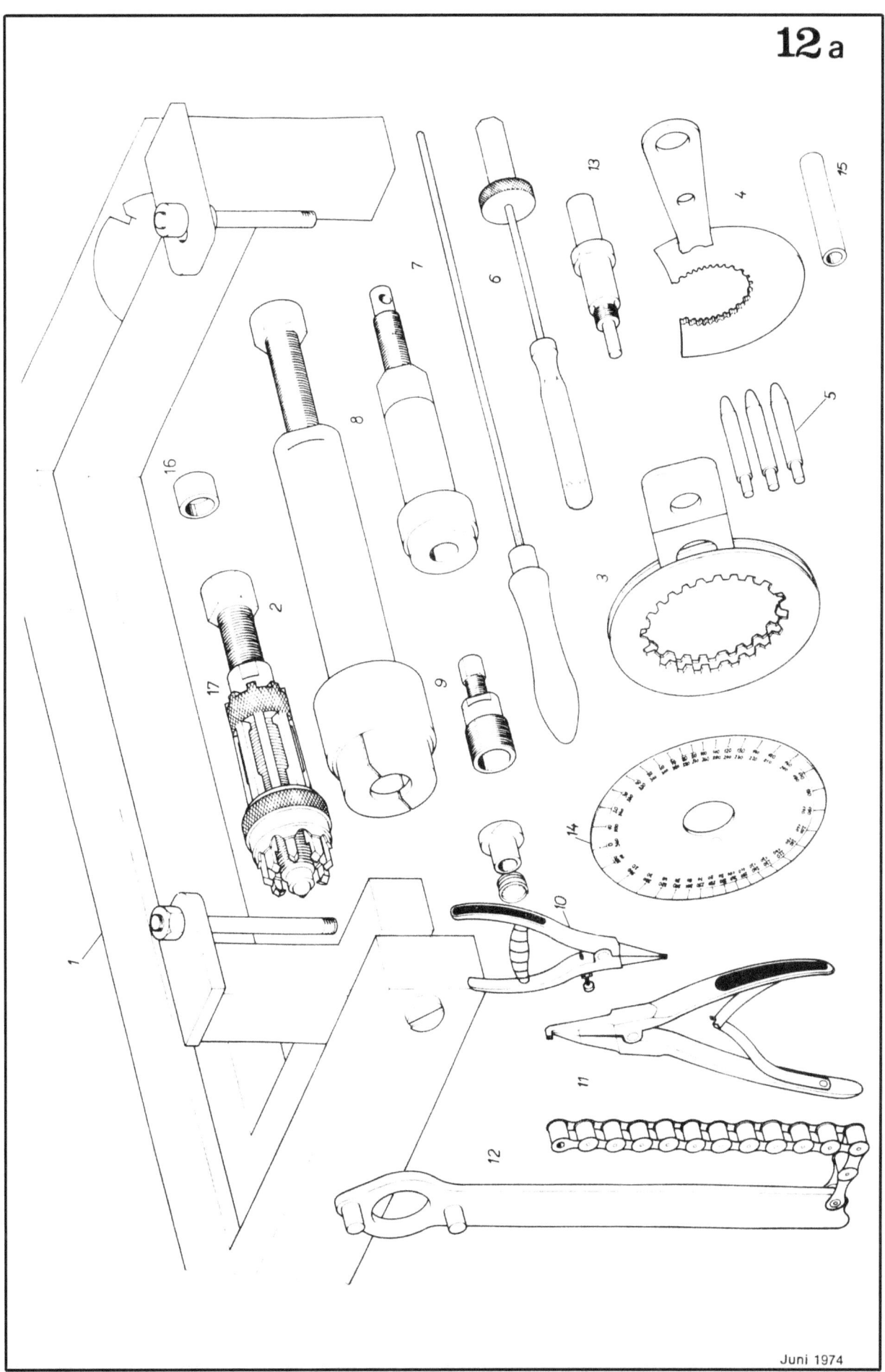

Gruppe 12a: Reparaturwerkzeuge und Montagevorrichtung für KTM 52 / 175 ccm
Group 12a: Repair tools and Jig for KTM 52 / 175 cc

Bild / Picture	Teil-Nr. / Part-No.	Benennung / Description	Stk./Motor Pos./Engine 175
1	51.12.001.000	Aufspannbock / Repair stand	1
2	51.12.002.000	Innenringabzieher / Extractor for inner races of main bearings M 20	1
3	51.12.003.000	Kupplungsschalter / Holding plate for clutch hub	1
4	51.12.004.000	Primärzahnradhalter / Holding plate for driving pinion	1
5	51.12.005.000	Zentrierbolzen / Guide pin	3
6	51.12.006.000	Spezialschraubenzieher / Special screw-driver	1
7	51.12.007.000	Spezialsechskantschraubenzieher / Special hexagon screw-driver	1
8	51.12.008.000	Einziehvorrichtung / Bearing inserting tool	1
9	51.12.009.000	Magnetabzieher / Puller for magneto flywheel	1
10	51.12.010.000	Spitzzange (verkehrt) / Needle nose pliers (opposite)	1
11	51.12.011.000	Spezial-Seegerringzange (verkehrt) / Special circlip pliers (opposite)	1
12	51.12.012.000	Halteschlüssel für Kettenrad und Schwungrad / Spanner for sprocket and flywheel	1
13	51.12.013.000	Einstellehre für Zündzeitpunkt / Adjusting gauge for ignition advance	1
14	51.12.014.000	Gradscheibe / Timing degree disc	1
15	51.12.015.000	Hilfskolbenbolzen / Wrist pin for fitting	1
16	51.12.016.000	Schutzkappe zum Schwungradabziehen / Protection cap for pulling the flywheel	1
17	51.12.017.000	Lagerabzieher / Bearing extractor	1

PENTON-KTM
Engine Parts Manual
1972 to 1975
PENTON Jackpiner - Hare & Mint
KTM MC & GS Models
(Motocross & Gelande Sport)

INDEX

Group		Page No.
30A	Crank Case	86
30B	Crankshaft - Piston	92
30C	Cylinder	99
31	Carburettor	104
31	Ignition	110
32	Clutch	112
33	Transmission	115
33	Kickstarter	120
34	Shifting Mechanism	124

A Floyd Clymer Publication - 2025 VelocePress.com

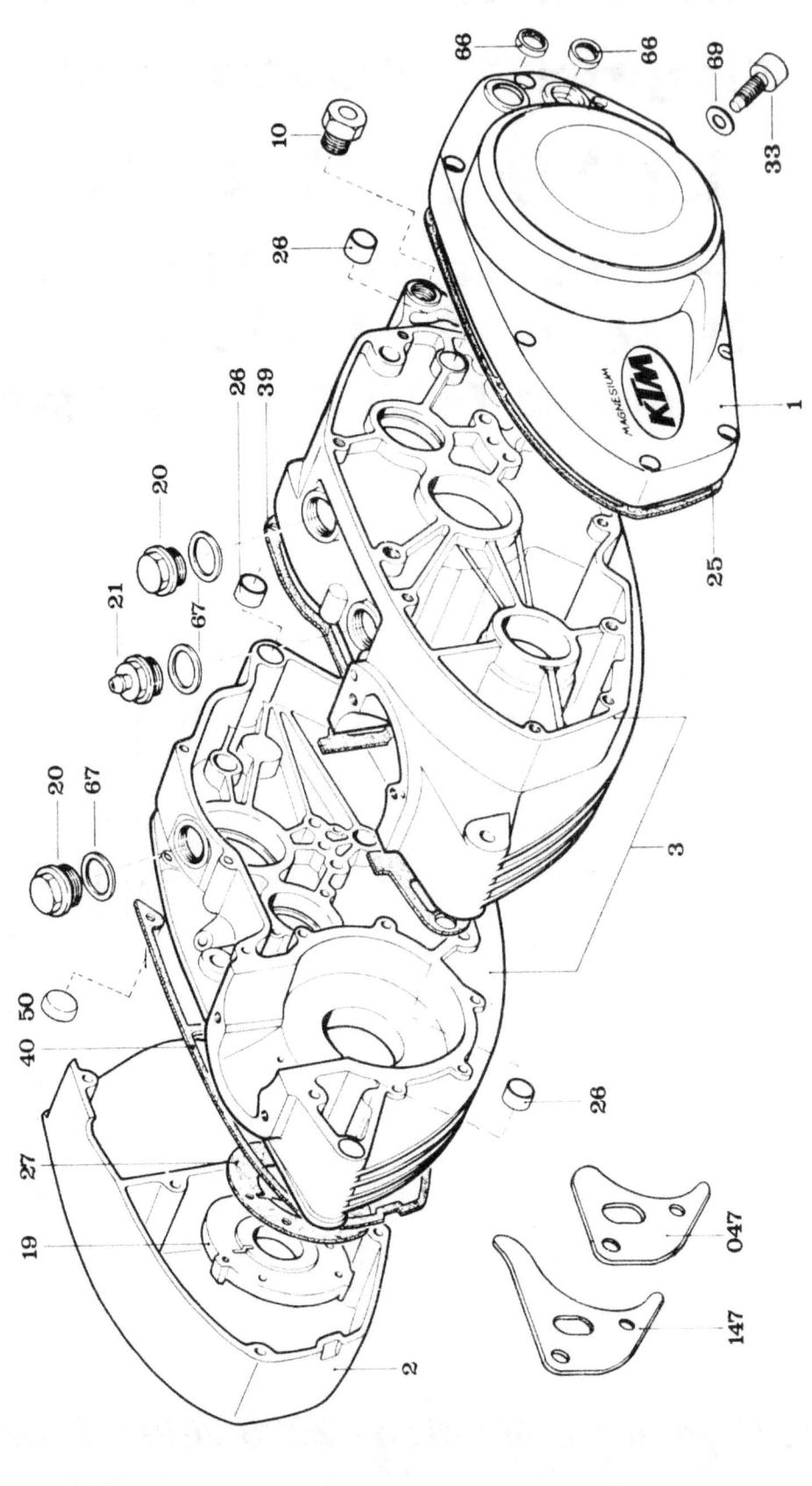

Gruppe 30: Motorgehäuse I
Group 30: Crank case I
Gruppo 30: Carter del motore I

Bild / Picture / Foto	Teil-Nr. / Part-No. / Parte-No	Benennung / Description / Descrizione	Stk./Motor Pos./Engine Pezzi/Motore 175	250	400
1	51.30.001.110	Kupplungsdeckel (für Kickstarterwelle 14 ⌀) / Clutch cover (for kickstarter shaft 14 ⌀) / Coperchio frizione (per albero pedale di avviamento 14 ⌀)	1	–	–
–	54.30.001.110	Kupplungsdeckel (für Kickstarterwelle 17 ⌀) / Clutch cover (for kickstarter shaft 17 ⌀) / Coperchio frizione (per albero pedale di aviamento 17 ⌀)	–	1	1
2	51.30.002.010	Zündgehäusedeckel / Ignition case cover / Coperchio accensione	1	–	–
–	51.30.002.110	Zündgehäusedeckel (ausgedreht) / Ignition case cover (for larger flywheel) / Coperchio accensione (per volano largo)	–	1	1
3	51.30.003.010	Motorgehäuse kpl. / Engine case cpl. / Carter motore cpl.	1	–	–
–	54.30.000.010 Sm / 54.30.000.110 Lg	Motorgehäuse kpl. / Engine case cpl. / Carter motore cpl.	–	1	–
–	55.30.000.010	Motorgehäuse kpl. / Engine case cpl. / Carter motore cpl.	–	–	1
10	52.30.010.100	Motoraugenverstärkung / Engine mount bushing / Bussola di sostegno motore	1	1	1
19	51.30.019.500	Dichtungsflansch rechts / Seal-retaining plate R/S / Piastra di tenuta destra	1	–	–
–	54.30.019.000	Dichtungsflansch rechts / Seal-retaining plate R/S / Piastra di tenuta destra	–	1	–
–	55.30.019.000	Dichtungsflansch rechts / Seal-retaining plate R/S / Piastra di tenuta destra	–	–	1
20	51.30.020.000	Verschlußschraube / Screw plug / Tappo di sfiato	2	2	2
21	51.30.021.000	Entlüftungsschraube / Breather plug / Tappo di sfiato	1	1	1
25	51.30.025.000	Kupplungsdeckeldichtung / Clutch case gasket / Guarnizione cassa frizione	1	1	1
26	51.30.026.100	Paßhülse 17 ⌀ / Dowel 17 ⌀ / Perno 17 ⌀	3	3	3
27	51.30.027.000	Flanschdichtung rechts / Flange gasket R/S / Guarnizione flangia destra	1	–	–
–	54.30.027.000	Flanschdichtung rechts / Flange gasket R/S / Guarnizione flangia destra	–	1	1
33	54.33.033.100	Anschlagschraube M 12 / Adjusting bolt / Vite di arresto	–	1	1
–	51.33.033.000	Anschlagschraube / Adjusting bolt / Vite di arresto	1	–	–
39	51.30.039.100	Motorgehäusedichtung / Engine case gasket / Guarnizione carter motore	1	1	1
40	51.30.040.000	Zündgehäusedichtung / Ignition case gasket / Guarnizione cassa accensione	1	1	1

Gruppe 30: Motorgehäuse I
Group 30: Crank case I
Gruppo 30: Carter del motore I

Bild Picture Foto	Teil-Nr. Part-No. Parte-No.	Benennung Description Descrizione	Stk./Motor Pos./Engine Pezzi/Motore 175/250/400		
147	51.30.047.200	Kettenausfallschutz 14-Z, MC für gekürzten Zündgehäusedeckel Crank case protector 14-T., MC for shortened ignition case Protezione carter 14 denti, MC per coperchio accensione accorciato	1	1	1
–	51.30.047.400	Kettenausfallschutz 13-Z, MC für gekürzten Zündgehäusedeckel Crank case protector 13-T., MC for shortened ignition case Protezione carter 13 denti, MC per coperchio accensione accorciato	1	1	1
047	51.30.047.300	Kettenausfallschutz 14-Z., GS für ungekürzten Zündgehäusedeckel Crank case protector 14-T., GS for unshortened ignition case Protezione carter 14 denti, GS per coperchio accensione non accorciato	1	1	1
–	51.30.047.500	Kettenausfallschutz 13-Z., GS für ungekürzten Zündgehäusedeckel Crank case protector 13-T., GS for unshortened ignition case Protezione carter 13-denti, GS per coperchio accensione non accorciato	1	1	1
–	51.30.047.600	Kettenausfallschutz 12-Z., GS + MC Crank case protector 12-T., GS + MC Protezione carter 12 denti, GS + MC	1	1	1
50	51.30.057.000	Verschlußkappe für Schaltwelle Sheet metal plug for shifting shaft chiusura per l'albero di comando	1	1	1
66	DIN 6504/	Simmerring BA 14x22x4 DIN 6504 Radial seal ring BA 14x22x4 DIN 6504 Anello di tenuta radiale BA 14x22x4 DIN 6504	2	1	1
67	DIN 7603/26x30x1.5	Dichtring 26x30x1,5 DIN 7603 Seal ring 26x30x1,5 DIN 7603 Anello di tenuta 26x30x1,5 DIN 7603	3	3	3
69	DIN 7603/12.2x20x1	Dichtring 12,2x20x1 DIN 7603 Seal ring 12,2x20x1 DIN 7603 Anello di tenuta 12,2x20x1 DIN 7603	1	1	1
–	52.30.100.000	Dichtungssatz für Motor 175 Gasket set for 175 cc engine Serie di guarnizione per motore KTM 175 cc	1	–	–
–	54.30.100.000	Dichtungssatz für Motor 250 Gasket set for 250 cc engine Serie di guarnizione per motore KTM 250 cc	–	1	–
–	55.30.100.000	Dchtungssatz für Motor 400 Gasket set for 400 cc engine Serie di guarnizione per motore KTM 400 cc	–	–	1

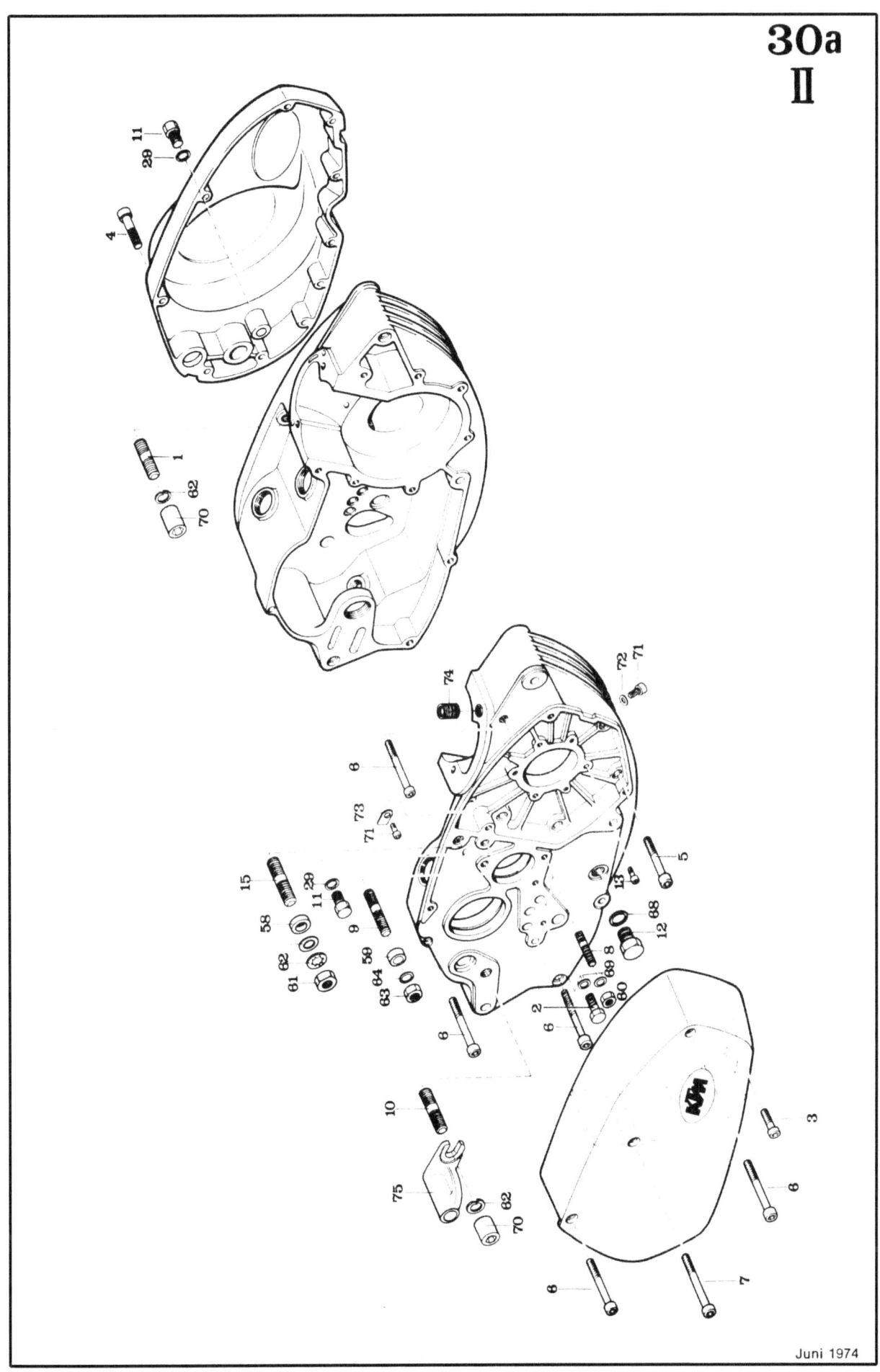

Gruppe 30: Motorgehäuse II
Group 30: Crank case II
Gruppo 30: Carter del motore II

Bild / Picture / Foto	Teil-Nr. / Part-No. / Parte-No.	Benennung / Description / Descrizione	Stk./Motor Pos./Engine Pezzi/Motore 175/250/400		
1	51.30.051.100	Stiftschraube M 10x20 (38 mm lang) / Stud M 10x20 (38 mm long) / Perno a vite M 10x20 (lunghezza 38 mm)	1	1	1
2	DIN 933/M6x15	Sechskantschraube M 6x16/8 G DIN 933 / Hexagon head screw M 6x16/8 G DIN 933 / Vite M 6x16/8 G DIN 933	1	1	1
3	DIN 912/M6x20/86	Innensechskantschraube M 6x20/8 G DIN 912 / Allen head screw M 6x20/8 G DIN 912 / Vite a testa esagonale interna M 6x20/8 G DIN 912	1	1	1
4	DIN 912/M6x35/86	Innensechskantschraube M 6x35/8 G DIN 912 / Allen head screw M 6x35/8 G DIN 912 / Vite a testa esagonale interna M 6x35/8 G DIN 912	10	10	10
5	DIN 912/M6x55/86	Innensechskantschraube M 6x55/8 G DIN 912 / Allen head screw M 6x55/8 G DIN 912 / Vite a testa esagonale interna M 6x55/8 G DIN 912	6	6	6
6	DIN 912/M6x65/86	Innensechskantschraube M 6x65/8 G DIN 912 / Allen head screw M 6x65/8 G DIN 912 / Vite a testa esagonale interna M 6x65/8 G DIN 912	7	7	7
7	DIN 912/M6x75/86	Innensechskantschraube M 6x75/8 G DIN 912 / Allen head screw M 6x75/8 G DIN 912 / Vite a testa esagonale interna M 6x75/8 G DIN 912	1	1	1
8	DIN 939/M6x20	Stiftschraube M 6x20 DIN 939 / Stud M 6x20 DIN 939 / Perno a vite M 6x20 DIN 939	2	2	2
9	DIN 939/M8x28	Stiftschraube M 8x28 DIN 940 / Stud M 8x28 DIN 940 / Perno a vite M 8x28 DIN 940	1	1	1
10	51.30.056.000	Stiftschraube M 10x45 / Stud M 10x45 / Perno a vite M 10x45	1	1	1
11	DIN 7604/AM8x1	Verschlußschraube AM 8x1x15/8 G DIN 7604 / Plug AM 8x1x15/8 G DIN 7604 / Tappo a vite AM 8x1x15/8 G DIN 7604	2	2	2
12	DIN 7604/AM12x15	Verschlußschraube AM 12x1,5/8 G DIN 7604 / Plug AM 12x1,5/8 G DIN 7604 / Tappo a vite AM 12x1,5/8 G DIN 7604	1	1	1
13	DIN 912/M5x15/86	Innensechskantschraube M 5x16/8 G DIN 912 / Allen head screw M 5x16/8 G DIN 912 / Tappo a vite M 5x16/8 G DIN 912	6	6	6
15	DIN 939/M10x30	Stiftschraube M 10x30 DIN 835 / Stud M 10x30 DIN 835 / Perno a vite M 10x30 DIN 835	1	1	1
29	DIN 7603/8x2x12x1	Dichtring 8,2x12x1 DIN 7603 / Seal ring 8,2x12x1 DIN 7603 / Guarnizione 8,2x12x1 DIN 7603	2	2	2
58	51.30.058.100	Scheibe für Kettenausfallschutz 20 mm ⌀ x 6,5 mm ≠ / Washer for crank case protector 20 mm ⌀ x 6,5 mm ≠ / Rondella per protezione carter 20 mm ⌀ x 6,5 mm ≠	1	1	1
59	51.30.059.000	Scheibe für Kettenausfallschutz 15 mm ⌀ x 7,5 mm ≠ / Washer for crank case protector 15 mm ⌀ x 7,5 mm ≠ / Rondella per protezione carter 15 mm ⌀ x 7,5 mm ≠	1	1	1
60	M6	Sechskantmutter M 6 DIN 934 / Hexagon nut M 6 DIN 934 / Dado M 6 DIN 934	2	2	2
61	M10	Sechskantmutter M 10 DIN 934 / Hexagon nut M 10 DIN 934 / Dado M 10 DIN 934	1	1	1

Gruppe 30: Motorgehäuse II
Group 30: Crank case II
Gruppo 30: Carter del motore II

Bild Picture Foto	Teil-Nr. Part-No. Parte No	Benennung Description Descrizione	Stk./Motor Pos./Engine Pezzi/Motore		
			175	250	400
62	DIN 137/B10	Federscheibe B 10 DIN 137 Spring washer B 10 DIN 137 Rondella elastica M 10 MIN 137	3	3	3
63	M8	Sechskantmutter M 8 DIN 934 Hexagon nut M 8 DIN 934 Dado M 8 DIN 934	1	1	1
64	DIN 137/B8	Federscheibe M 8 DIN 137 Spring washer M 8 DIN 137 Rondella elastica M 8 DIN 137	1	1	1
68	DIN 7603/12.2x17x1	Dichtring 12,2x17x1 DIN 7603 Seal ring 12,2x17x1 DIN 7603 Guarnizione 12,2x17x1 DIN 7603	1	1	1
69	DIN 137/B6	Federscheibe B 6 DIN 137 Spring washer B 6 DIN 137 Rondella elastica B 6 DIN 137	3	3	3
70	51.30.048.000	Innensechskantmutter M 10 Inside hexagon nut Dado esagonale interna M 10	1	1	1
—	51.30.148.000	Sechskantmutter M 10, 25 mm lang Hexagon nut M 10 Dado M 10	1	1	1
71	DIN 912/M5x8/86	Innensechskantschraube M 5x8 DIN 912 Allen head screw M 5x8 DIN 912 Vite a testa esagonale interna M 5x8 DIN 912	2	2	2
72	DIN 7603/5x10x1.5	Dichtring 5x10x1,5 DIN 7603 Seal ring 5x10x1,5 DIN 7603 Guarnizione 5x10x1,5 DIN 7603	1	1	1
73	51.30.049.000	Halteplättchen Retaining plate Piastra di tenuta	1	1	1
74	51.30.054.000	Gewindebüchse M 12/M 8 Threaded bushing Ghiera	1	1	1
75	52.03.052.400	Distanzstück Spacer Spessore	1	1	1

30b
175

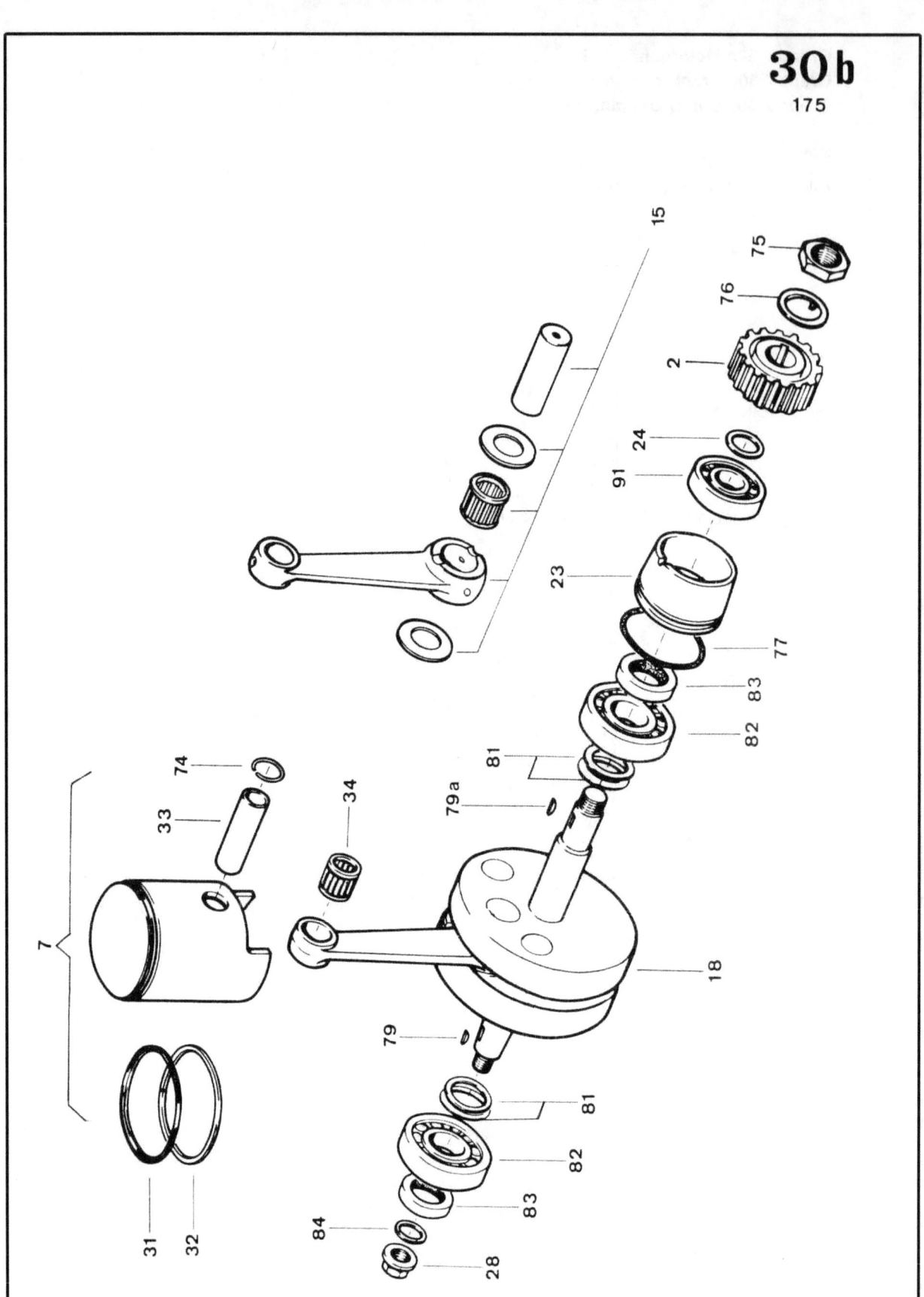

Gruppe 30: Kurbeltrieb — 175 ccm
Group 30: Crankshaft, piston — 175 cc
Gruppo 30: Albero a gomiti — 175 cc

Bild / Picture / Foto	Teil-Nr. / Part-No. / Parte No	Benennung / Description / Descrizione		Stk./Motor Pos./Engine Pezzi/Motore 175
2		Primärzahnrad, 25 Zähne, Flanken geschliffen, nur in Verbindung mit Kupplungskorb lieferbar Pinion 25-T., only available together with outer clutch hub Pignone 25 denti fornibile solo con portafrizione		
7	52.30.007.000	Kolben 63,5 mm ⌀ kpl. Piston 63,5 mm ⌀ cpl. Pistone ⌀ 63,5 mm cpl.		1
–	52.30.007.200	Kolben 63,75 mm ⌀ kpl. Piston 63,75 mm ⌀ cpl. Pistone ⌀ 63,75 mm cpl.		nB ar
–	52.30.007.300	Kolben 64,00 mm ⌀ kpl. Piston 64,00 mm ⌀ cpl. Pistone ⌀ 64,00 mm cpl.	52.30.007.500 Piston 64.75mm ⌀ cpl.	nB ar
–	52.30.007.400	Kolben 64,45 mm ⌀ kpl. Piston 64,45 mm ⌀ cpl. Pistone ⌀ 64,45 mm cpl.	52.30.007.600 Piston 65.0 mm ⌀ cpl.	nB ar
15	1.51.30.015.000	Pleuellager-Reparatursatz Connecting rod repair kit Gruppo per la riparazione del cuscinetto a biella		1
18	51.30.018.200	Kurbelwelle (Zapfen beiderseits 25 ⌀) kpl. Crankshaft cpl. (Pin on both sides 25 ⌀) Gruppo albero a gomiti perno, ambedue i lati ⌀ 25		1
23	51.30.023.600	Simmerringträger Spacer Spessore		1
24	51.30.024.000	Zwischenscheibe Spacer Spessore		1
28	51.30.028.100	Bundmutter M 12x1 links Magneto nut M 12x1 L/S Dado magneto M 12x1 sinistra		1
31	52.30.031.000	L-Ring 63,5 mm ⌀ x 2 L-ring 63,5 mm ⌀ x 2 Anello a L 63,5 mm ⌀ x 2		1
–	52.30.031.200	L-Ring 63,75 mm ⌀ x 2 L-ring 63,75 mm ⌀ x 2 Anello a L 63,75 mm ⌀ x 2		nB ar
–	52.30.031.300	L-Ring 64,00 mm ⌀ x 2 L-ring 64,00 mm ⌀ x 2 Anello a L 64,00 mm ⌀ x 2	52.30.031.500 L-Ring 64.75mm ⌀ x 2	nB ar
–	52.30.031.400	L-Ring 64,45 mm ⌀ x 2 L-ring 64,45 mm ⌀ x 2 Anello a L 64,45 mm ⌀ x 2	52.30.031.600 L-Ring 65.0 mm ⌀ x 2	nB ar
32	52.30.032.000	Rechteckring 63,5 mm ⌀ x 2 Square ring 63,5 mm ⌀ x 2 Anello quadro 63,5 mm ⌀ x 2		1
–	52.30.032.200	Rechteckring 63,75 mm ⌀ x 2 Square ring 63,75 mm ⌀ x 2 Anello quadro 63,75 mm ⌀ x 2		nB ar
–	52.30.032.300	Rechteckring 64,00 mm ⌀ x 2 Square ring 64,00 mm ⌀ x 2 Anello quadro 64,00 mm ⌀ x 2	52.30.032.500 Square ring 64.75 mm ⌀ x 2	ar nB
–	52.30.032.400	Rechteckring 64,45 mm ⌀ x 2 Square ring 64,45 mm ⌀ x 2 Anello quadro 64,45 mm ⌀ x 2	52.30.032.600 Square ring 65.0 mm ⌀ x 2	nB ar
33	52.30.033.000	Kolbenbolzen 15 ⌀ x 56,4 Wrist-pin 15 ⌀ x 56,4 Spinotto 15 ⌀ x 56,4		1
34	51.30.034.000	Nadellager 15 ⌀ x 19 ⌀ x 20 Needle bearing 18 ⌀ x 22 ⌀ x 20 Cuscinetto a spillo 18 ⌀ x 22 ⌀ x 20		1

Gruppe 30: Kurbeltrieb   175 ccm
Group 30: Crankshaft, piston   175 cc
Gruppo 30: Albero a gomiti   175 cc

Bild / Picture / Foto	Teil-Nr. / Part-No. / Parte No	Benennung / Description / Descrizione	Stk./Motor Pos./Engine Pezzi/Motore 175
74	C 15	Drahtsprengring C 15 DIN 73123 Retaining clip C 15 DIN 73123 Pinza di ritenuta C 18 DIN 73123	2
75	DIN 936/M14x1.5	Sechskantmutter M 14x1,5 DIN 936 Hexagon head screw M 14x1,5 DIN 936 Vite M 14x1,5 DIN 936	1
76	52.30.048.000	Sicherungsblech 15 mm ⌀ Flat washer 15 mm ⌀ Rondella piatta 15 mm ⌀	1
77	OR 2-224	O-Ring 2-224 O-ring 2-224 Anello a O 2-224	1
79	DIN 6888/3x5	Scheibenfeder 3x5 DIN 6888 Woodruff key 3x5 DIN 6888 Chiave Woodruf 3x5 DIN 6888	1
79a	DIN 6888/4x5	Scheibenfeder 4x5 DIN 6888 Woodruff key 4x5 DIN 6888 Chiave Woodruff 4x5 DIN 6888	1
81	PS 25x35x0,1	Paßscheibe Shim washer Rondella	nB ar
—	PS 25x35x0,15	Paßscheibe Shim washer Rondella	nB ar
—	PS 25x35x0,3	Paßscheibe Shim washer Rondella	nB ar
82	L 25	Schulterlager L 25 DIN 615 Shoulder bearing L 25 DIN 615 Cuscinetto spalla L 25 DIN 615	2
83	DIN 6504/	Simmerring 25x35x7 Radial seal ring 25x35x7 Anello di tenuta radiale 25x35x7	2
84	DIN 137/B12	Federscheibe B 12 DIN 137 Spring washer B 12 DIN 137 Rondella elastica B 12 DIN 137	1
91	RB 6302	Rillenlager 6302 C 3 SV 41 DIN 625 Ball bearing 6302 C 3 SV 41 DIN 625 Cuscinetto a sfera 6302 C 3 SV 41 DIN 625	1

TEILE FÜR ALTE AUSFÜHRUNG MIT 20 ⌀ KURBELWELLE:
PARTS FOR OLD EXECUTION WITH 20 ⌀ CRANKSHAFT:
PEZZI PER TIPO VECCHIO COI ALBERO A GOMITI 20 ⌀:

Bild	Teil-Nr.	Benennung	Stk./Motor
—	PS 20x28x0,1	Paßscheibe Shim washer Rondella	nB ar
—	PS 20x28x0,15	Paßscheibe Shim washer Rondella	nB ar
—	PS 20x28x0,3	Paßscheibe Shim washer Rondella	nB ar
—	DIN 615/M20 R40 55SU6	Hauptlager M 20 R 40 DIN 615 Main bearing M 20 R 40 DIN 615 Cuscinetto M 20 R 40 DIN 615	2

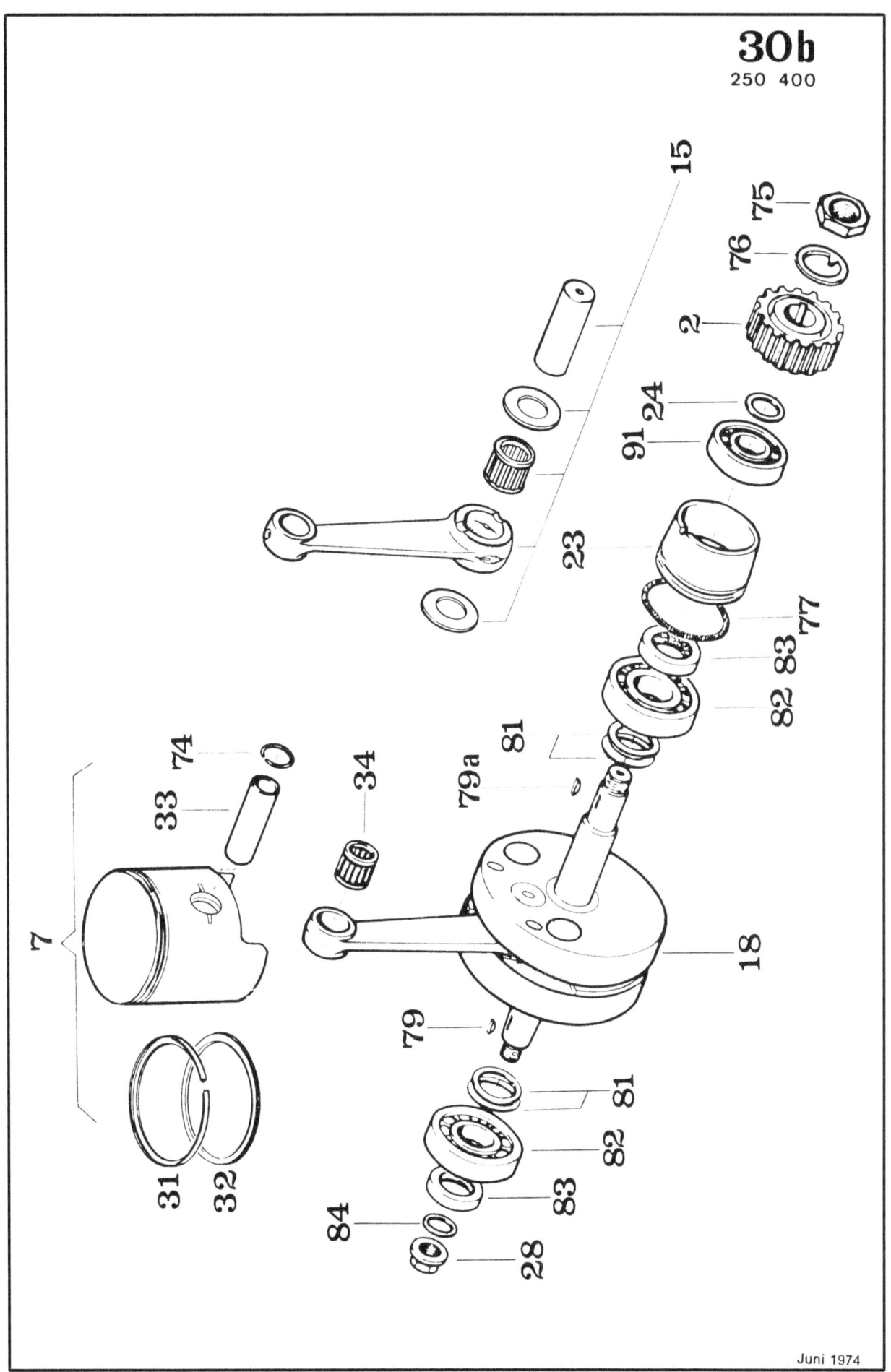

Gruppe 30: Kurbeltrieb   250/400 ccm
Group 30: Crankshaft, piston   250/400 cc
Gruppo 30: Albero a gomiti   250/400 cc

Bild / Picture / Foto	Teil-Nr. / Part-No. / Parte-No	Benennung / Description / Descrizione	Stk./Motor Pos./Engine Pezzi/Motore 250/400	
2		Primärzahnrad, 25 Zähne, Flanken geschliffen, nur in Verbindung mit Kupplungskorb lieferbar Pinion 25-T., only available together with outer clutch hub Pignone 25 denti fornibile solo con portafrizione		
7	54.30.007.000	Kolben 71,00 mm ⌀ kpl. Piston 71,00 mm ⌀ cpl. Pistone ⌀ 71,00 mm kpl.	1	—
—	54.30.007.200	Kolben 71,25 mm ⌀ kpl. Piston 71,25 mm ⌀ cpl. Pistone ⌀ 71,25 mm cpl.	nB ar	— — —
—	54.30.007.300	Kolben 71,50 mm ⌀ kpl. Piston 71,50 mm ⌀ cpl. Pistone ⌀71,50 mm cpl.	nB ar	— — —
—	54.30.007.400	Kolben 72,00 mm ⌀ kpl. Piston 72,00 mm ⌀ cpl. Pistone ⌀ 72,00 mm cpl.	nB ar	— — —
—	55.30.007.400	Kolben 81,00 mm ⌀ kpl. Piston 81,00 mm ⌀ cpl. Pistone ⌀ 81,00 mm cpl.	—	1
—	55.30.007.500	Kolben 81,25 mm ⌀ kpl. Piston 81,25 mm ⌀ cpl. Pistone ⌀ 81,25 mm cpl.	— — —	nB ar —
—	55.30.007.600	Kolben 81,50 mm ⌀ kpl. Piston 81,50 mm ⌀ cpl. Pistone ⌀ 81,25 mm cpl.	— — —	nB ar —
—	55.30.007.700	Kolben 82,00 mm ⌀ kpl. Piston 82,00 mm ⌀ cpl. Pistone ⌀ 82,00 mm cpl.	— — —	nB ar —
—	55.30.007.800	Kolben 82,50 mm ⌀ kpl. Piston 82,50 mm ⌀ cpl. Pistone ⌀ 82,50 mm cpl.	— — —	nB ar —
15	1.54.30.015.000	Pleuellager-Reparatursatz Connecting rod repair kit Gruppo per la riparazione del cuscinetto a biella	1	—
—	1.55.30.015.000	Pleuellager-Reparatursatz Connecting rod repair kit Gruppo per la riparazione del cuscinetto a biella	—	1
18	54.30.018.200	Kurbelwelle kpl. Crankshaft assy. Gruppo albero a gomiti	1	—
—	55.30.018.000	Kurbelwelle kpl. Crankshaft assy. Gruppo albero a gomiti	—	1
23	54.30.023.300	Simmerringträger Spacer Spessore	1	—
—	55.30.023.000	Simmerringträger Spacer Spessore	—	1
24	54.30.024.000	Zwischenscheibe Spacer Spessore	2	2
28	51.30.028.100	Bundmutter M 12x1 links Magneto nut M 12x1 L/S Dado magneto M 12x1 sinistra	1	1

nB = nach Bedarf — ar = as requested

Bild Picture Foto	Teil-Nr. Part-No. Parte No	Benennung Description Descrizione	Stk./Motor Pos./Engine Pezzi/Motore	
			250	400
	54.30.031.000	L-Ring 71,00 mm ⌀ x 2 L-ring 71,00 mm ⌀ x 2 Anello a L 71,00 mm ⌀ x 2	1	—
—	54.30.031.200	L-Ring 71,25 mm ⌀ x 2 L-ring 71,25 mm ⌀ x 2 Anello a L 71,25 mm ⌀ x 2	nB ar	— —
—	54.30.031.300	L-Ring 71,50 mm ⌀ x 2 L-ring 71,50 mm ⌀ x 2 Anello a L 71,50 mm ⌀ x 2	nB ar	— —
—	54.30.031.400	L-Ring 72,00 mm ⌀ x 2 L-ring 72,00 mm ⌀ x 2 Anello a L 72,00 mm ⌀ x 2	nB ar	— —
—	55.30.031.400	L-Ring 81,00 mm ⌀ x 2 L-ring 81,00 mm ⌀ x 2 Anello a L 81,00 mm ⌀ x 2	—	1
—	55.30.031.500	L-Ring 81,25 mm ⌀ x 2 L-ring 81,25 mm ⌀ x 2 Anello 81,25 mm ⌀ x 2	— —	nB ar
—	55.30.031.600	L-Ring 81,50 mm ⌀ x 2 L-ring 81,50 mm ⌀ x 2 Anello a L 81,50 mm ⌀ x 2	— —	nB ar
—	55.30.031.700	L-Ring 82,00 mm ⌀ x 2 L-ring 82,00 mm ⌀ x 2 Anello a L 82,00 mm ⌀ x 2	— —	nB ar
—	55.30.031.800	L-Ring 82,50 mm ⌀ x 2 L-ring 82,50 mm ⌀ x 2 Anello a L 82,50 mm ⌀ x 2	— —	nB ar
32	54.30.032.000	Rechteckring 71,00 x 2 Square ring 71,00 x 2 Anello quadro 71,00 x 2	1	—
—	54.30.032.200	Rechteckring 71,25 x 2 Square ring 71,25 x 2 Anello quadro 71,25 x 2	nB ar	— —
—	54.30.032.300	Rechteckring 71,50 x 2 Square ring 71,50 x 2 Anello quadro 71,50 x 2	nB ar	— —
—	54.30.032.400	Rechteckring 72,00 x 2 Square ring 72,00 x 2 Anello quadro 72,00 x 2	nB ar	— —
—	55.30.032.400	Rechteckring 81,00 x 2 Square ring 81,00 x 2 Anello quadro 81,00 x 2	— —	nB ar
—	55.30.032.500	Rechteckring 81,25 x 2 Square ring 81,25 x 2 Anello quadro 81,25 x 2	— —	nB ar
—	55.30.032.600	Rechteckring 81,50 x 2 Square ring 81,50 x 2 Anello quadro 81,50 x 2	— —	nB ar

Gruppe 30: Kurbeltrieb — 250/400 ccm
Group 30: Crankshaft, piston — 250/400 cc
Gruppo 30: Albero a gomiti — 250/400 cc

nB = nach Bedarf — ar = as requested

Gruppe 30: Kurbeltrieb   250/400 ccm
Group 30: Crankshaft, piston   250/400 cc
Gruppo 30: Albero a gomiti   250/400 cc

Bild / Picture / Foto	Teil-Nr. / Part-No. / Parte No	Benennung / Description / Descrizione	Stk./Motor Pos./Engine Pezzi/Motore 250/400	
–	55.30.032.700	Rechteckring 82,00 x 2 / Square ring 82,00 x 2 / Anello quadro 82,00 x 2	– / – /	nB / ar /
–	55.30.032.800	Rechteckring 82,50 x 2 / Square ring 82,50 x 2 / Anello quadro 82,50 x 2	– / – /	nB / ar /
33	54.30.033.000	Kolbenbolzen 18 ⌀ x 60,3 / Wrist pin 18 ⌀ x 60,3 / Spinotto rinforzato 18 ⌀ x 60,3	1	–
–	55.30.033.000	Kolbenbolzen 18 ⌀ x 72,2 / Wrist pin 18 ⌀ x 72,2 / Spinotto rinforzato 18 ⌀ x 72,2	–	1
34	54.30.034.000	Nadellager 10 ⌀ x 22 ⌀ x 25 / Needle bearing 18 ⌀ x 22 ⌀ x 25 / Cuscinetto a spillo 18 ⌀ x 22 ⌀ x 25	1	1
74	C 18	Drahtsprengring C 18 DIN 73123 / Retaining clip C 18 DIN 73123 / Pinza di ritenuta C 18 DIN 73123	2	2
75	DIN 936/M18x1.5	Sechskantmutter M 18x1,5 DIN 936 / Hexagon head screw M 18x1,5 DII 936 / Vite M 18x1,5 DII 936	1	1
76	54.30.048.000	Sicherungsblech 22 mm ⌀ / Flat washer 22 mm ⌀ / Rondella piatta 22 mm ⌀	1	1
77	OR 2-227	O-Ring 2-227 / O-ring 2-227 / Anello a O 2-227	1	–
–	OR 2-139	O-Ring 2-139 / O-ring 2-139 / Anello a O 2-139	–	1
79	DIN 6888/3x5	Scheibenfeder 3x5 DIN 6888 / Woodruff key 3x5 DIN 6888 / Chiave Woodruff 3x5 DIN 6888	1	1
79a	DIN 6888/4x5	Scheibenfeder 4x5 DIN 6888 / Woodruff key 4x5 DIN 6888 / Chiave Woodruff 4x5 6888	1	1
81	PS 25x35x0,1	Paßscheibe / Shim washer / Rondella	nB / ar	nB / ar
–	PS 25x35x0,15	Paßscheibe / Shim washer / Rondella	nB / ar	nB / ar
–	PS 25x35x0,3	Paßscheibe / Shim washer / Rondella	nB / ar	nB / ar
82	DIN 615/M25	Schulterlager M 25 DIN 615 / Shoulder bearing M 25 DIN 615 / Cuscinetto spalla M 25 DIN 615	2	2
83	DIN 6504/	Simmerring 25x35x7 / Radial seal ring 25x35x7 / Anello di tenuta radiale 25x35x7	2	2
84	DIN 137/B12	Federscheibe B 12 DIN 137 / Spring washer B 12 DIN 137 / Rondella elastica B 12 DIN 137	1	1
91	RB 6204	Rillenlager 6204 C 3 SV 41 DIN 625 / Ball bearing 6204 C 3 SV 41 DIN 625 / Cuscinetto a sfera 6204 C 3 SV 41 DIN 625	1	1

nB = nach Bedarf — ar = as requested

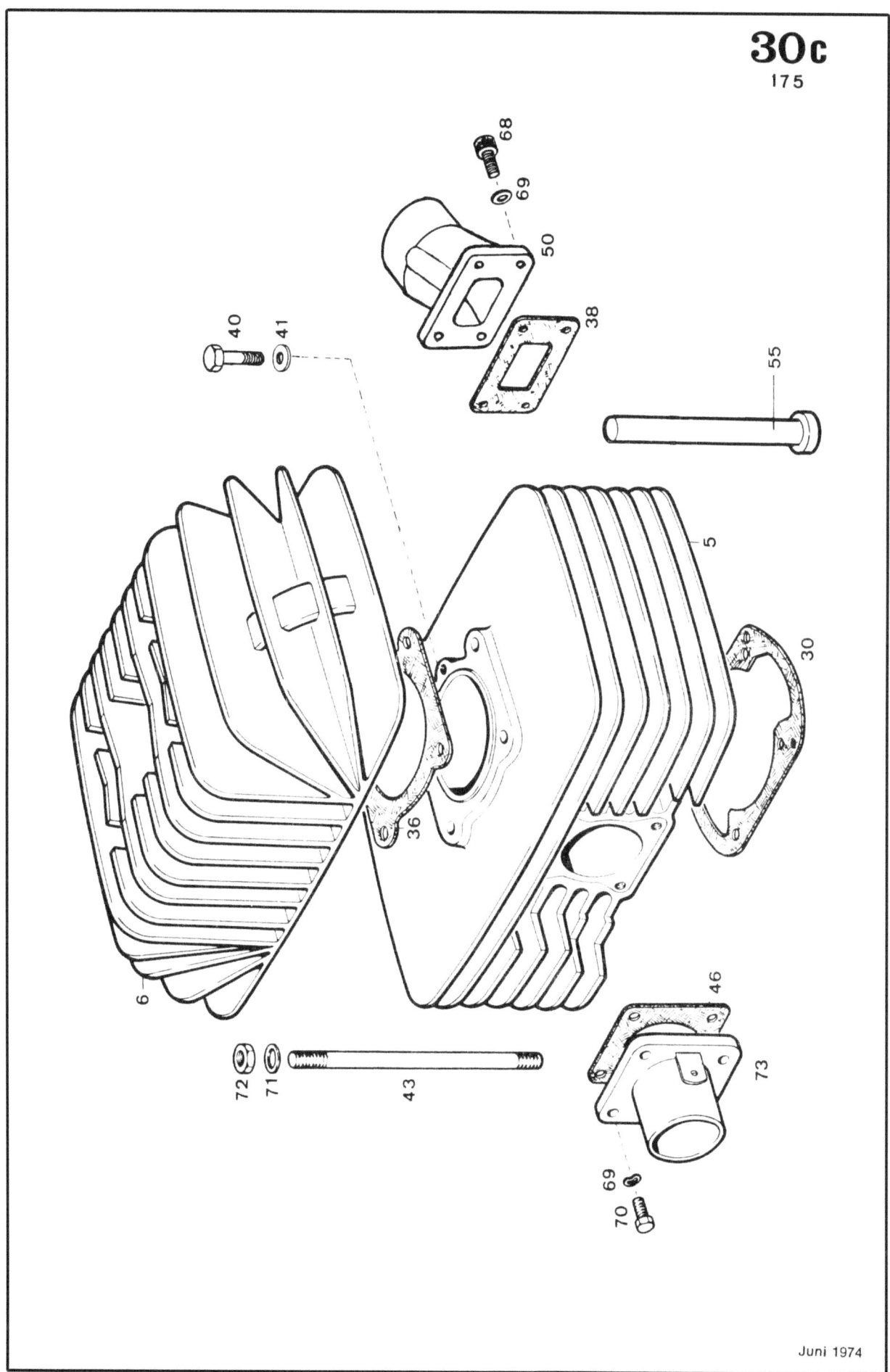

Gruppe 30: Zylinder   **175 ccm**
Group 30: Cylinder   **175 cc**
Gruppo 30: Cilindro   **175 cc**

Bild / Picture / Foto	Teil-Nr. / Part-No. / Parte No	Benennung / Description / Descrizione	Stk./Motor Pos./Engine Pezzi/Motore 175
5	52.30.005.000	Zylinder 63,5 ⌀ / Cylinder barrel 63,5 ⌀ / Corpo del cilindro ⌀ 63,5	1
6	52.30.006.100	Zylinderkopf / Cylinder head / Testa del cilindro	1
30	52.30.030.000	Zylinderfußdichtung 0,2 mm / Cylinder base gasket 0,2 mm / Guarnizione base cilindro 0,2 mm	nB ar
–	52.30.030.100	Zylinderfußdichtung 0,3 mm / Cylinder base gasket 0,3 mm / Guarnizione base cilindro 0,3 mm	nB ar
–	52.30.030.200	Zylinderfußdichtung 0,5 mm / Cylinder base gasket 0,5 mm / Guarnizione base cilindro 0,5 mm	nB ar
–	52.30.030.300	Zylinderfußdichtung 0,75 mm / Cylinder base gasket 0,75 mm / Guarnizione base cilindro 0,75 mm	nB ar
–	52.30.030.400	Zylinderfußdichtung 1,0 mm / Cylinder base gasket 1,0 mm / Guarnizione base cilindro 1,0 mm	nB ar
36	52.30.036.100	Zylinderkopfdichtung 1,0 mm / Cylinder head gasket 1,0 mm / Guarnizione testa cilindro 1,0 mm	1
38	52.30.038.000	Ansaugstutzendichtung / Induction manifold gasket / Guarnizione percollettore d'ammissione	1
40	DIN 931/M7x40/86	Sechskantschraube M 7x40 DIN 931 / Hexagon head screw M 7x40 DIN 931 / Vite M 7x40 DIN 931	1
41	DIN 125/7.4	Scheibe 7,4 DIN 125 / Flat washer 7,4 DIN 125 / Rondella 7,4 DIN 125	1
43	51.30.043.000	Zylinderstehbolzen M 8, 152 mm lang / Cylinder stud M 8, 152 mm long / Perno cilindro M 8, lunghezza 152 mm	4
46	52.30.046.000	Auspuffstutzendichtung / Exhaust adapter gasket / Guarnizione attacco di scarica	1
50	52.30.050.000	Ansaugstutzen / Intake adapter / Attacco aspirazione	1
55	54.30.055.000	Dämpfergummi / Rubber / Gomma	4
68	DIN 912/M6x15/86	Innensechskantschraube M 6x16 DIN 912 / Allen head screw M 6x16 DIN 912 / Vite a testa esagonale interna M 6x16 DIN 912	1
69	DIN 137/B6	Federscheibe B 6 DIN 137 / Spring washer B 6 DIN 137 / Rondella elastica B 6 DIN 137	8
70	DIN 933/M6x15/86	Sechskantschraube M 6x16 / Hexagon head screw M 6x16 / Vite M 6x16	4
71	DIN 125/8.4	**Scheibe 8,4 DIN 125** / Flat washer 8,4 DIN 125 / Rondella 8,4 DIN 125	4
72	M8	Sechskantmutter M 8 DIN 934 / Hexagon nut M 8 DIN 934 / Dado M 8 DIN 934	4
73	52.05.073.000	**Auspufflansch (2 Federlaschen)** / Exhaust flange / Flangia di scarico	1

nB = nach Bedarf – ar = as requested

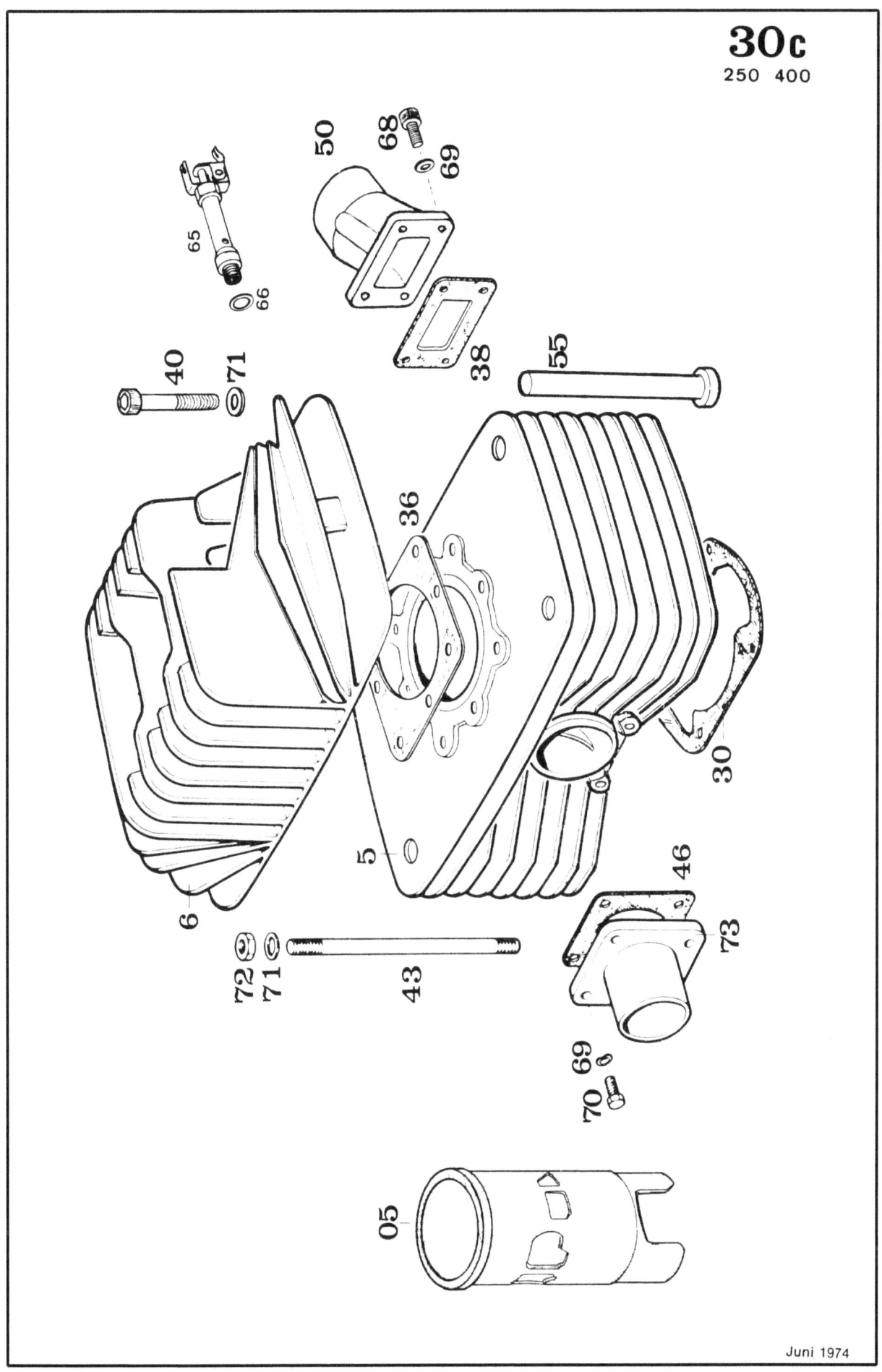

Gruppe 30: Zylinder 250/400 ccm
Group 30: Cylinder 250/400 cc
Gruppo 30: Cilindro 250/400 cc

Bild/Picture/Foto	Teil-Nr./Part-No./Parte No	Benennung/Description/Descrizione	Stk./Motor Pos./Engine Pezzi/Motore 250/400	
5	54.30.005.000	Zylinder 71,0 ⌀ / Cylinder barrel 71,0 ⌀ / Corpo del cilindro 71,0 ⌀	1	—
—	55.30.005.000	Zylinder 80,0 ⌀ / Cylinder barrel 80,0 ⌀ / Corpo del cilindro ⌀ 80,0	—	1
—	55.30.005.100	Zylinder 81,0 ⌀ / Cylinder barrel 81,0 ⌀ / Corpo del cilindro ⌀ 81,0	1	—
—	54.30.005.050	Zylinder-Laufbüchse 71,0 ⌀ / Cylinder liner 71,0 ⌀ / Canna cilindro	—	1
05	55.30.005.150	Zylinder-Laufbüchse 81,0 ⌀ / Cylinder liner 81,0 ⌀ / Canna cilindro	—	1
6	54.30.006.000	Zylinderkopf / Cylinder head / Testa del cilindro	1	—
—	55.30.006.000	Zylinderkopf / Cylinder head / Testa del cilindro	—	1
30	54.30.030.000	Zylinderfußdichtung 0,2 mm / Cylinder base gasket 0,2 mm / Guarnizione base cilindro 0,2 mm	nB / ar	—
—	54.30.030.100	Zylinderfußdichtung 0,3 mm / Cylinder base gasket 0,3 mm / Guarnizione base cilindro 0,3 mm	nB / ar	—
—	54.30.030.200	Zylinderfußdichtung 0,5 mm / Cylinder base gasket 0,5 mm / Guarnizione base cilindro 0,5 mm	nB / ar	—
—	54.30.030.300	Zylinderfußdichtung 0,75 mm / Cylinder base gasket 0,75 mm / Guarnizione base cilindro 0,75 mm	nB / ar	—
—	54.30.030.400	Zylinderfußdichtung 1 mm / Cylinder base gasket 1 mm / Guarnizione base cilindro 1 mm	nB / ar	—
30	55.30.030.000	Zylinderfußdichtung 0,2 mm / Cylinder base gasket 0,2 mm / Guarnznone base cilindro 0,2 mm	—	nB / ar
—	55.30.030.100	Zylinderfußdichtung 0,3 mm / Cylinder base gasket 0,3 mm / Guarnizione base cilindro 0,3 mm	—	nB / ar
—	55.30.030.200	Zylinderfußdichtung 0,5 mm / Cylinder base gasket 0,5 mm / Guarnizione base cilindro 0,5 mm	—	nB / ar
—	55.30.030.300	Zylinderfußdichtung 0,75 mm / Cylinder base gasket 0,75 mm / Guarnizione base cilindro 0,75 mm	—	nB / ar
—	55.30.030.400	Zylinderfußdichtung 1 mm / Cylinder base gasket 1 mm / Guarnizione base cilindro 1 mm	—	nB / ar
36	54.30.036.100	Zylinderkopfdichtung 1 mm / Cylinder head gasket 1 mm / Guarnizione testa cilindro 1 mm	1	—
—	55.30.036.000	Zylinderkopfdichtung 1 mm / Cylinder head gasket 1 mm / Guarnizione testa cilindro 1 mm	—	1
38	54.30.038.000	Ansaugstutzendichtung / Induction manifold gasket / Guarnizione per collettore d' ammissione	1	—

nB = nach Bedarf — ar = as requested

Gruppe 30: Zylinder
Group 30: Cylinder
Gruppo 30: Cilindro

250/400 ccm
250/400 cc
250/400 cc

Bild / Picture / Foto	Teil-Nr. / Part-No. / Parte-No	Benennung / Description / Descrizione	Stk./Motor 250/400	Pos./Engine Pezzi/Motore
—	55.30.038.000	Ansaugstutzendichtung / Induction manifold gasket / Guarnizione per collettore d'ammissione	—	1
40	DIN 912/M8x45	Innensechskantschraube M 8x45 DIN 912 / Allen head screw M 8x45 DIN 912 / Vite a testa esagonale interna M 8x45 DIN 912	4	4
43	54.30.043.000	Zylinderstehbolzen M 8, 169 mm lang / Cylinderstud M 8, 169 mm long / Perno cilindro M 8, lunghezza 169 mm	4	—
—	55.30.043.000	Zylinderstehbolzen M 8, 173 mm lang / Cylinder stud M 8, 173 mm long / Perno cilindro M 8, 173 mm lunghezza	—	4
46	52.30.046.000	Auspuffstutzendichtung / Exhaust adapter gasket / Guarnizione attaco di scarica	1	1
50	54.30.050.000 / 54.30.150.000 new	Ansaugstutzen / Intake adapter / Attacco aspirazione	1	—
—	55.30.050.000	Ansaugstutzen / Intake adapter / Attacco aspirazione	—	1
55	54.30.055.000	Dämpfergummi / **Rubber** / Gomma	4	4
68	DIN 912/M6x20/86	Innensechskantschraube M 6x20 DIN 912 / Allen head screw M 6x20 DIN 912 / Vite a testa esagonale interna M 6x20 DIN 912	4	4
69	DIN 137/B6	Federscheibe B 6 DIN 137 / **Spring washer B 6 DIN 137** / Rondella elastica B 6 DIN 137	8	8
70	DIN 933/M6x15/86	Sechskantschraube M 6x16 / Hexagon head screw M 6x16 / Vite M 6x16	4	4
71	DIN 125/8.4	Scheibe 8,4 DIN 125 / Flat washer 8,4 DIN 125 / Rondella 8,4 DIN 125	8	8
72	M8	Sechskantmutter M 8 DIN 934 / Hexagon nut M 8 DIN 934 / Dado M 8 DIN 934	4	4
73	52.05.073.000	Auspufflansch (1 Federlasche) / Exhaust flange / Flangia di scarico	1	1
65	55.30.065.000	Dekompressor kpl. / Decompressor cpl. / Starter cpl.	1	1
66	55.30.066.000	Dichtring / Seal ring / Guarnizione	1	1

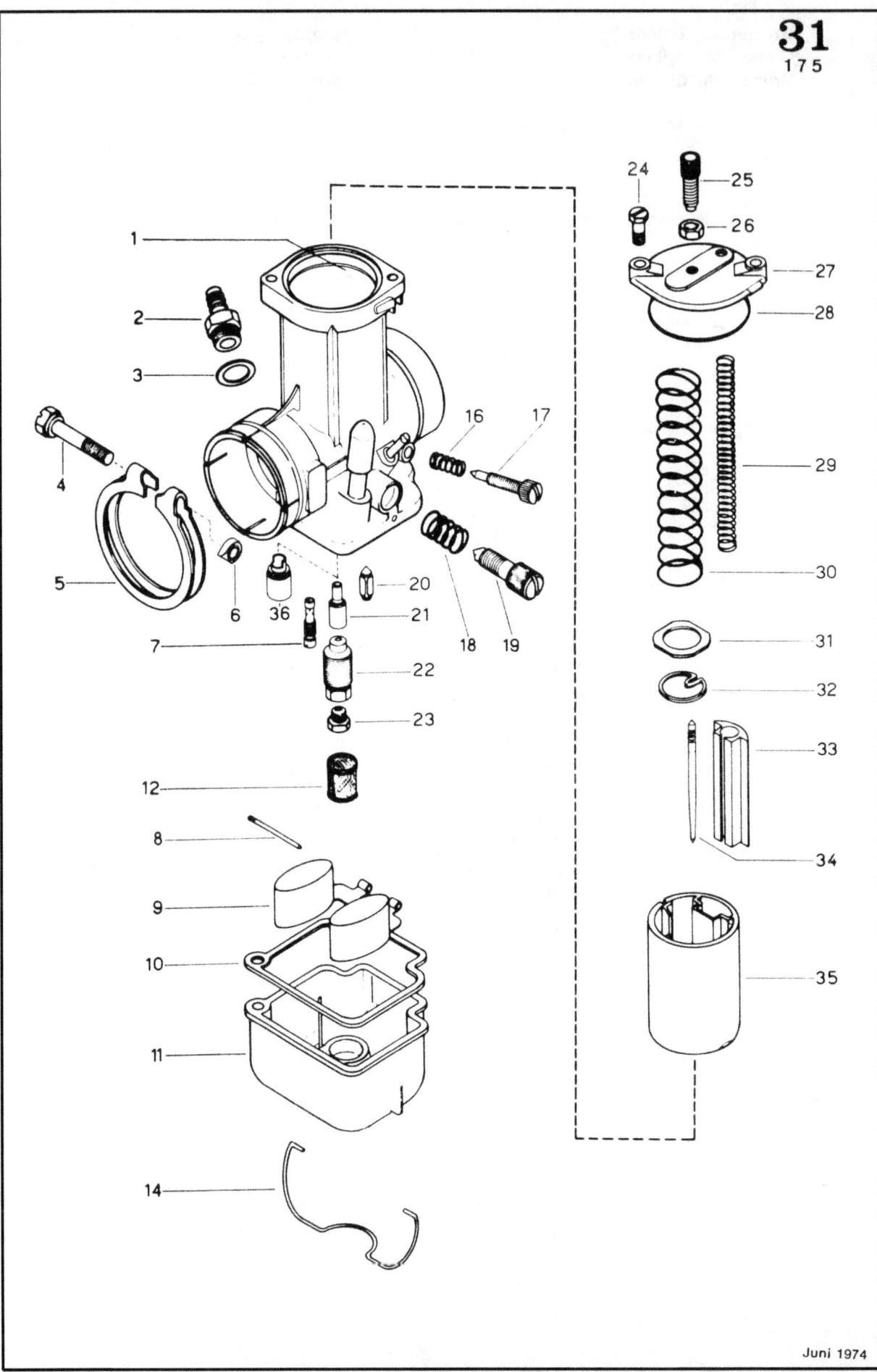

Gruppe 31: Vergaser
Group 31: Carburettor
Gruppo 31: Carburatore

Bild Picture Foto	Teil-Nr. Part-No. Parte No	Benennung Description Descrizione	Stk./Motor Pos./Engine Pezzi/Motore 175
—	2/30/101	Vergaser 30 ⌀, kpl. Carburettor cpl. Carburatore cpl.	1
1	2/30/101	Vergasergehäuse 30 ⌀, kpl. Body Only Corpo carburatore	1
2	51-323	Schlauchtülle Fuel line adapter Condotta	1
3	65-171	Dichrting Seal ring Guarnizione	1
4	40-626	Klemmschraube Pinch bolt Vite di fermo	1
5	59-114	Klemmring Clamp Anello di fermo	1
6	42-611	Mutter Nut Dado	1
7	44-350	△ Leerlaufdüse Pilot jet Getto del minimo	1
8	52-058	Stift Spindle Astina	1
9	35-300	Schwimmer Float Galleggiante	1
10	65-584	Dichtung Seal Guarnizione	1
11	30-563	Schwimmergehäuse Float chamber body Vaschetta	1
12	57-701	Siebhülse Fuel filter Filtro del combustibile	1
14	61-479	Federbügel Float chamber clamp Boccola	1
16	60-160	Feder Spring Molla	1
17	50-023	Luftregulierschraube Pilot air adjusting screw Vite registro aria	1
18	60-322	Feder Spring Molla	1
19	50-072	Stellschraube Throttle stop adjusting screw Vite di registro	1
20 —	47-953 40-405 Neoprene Tip	Schwimmernadel Float needle Ago galleggiante	1
21	45-196	△ Nadeldüse Needle jet Getto ad ago	1

△ Aufgestempelte Nummer zusätzlich bekanntgeben, bei Düsennadeln Zahl der feinen Rillen.
  Please quoto printed number
  Indicare anche il numero stampigliato sul pezzo

Gruppe 31: Vergaser
Group 31: Carburettor
Gruppo 31: Carburatore

Bild Picture Foto	Teil-Nr. Part-No. Parte No	Benennung Description Descrizione	Stk./Motor Pos./Engine Pezzi/Motore 175
22	45-420	Mischrohr Jet holder Tubetto miscelatore	1
23	44-051	△ Hauptdüse Jet Getto principale	1
24	40-518	Befestigungsschraube Top securing screw Vite	2
25	50-050	Stellschraube cable adjusting screw Vite di registro	2
26	42-605	Mutter Nut Dado	2
27	20-642	Deckelplatte Cover Coperchio	
28	65-740	Gummidichtring Rubber seal ring Anello gomma	1
29	60-194	Schieberfeder Spring Molla valvola dell aria	1
30	60-370	Schieberfeder Spring Chiavella	1
31	57-257	**Scheibe** Washer Rondella	1
32	57-253	Halteplättchen Needle clip Piastrina	1
33	24-056	Luftschieber Air valve Valvota dell aria	1
34	46-291	△ Düsennadel Jet needle Ago del getto	1
35	22-736-2	Gasschieber Throttle valve Valvola gas	1
36	40-404	Zerstäuber Vaporizer Polverizzatore	1
—	80-708	Entlüftungsschlauch Breather tube Otre	1
—	65-851	Gummitülle Plug (rubber) Bussola di gomma	2

△ Aufgestempelte Nummer zusätzlich bekanntgeben, bei Düsennadeln Zahl der feinen Rillen.
Please quote printed number
Indicare anche il numero stampigliato sul pezzo

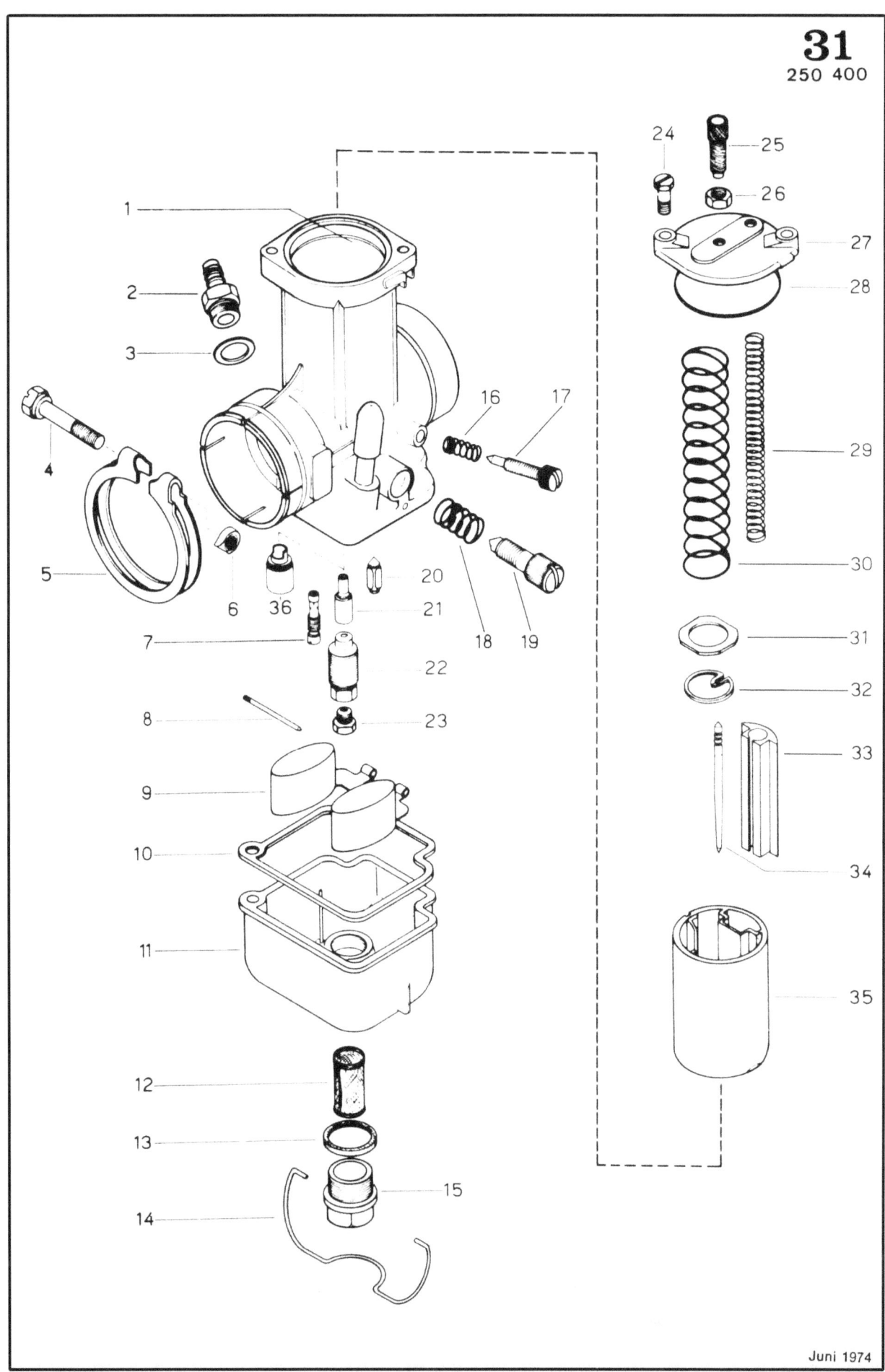

Gruppe 31: Vergaser
Group 31: Carburettor
Gruppo 31: Carburatore

Bild / Picture / Foto	Teil-Nr. / Part-No. / Parte No	Benennung / Description / Descrizione	Stk./Motor Pos./Engine Pezzi/Motore 250/400	
–	2/36/102	Vergaser 36 ⌀ kpl. / Carburettor cpl. / Carburatore cpl.	1	1
1	2/36/102	Vergasergehäuse 36 ⌀ / Carburetor Only / Corpo carburatore	1	1
–	2/38/102	Vergaser 38 ⌀ kpl. / Carburettor cpl. / Carburatore cpl.	1	1
1	2/38/102	Vergasergehäuse 38 ⌀ / Carburetor Only / Corpo carburatore	1	1
2	51-323	Schlauchtülle / Fuel line adapter / Condotta	1	1
3	65-171	Dichtring / Seal ring / Guarnizione	1	1
4	40-626	Klemmschraube / Pinch bolt / Vite di fermo	1	1
5	59-115	Klemmring / Clamp / Anello di fermo	1	1
6	42-611	Mutter / Nut / Dado	1	1
7	44-350	△ Leerlaufdüse / Pilot jet / Getto del minimo	1	1
8	52-058	Stift / Spindle / Astina	1	1
9	35-300	Schwimmer / Float / Galleggiante	1	1
10	65-584	**Dichtung** / Seal / Guarnizione	1	1
11	30-569	Schwimmergehäuse / Float chamber body / Vaschetta	1	1
12	57-702	Siebhülse / Fuel filter / Filtro del combustibile	1	1
13	65-221	**Dichtring** / Seal ring / Guarnizione	1	1
14	61-479	Federbügel / Float chamber clamp / Boccola	1	1
15	50-286	Abschlußschraube / Plug / Tappo a vite	1	1
16	60-160	**Feder** / Spring / Molla	1	1
17	50-023	**Luftregulierschraube** / Pilot air adjusting screw / Vite registro aria	1	1
18	60-322	Feder / Spring / Molla	1	1
19	50-072	Stellschraube / Throttle stop adjusting screw / Vite di registro	1	1

△ Aufgestempelte Nummer zusätzlich bekanntgeben, bei Düsennadeln Zahl der feinen Rillen.
Please quote printed number
Indicare anche il numero stampigliato sul pezzo

Gruppe 31: Vergaser
Group 31: Carburettor
Gruppo 31: Carburatore

Bild / Picture / Foto	Teil-Nr. / Part-No. / Parte-No.	Benennung / Description / Descrizione	Stk./Motor Pos./Engine Pezzi/Motore 250 / 400	
20	47-953	Schwimmernadel / Float needle / Ago galleggiante	1	1
–	40-405 Neoprene Tip			
21	45-118	△ Nadeldüse / Needle jet / Getto ad ago	1	1
22	45-420	Mischrohr / Jet holder / Tubetto miscelatore	1	1
23	44-051	△ Hauptdüse / Jet / Getto principale	1	1
24	40-518	Befestigungsschraube / Top securing screw / Vite	2	2
25	50-050	Stellschraube / Cable adjusting screw / Vite di registro	2	2
26	42-605	Mutter / Nut / Dado	2	2
27	20-650	Deckelplatte / Cover / Coperchio	1	1
28	65-745	Gummidichtring / Rubber seal ring / Anello gomma	1	1
29	60-195	Schieberfeder / Spring / Molla valvola dell aria	1	1
30	60-432	Schieberfeder / Spring / Chiavella	1	1
31	57-028	Scheibe / Washer / Rondella	1	1
32	57-251	Halteplättchen / Needle clip / Piastrina	1	1
33	24-055	Luftschieber / Air valve / Valvola dell aria	1	1
34	46-281	△ Düsennadel / Jet needle / Ago del getto	1	1
35	22-746-1	Gasschieber / Throttle valve / Valvola gas	1	1
36	40-404	Zerstäuber / Vaporizer / Polverizzatore	1	1
–	80-708	Entlüftungsschlauch / Breather tube / Otre	1	1
–	65-851	Gummitülle / Plug (rubber) / Bussola di gomma	2	2

△ Aufgestempelte Nummer zusätzlich bekanntgeben, bei Düsennadeln Zahl der feinen Rillen.
  Please quote printed number
  Indicare anche il numero stampigliato sul pezzo

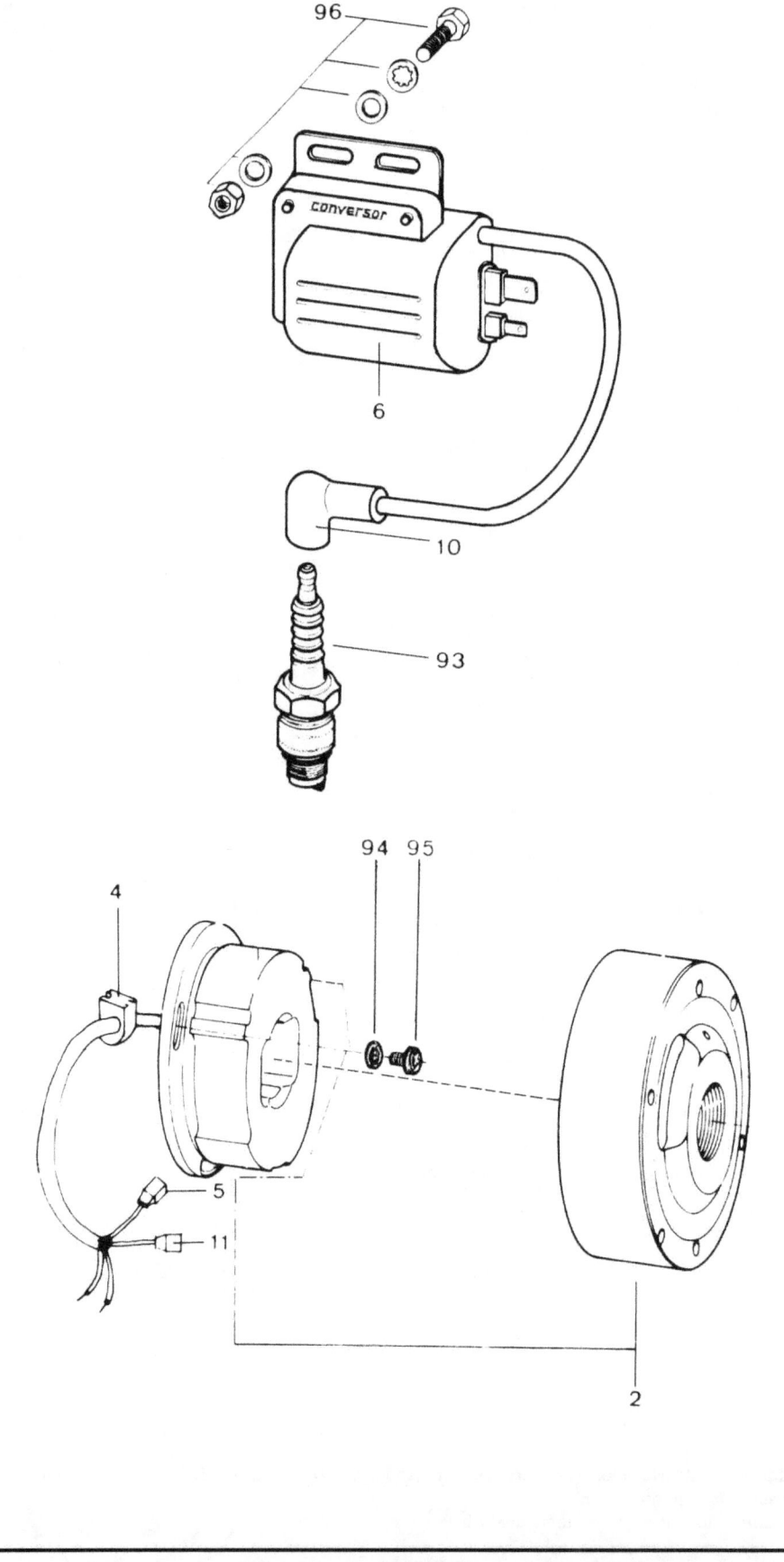

Juni 1974

Gruppe 31: Zündanlage
Group 31: Ignition
Gruppo 31: Accensione

Bild Picture Foto	Teil-Nr. Part-No. Parte No	Benennung Description Descrizione	Stk./Motor Pos./Engine Pezzi/Motore		
			175	250	400
–	52.31.001.000	Zündanlage kpl., 6 V 35/4/18 W mit Zündspule (Type 9600 162-1) Schwungrad 116 mm ⌀ Ignition cpl., 6 V 35/4/18 W with ignition coil (type 9600 162-1) Flywheel 116 mm ⌀ Accensione cpl., 6 V 35/4/18 W con Bobina di accensione (tipo 9600 162-1) Volano ⌀ 116 mm	1	1	–
–	55.31.001.000	Zündanlage kpl., 6 V 35/4/18 W mit Zündspule (Type 9600 180-1) Ignition cpl., 6 V 35/4/18 W with ignition coil (type 9600 180-1) Accensione cpl., 6 V 35/4/18 W con bobina di accensione (tipo 9600 180-1)	–	–	1
2	52.31.001.100	Zündanlage kpl., ohne Zündspule Diode im Stator) Ignition cpl., without ignitionn coil Accensione cpl., senza bobina di accensione	1	1	–
–	51.31.002.200	Zündanlage kpl., ohne Zündspule (rote Schutzkappen) Ignition cpl., without ignition coil (red protection caps) Accensione cpl., senza bobina di accensione (coperchietti rossi di protezione)	1	1	–
–	55.31.002.000	Zündanlage kpl., ohne Zündspule (rote Schutzkappen) Ignition cpl., without ignition coil (red protection caps) Accensione cpl., senza bobina di accensione (coperchietti rossi di protezione)	–	–	1
4	51.31.004.000	Kabeldurchführung Rubber cable grommet Anello per cavo di gomma	1	1	1
5	51.31.005.000	Steckverbinder (klein) Receptacle, small Presa, piccola	1	1	1
6	51.31.006.200	Zündspule, rotes Zündkabel (passend für alle Zündanlagen) Ignition coil, red ignition cable (suitable for all ignitions) adatti per tutti gli impianti di accensione	1	1	1
10	51.31.010.100	Kerzenstecker Sparking plug protector Protezione candela	1	1	1
11	51.31.011.000	Steckverbinder (groß) Receptacle (large) Presa, grande	1	1	1
93	51.31.093.100	○ Zündkerze Sparking plug W 290 R 116 or W 310+16 Candela	1	1	1
94	DIN 137/A4	Federscheibe A 4 Spring washer A 4 Rondella elastica A 4	3	3	3
95	DIN 7985/AM 4x12	Linsenschraube AM 4x12 Flat head screw AM 4x12 Vite atesta piana AM 4x12	3	3	3
96	51.31.096.000	Sechskantschraube M 6x20 kpl. Hexagon head screw M 6x20 cpl. Vite M 6x20 cpl.	2	2	2

○ Wärmewert bekanntgeben
Please quote heat value
Indicare il valore termico

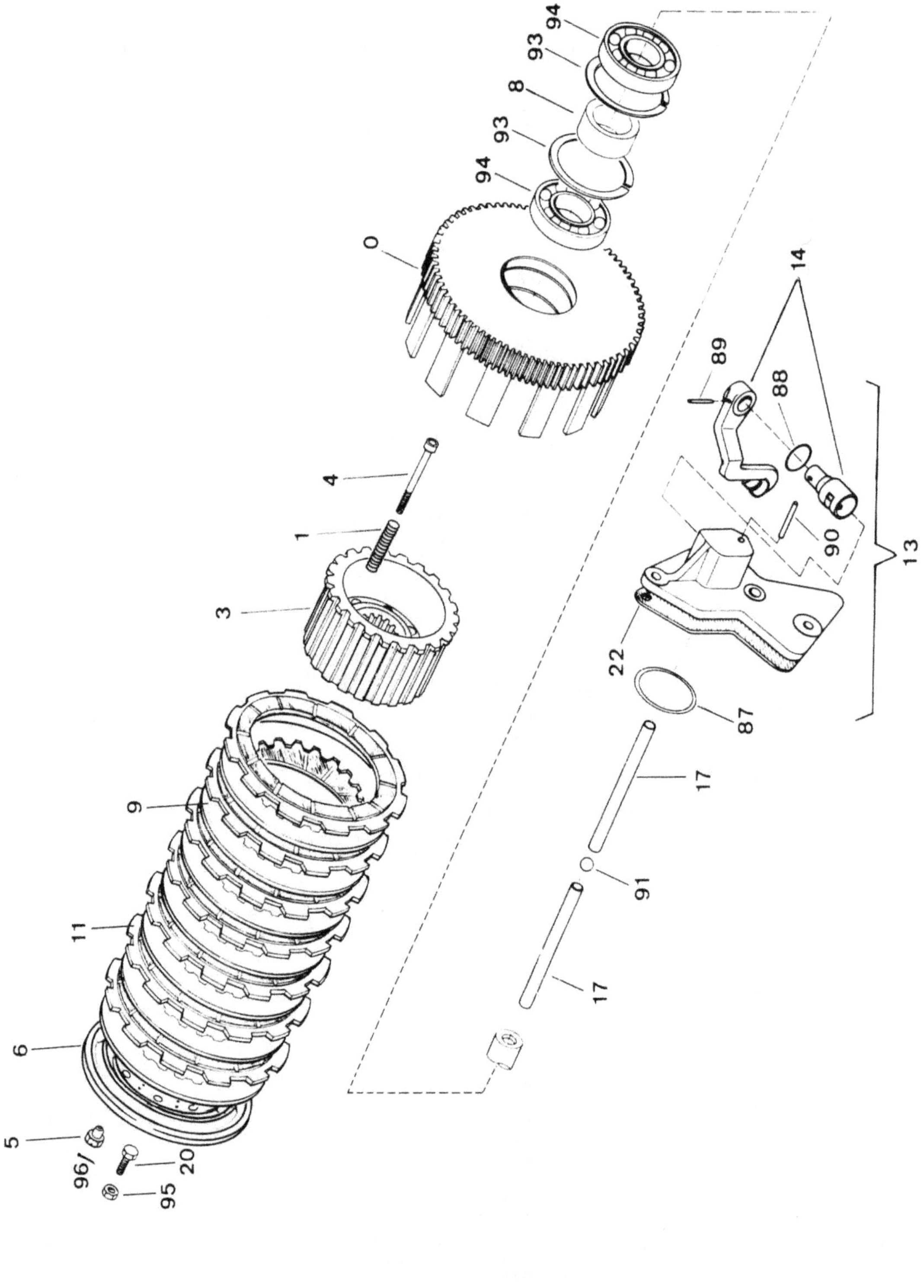

Gruppe 32: Kupplung
Group 32: Clutch
Gruppo 32: Frizione

Bild / Picture / Foto	Teil-Nr. / Part-No. / Parte No	Benennung / Description / Descrizione	Stk./Motor Pos./Engine Pezzi/Motore 175/250/400		
0	1.51.32.000.570	Kupplungskorb, 69 Zähne, mit Primärzahnrad, 25 Zähne (geschliffen) / Outer clutch hub 69-T with pinion 25-T (grinded) / Mozzo frizione esterna 69 denti con pignone 25 denti, rettificato su richiesta	1	–	–
0	1.54.32.000.570	Kupplungskorb, 69 Zähne, mit Primärzahnrad, 25 Zähne (geschliffen) / Outer clutch hub 69-T with pinion 25-T (grinded) / Mozzo frizione esterna 69 denti con pignone 25 denti, rettificato su richiesta	–	1	1
1	51.32.001.120	Kupplungsfeder 1,5 ⌀ / Clutch spring 1,5 ⌀ / Molla frizione 1,5 ⌀	8	–	–
–	51.32.001.130	Kupplungsfeder 1,6 ⌀ / Clutch spring 1,6 ⌀ / Molla frizione 1,6 ⌀	–	8	–
–	51.32.001.140	Kupplungsfeder 1,7 ⌀ / Clutch spring 1,7 ⌀ / Molla frizione 1,7 ⌀	–	–	8
3	51.32.003.200	Mitnehmer / Inner clutch hub / Mozzo frizione interna	1	1	1
4	51.32.004.100	Federschraube / Spring bolt / Bullone elastico	8	8	8
5	51.32.005.100	Federmutter / Spring nut / Dado per molla	8	8	8
6	51.32.006.130	Druckkappe / Pressure plate / Piastra di puessione	1	–	–
–	54.32.006.100	Druckkappe / Pressure plate / Piastra di puessione	–	1	1
8	51.32.008.000	Distanzbüchse / Distance bushing / Spessore	1	1	1
9	51.32.009.100	Stahllamelle / Steel disc / Disco in acciaio	5	7	7
11	51.32.011.011	Belaglamelle, organisch / Clutch disc, organic / Disco frizione cpl. di rivestimento	5	–	–
–	54.32.011.250	Belaglamelle / Clutch disc. / Disco frizione cpl. di rivestimento	–	7	7
13	51.32.013.300	Lagerdeckel kpl., montiert / Bearing cover cpl. / Coperchio cuscinetti cpl.	1	1	1
14	51.32.014.200	Ausrückhebel kpl. mit Welle / Disengaging levter cpl. with shaft / Leva di disinnesto cpl. con albero	1	1	1
17	51.32.017.100	Druckstange / Pushrod / Asta di spinta	2	2	2
20	51.32.020.100	Druckschraube, gehärtet / Pressure bolt, heat-treated / Bullone di pressione	1	1	1
22	51.32.022.200	Lagerdeckeldichtung / Gasket for bearing cover / Guarnizione per coperchio cuscinetti	1	1	1
87	OR 2-126	O-Ring 2-126 / O-ring 2-126 / Anello a O 2-112	1	1	1

Gruppe 32: Kupplung
Group 32: Clutch
Gruppo 32: Frizione

Bild Picture Foto	Teil-Nr. Part-No. Parte-No	Benennung Description Descrizione	Stk./Motor Pos./Engine Pezzi/Motore		
			175	250	400
88	OR 2-112	O-Ring 2-112 O-ring 2-112 Anello a o 2-112	1	1	1
89	DIN 5402/4x15.8	Lagernadel 4 ⌀ DIN 5402 **Bearing needle 4 ⌀ DIN 5402** Ago cuscinetto 4⌀ DIN 5402	1	1	1
90	DIN 5402/4x23.8	Lagernadel 4 ⌀ **DIN 5402** Bearing needle 4 ⌀ DIN 5402 Ago cuscinetto 4⌀ DIN 5402	1	1	1
91	DIN 5401/6	Kugel 6 ⌀ **DIN 5401** Ball 6 ⌀ DIN 5401 Sfera 6 ⌀ DIN 5401	1	1	1
93	Sb 47	Seeger-Sprengring Sb 47 Circlip Sb 47 Anello elastico di sicurezza	2	2	2
94	DIN 625/16005 C3 SV41	Rillenkugellager 16005 C 3 SV 41 Ball bearing 16005 C 3 SV 41 Cuscinetto a sfera 16005 C 3 SV 41	2	2	2
05	DIN 439/BM5	Flache Sechskantmutter M 5 DIN 439 Lock nut M 5 DIN 439 Dado di serraggio M 5 DIN 439	1	1	1
96	PIN 1x15	Splint 1x15 Pin 1x15 Cupiglia 1x15	8	8	8

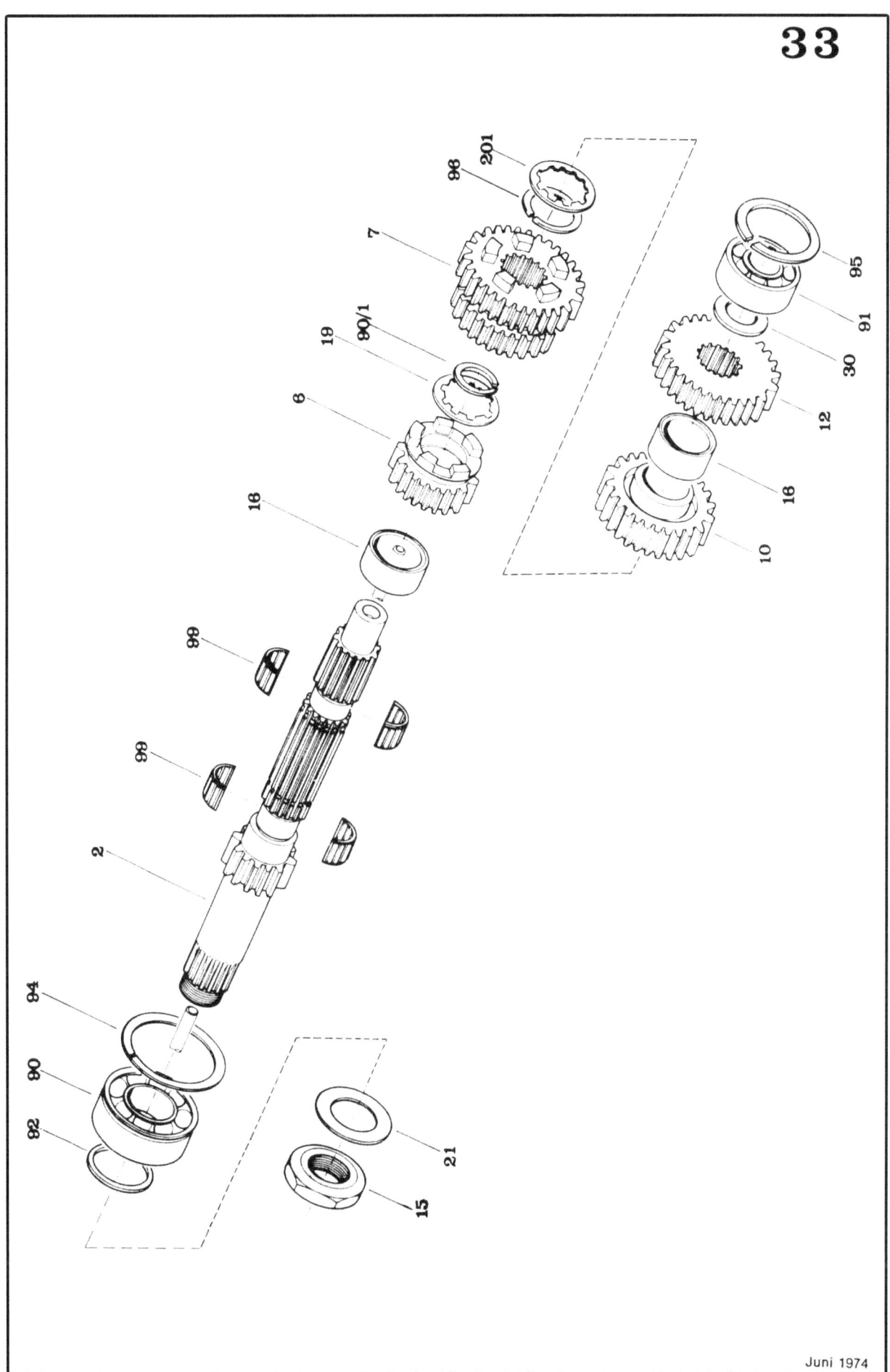

Gruppe 33: Getriebe I
Group 33: Transmission I
Gruppo 33: Trasmissione I

Bild Picture Foto	Teil-Nr. Part-No. Parte No	Benennung Description Descrizione	Stk./Motor Pos./Engine Pezzi/Motore 175	250	400
2	54.33.002.000	Antriebswelle Mainshaft Albero principale	1	1	1
6	54.33.006.000	2. Gang – Losrad 2nd gear – mainshaft 2a marcia – albero principale	1	1	1
7	54.33.007.000	3./5. Gang – Schieberad 3rd/5th gear – mainshaft 3a/5a marcia – albero principale	1	1	1
10	54.33.010.000	4. Gang – Losrad 4th gear – mainshaft 4a marcia – albero principale	1	1	1
12	54.33.012.000	6. Gang – Festrad 6th gear – mainshaft 6a marcia – albero principale	1	1	1
15	51.32.015.100	Mutter M 22x1,5 Nut M 22x1,5 Spessore 22x1,5	1	1	1
16	51.33.016.200	Distanzbüchse Spacer Spessore	2	2	2
19	51.33.019.100	Anlaufring Thrust washer Rondella di spinta	1	1	1
201	51.33.020.100	Anlaufring Thrust washer Rondella di spinta	1	1	1
21	51.32.021.000	Sicherungsblech Flat washer Rondella piana	1	1	1
30	51.33.030.000	Anlaufscheibe Thrust washer Rondella di spinta	1	1	1
90	DIN 625/6205 NC35 SV41	Rillenlager 6205 N C 3 SV 41 Ball bearing 6205 N C 3 SV 41 Cuscinetto a sfera 6205 N C 3 SV 41	1	1	1
90/1	SW 25	Seeger-Sprengring SW 25 Circlip SW 25 Anello di sicurezza di arresto	1	1	1
92	51.33.020.000	Stützscheibe 32 ⌀ Spacer washer 32 ⌀ Spessore 32 ⌀	1	1	1
91	DIN 625/6203 C3 SV41	Rillenlager 6203 C 3 SV 41 DIN 625 Ball bearing 6203 C 3 SV 41 DIN 625 Cuscinetto a sfera 6203 C 3 SV 41 DIN 625	1	1	1
94	Sp 52	Seeger-Sprengring Sp 52 DIN 5417 Circlip Sp 52 DIN 5417 Anello di sicurezza **Sp 52**	1	1	1
95	Sb 40	Seeger-Sprengring Sb 40 Circlip Sb 40 Anello di sicurezza Sb 40	1	1	1
96	WA 985	Seeger-Sprengring WA 985 Circlip WA 985 Anello di sicurezza WA 985	1	1	1
99	K 21x25x13 D	Nadelkäfig 2teilig Needle cage Gabbia degli aghi.	2	2	2

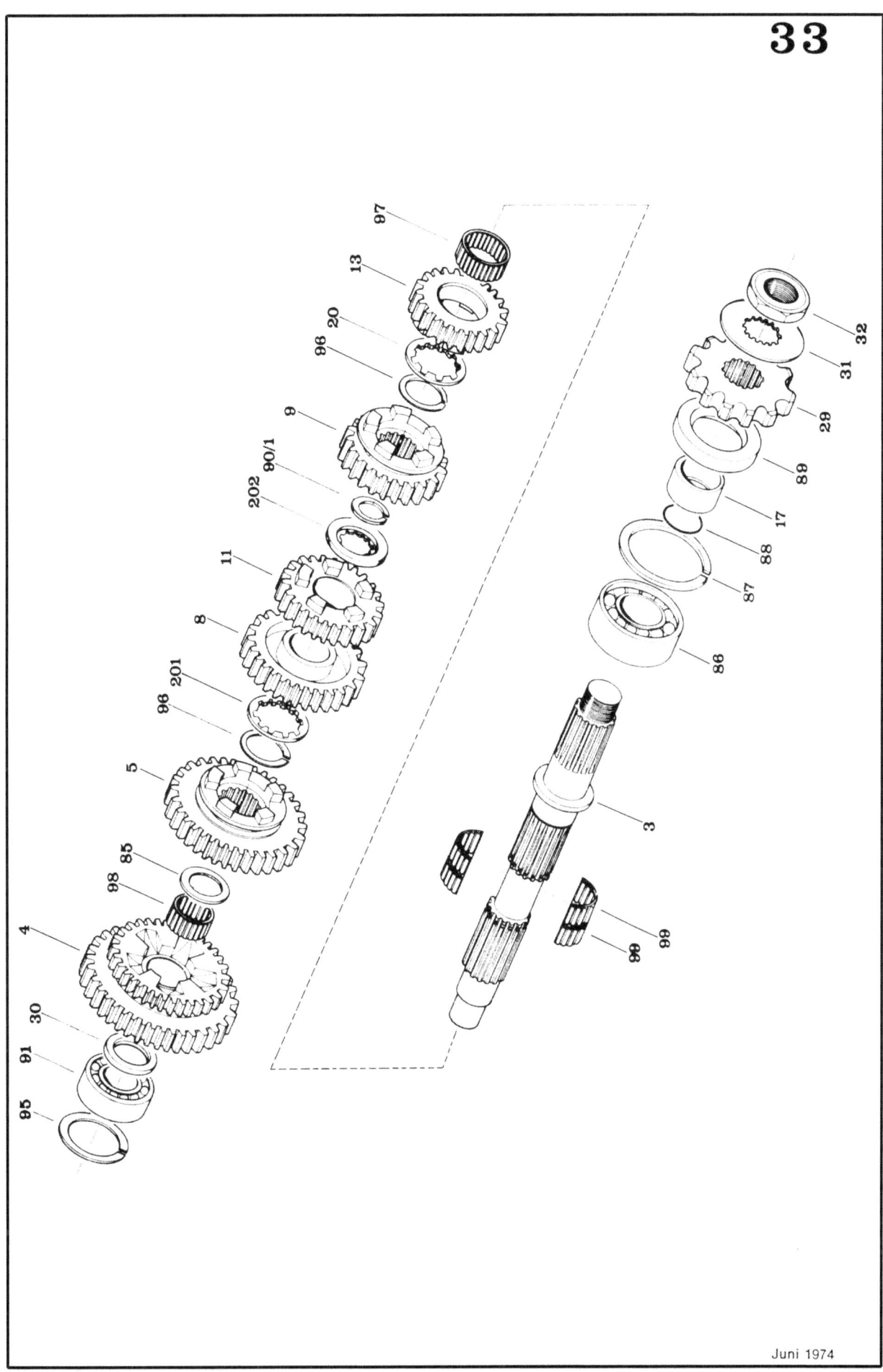

Gruppe 33: Getriebe II
Group 33: Transmission II
Gruppo 33: Trasmissione II

Bild Picture Foto	Teil-Nr. Part-No. Parte No	Benennung Description Descrizione		Stk./Motor Pos./Engine Pezzi/Motore 175/250/400		
3	54.33.003.000	Antriebswelle Counter shaft Contralbero		1	1	1
4	54.33.004.100	1. Gang – Losrad 1st gear – counter shaft 1a marcia – contralbero		1	1	1
5	54.33.005.000	2. Gang – Schieberad 2nd gear – counter shaft 2a marcia – contralbero		1	1	1
8	54.33.008.000	3. Gang – Losrad 3rd gear – counter shaft 3a marcia – contralbero		1	1	1
9	54.33.009.000	4. Gang – Schieberad 4th gear – counter shaft 4a marcia – contralbero		1	1	1
11	54.33.011.000	5. Gang – Losrad 5th gear – counter shaft 5a marcia – contralbero		1	1	1
13	54.33.013.000	6. Gang – Losrad 6th gear – counter shaft 6a marcia – contralbero		1	1	1
17	51.33.017.000	Distanzbüchse Spacer Spessore		1	1	1
201	51.33.020.100	Anlaufring Thrust washer Rondella di spinta		1	1	1
202	51.33.020.200	Anlaufring Thrust washer Rondella di spinta		1	1	1
20	51.33.020.000	Stützscheibe 32 ⌀ Supporting disc 32 ⌀ Disco di sostegno 32 ⌀		1	1	1
29	54.33.029.050	Kettenrad 12-Z. Sprocket 12-T. Ruota dentata 12 denti		nB ar sr	nB ar sr	nB ar sr
–	54.33.029.060	Kettenrad 13-Z. Sprocket 13-T. Ruota dentata 13 denti		nB ar sr	nB ar sr	nB ar sr
–	54.33.029.070	Kettenrad 14-Z. Sprocket 14-T. Ruota dentata 14 denti	54.33.029.080 15 – T	nB ar sr	nB ar sr	nB ar sr
30	51.33.030.000	Anlaufscheibe Thrust washer Rondella di spinta		1	1	1
31	51.33.031.000	Sicherungsblech Sheet metal lock washer Rondella in lamicra		1	1	1
32	51.33.032.000	Kettenradmutter M 20x1,5 Nut M 20x1,5 Dado M 20x1,5		1	1	1
85	SS 20x28x2	Stützscheibe Supporting disc Disco di sostegno		1	1	1
86	DIN 625/6205 C3 SV41	Rillenlager 6205 C 3 SV 41 DIN 615 Ball bearing 6205 C 3 SV 41 DIN 615 Cuscinetto a sfera 6205 C 3 SV 41 DIN 615		1	1	1
87	Sb 52	Seeger-Sprengring Sb 52 Circlip Sb 52 Anello di sicurezza Sb 52		1	1	1
88	OR 2-22	O-Ring 2-22 O-ring 2-22 Anello a O 2-22		1	1	1

nB = nach Bedarf – ar = as requested – sr = su richiesta

Gruppe 33: Getriebe II
Group 33: Transmission II
Gruppo 33: Trasmissione II

Bild / Picture / Foto	Teil-Nr. / Part-No. / Parte No	Benennung / Description / Descrizione	Stk./Motor Pos./Engine Pezzi/Motore 175/250/400
89	DIN 6504/	Simmerring / Radial seal ring / Anello di tenuta radiale	1 1 1
90/1	SW 25	Seeger-Sprengring SW 25 / Circlip / Anello di sicurerzza	1 1 1
91	DIN 625/6203 C3 SV41	Rillenlager 6203 C 3 SV 41 DIN 625 / Ball bearing 6203 C 3 SV 41 DIN 625 / Cuscinetto a sfera 6203 C 3 SV 41 DIN 625	1 1 1
95	Sb 40	Seeger-Sprengring / Circlip / Anello di sicurezza	1 1 1
96	WA 985	Seeger-Sprengring / Circlip / Anello di sicurezza	2 2 2
97	K 25x29x10	Nadelkäfig / Needle cage / Gabbia degli aghi	1 1 1
98	K 20x24x13	Nadelkäfig / Needle cage / Gabbia degli aghi	1 1 1
99	K 21x25x13 D	Nadelkäfig 2teilig / Needle cage / Gabbia degli aghi	2 2 2

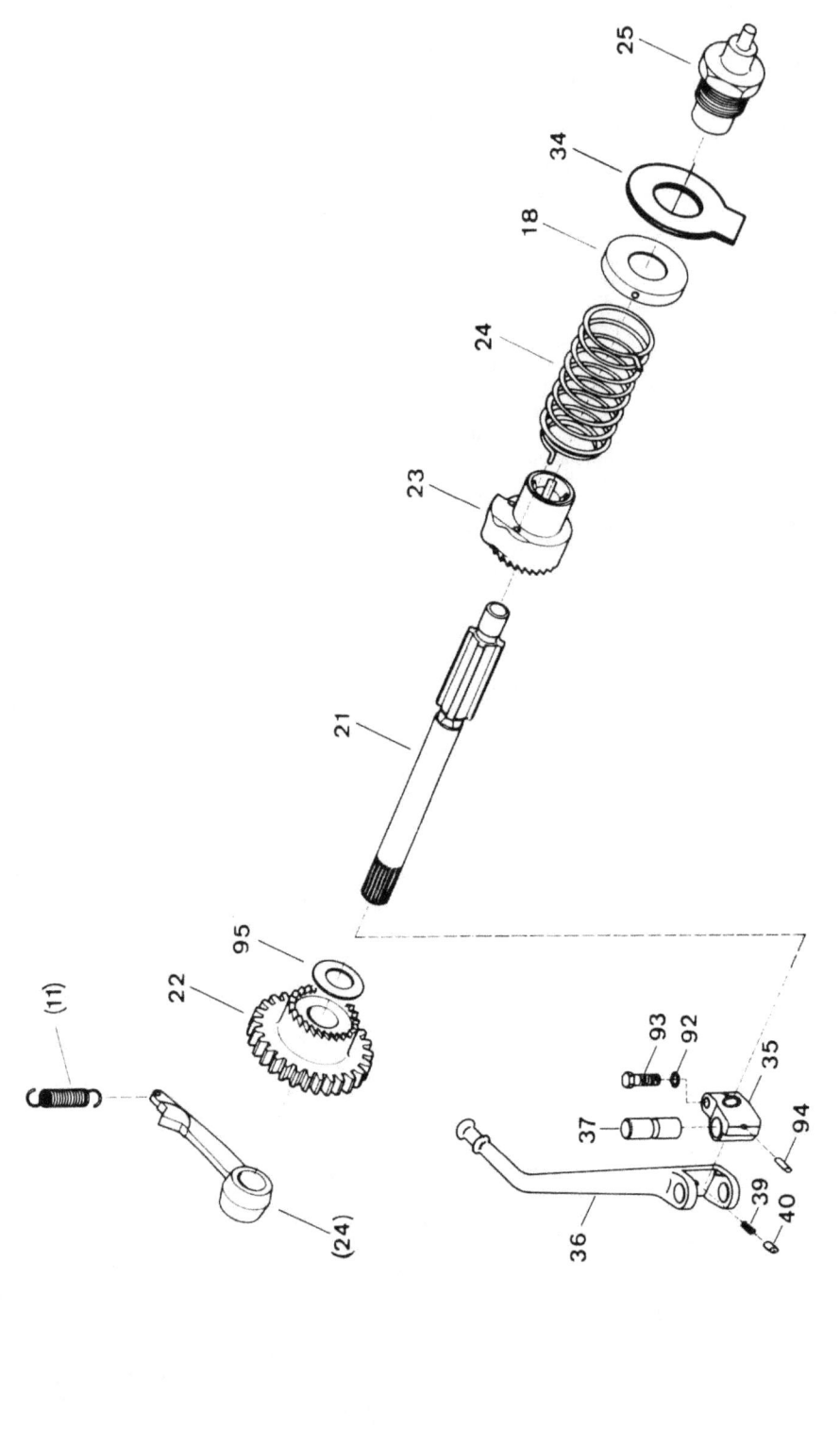

Gruppe 33: Kickstarter   **175 ccm**
Group 33: Kickstarter   **175 cc**
Gruppo 33: Dispositivo di avviamento   **175 cc**

Bild Picture Foto	Teil-Nr. Part-No. Parte No	Benennung Description Descrizione	Stk./Motor Pos./Engine Pezzi/Motore 175
18	51.33.018.000	Federunterlage Spring cup Base molla	1
21	51.33.021.000	Kickstarterwelle Kickstarter rubber Gomma pedale di avviamento	1
22	51.33.022.000	Kickstarterrad Kickstarter gear Ingranaggio pedale di avviamento	1
23	51.33.023.000	Kickstartersperrad Kickstarter ratchet Nottolino di arrest pedale di avviamento	1
24	51.33.024.100	Kickstarterfeder Kickstarter spring Molla pedale di avviamento	1
25	51.33.025.000	Schraubbüchse Screw plug Bussola a vite	1
34	51.33.034.000	Sicherungsblech 1mm Sheetmetal lock washer 1 mm Rondella in lamiera 1 mm	nB ar
—	51.33.034.100	Sicherungsblech 0,75 mm Sheetmetal lock washer 0,75 mm Rondella in lamiera 0,75 mm	nB ar
—	51.33.034.200	Sicherungsblech 0,5 mm Sheetmetal lock washer 0,5 mm Rondella in lamiera 0,5 mm	nB ar
—	1.51.33.036.000	Kickstarter kpl. Kickstarter cpl. Pedale di avviamento cpl.	1
35	51.33.035.200	Kickstarternabe Kickstarter hub Mozzo pedale di avviamento	1
36	51.33.036.100	Kickstarterhebel Kickstarter lever Leva pedale di avviamento	1
37	51.33.037.100	Kickstarterbolzen Kickstarter pin Perno pedale di avviamento	1
39	20.05.021.000	Schnapperfeder Locating spring Molla di posizionamento	1
40	20.05.022.000	Schnapper Locating pin Perno di posizionamento	1
92	DIN 137/B6	Federring B 6 Spring washer B 6 Rondella di fermo B 6	1
93	279.00	Sechskantschraube M 6x20 DIN 601 Hexagon head screw M 6x20 DIN 601 Vite M 6x20 DIN 601	1
94	DIN 1481x4x10	Spannstift 4x10 DIN 1481 Pin 4x10 DIN 1481 Perno 4x10 DIN 1481	1
95	51.33.095.000	Anlaufscheibe Thrust washer Rondella di spinta	1
—	20.05.018.000	Kickstartergummi Kickstarter rubber Gomma pedale di avviamento	1

nB = nach Bedarf — ar = as requested

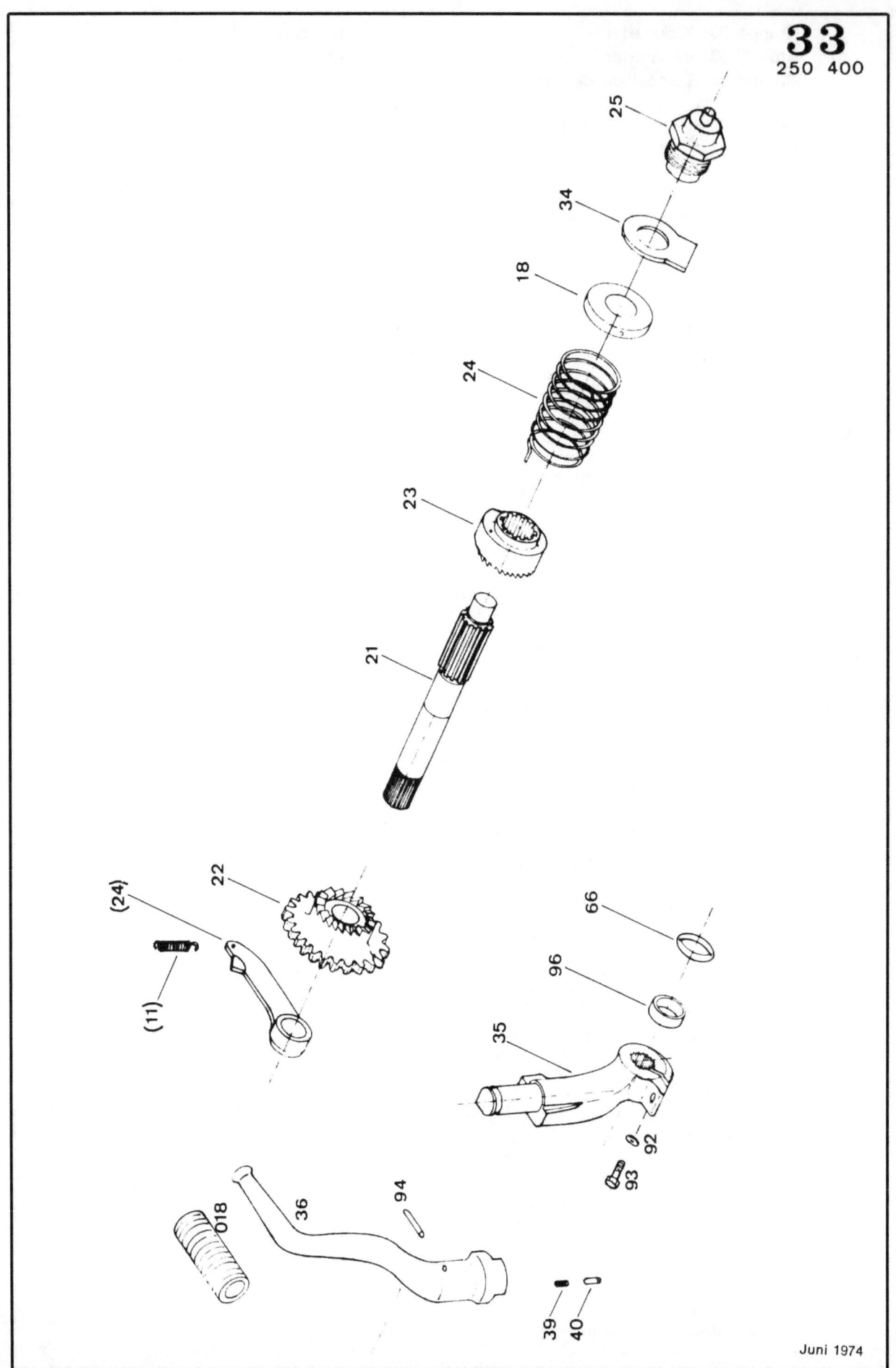

Gruppe 33: Kickstarter
Group 33: Kickstarter
Gruppo 33: Dispositivo di avviamento

250/400 ccm
250/400 cc
250/400 cc

Bild / Picture / Foto	Teil-Nr. / Part-No. / Parte No	Benennung / Description / Descrizione	Stk./Motor Pos./Engine Pezzi/Motore 250 / 400	
18	55.33.018.000	Federunterlage / Spring cup / Base mola	1	1
018	20.05.018.000	Kickstartergummi / Kickstarter rubber / Gomma pedale di avviamento	1	1
21	55.33.021.100	Kickstarterwelle / Kickstarter shaft / Albero pedale di avviamento	1	1
—	55.33.022.100	Kickstarterrad / Kickstarter gear / Ingranaggio pedale di avviamento	1	1
23	55.33.023.200	Kickstarter-Sperrad / Kickstarter ratchet / Nottolino di arrest pedale di avviamento	1	1
24	51.33.024.100	Kickstarterfeder / Kickstarter spring / Molla pedale di avviamento	1	1
25	55.33.025.000	Schraubbüchse / Screw plug / Bussola a vite	1	1
34	51.33.034 000	Sicherungsblech 1 mm / Sheetmetal lock washer 1 mm / Rondella in lamiera 1 mm	nB ar	nB ar
—	51.33.034.100	Sicherungsblech 0,75 mm / Sheetmetal lock washer 0,75 mm / Rondella in lamiera 0,75 mm	nB ar	nB ar
—	51.33.034.200	Sicherungsblech 0,5 mm / Sheetmetal lock washer 0,5 mm / Rondella in lamiera 0,5 mm	nB ar	nB ar
—	1.55.33.036.000	Kickstarter kpl. / Kickstarter cpl. / Pedale di avviamento cpl.	1	—
35	54.33.035.000	Kickstarterunterteil / Lower part of kickstarter / Parte inferiore del pedale di avviamento	1	—
36	54.33.036.000	Kickstarteroberteil / Upper part of kickstarter / Parte superiore del pedale di avviamento	1	—
39	20.05.021.000	Schnapperfeder / Locating spring / Molla di posizionamento	1	1
40	20.05.022.000	Schnapper / Locating pin / Perno di posizionamento	1	1
66	DIN 3770/16x3	O-Ring 16x3 DIN 3770 / O-ring 16x3 DIN 3770 / Anello a O 16x3 DIN 3770	1	1
92	DIN 127/B6	Federscheibe B 6 DIN 127 / Spring washer B 6 DIN 127 / Rondella di fermo B 6 DIN 127	1	1
93	2.63.00	Sechskantschraube M 6x25 / Hexagon head screw M 6x25 / Vite M 6x25	1	1
94	DIN 1481/4x18	Spannstift 4x18 DIN 1481 / Pin 4x18 DIN 1481 / Perno 4x18 DIN 1481	1	1
96	55.33.096.000	Distanzrohr / Bushing / **Bussola**	1	1
—	1.55.33.036.100	Kickstarter kpl. / Kickstarter cpl. / Pedale di avviamento	—	1
35	54.33.035.100	Kickstarter-Unterteil / Lower part of Kickstarter / Parte inferiore del pedale di avviamento	—	1
36	54.33.036.100	Kickstarter-Oberteil / Upper part of Kickstarter / Parte superiore del pedale di avviamento	—	1

nB = nach Bedarf — ar = as requested

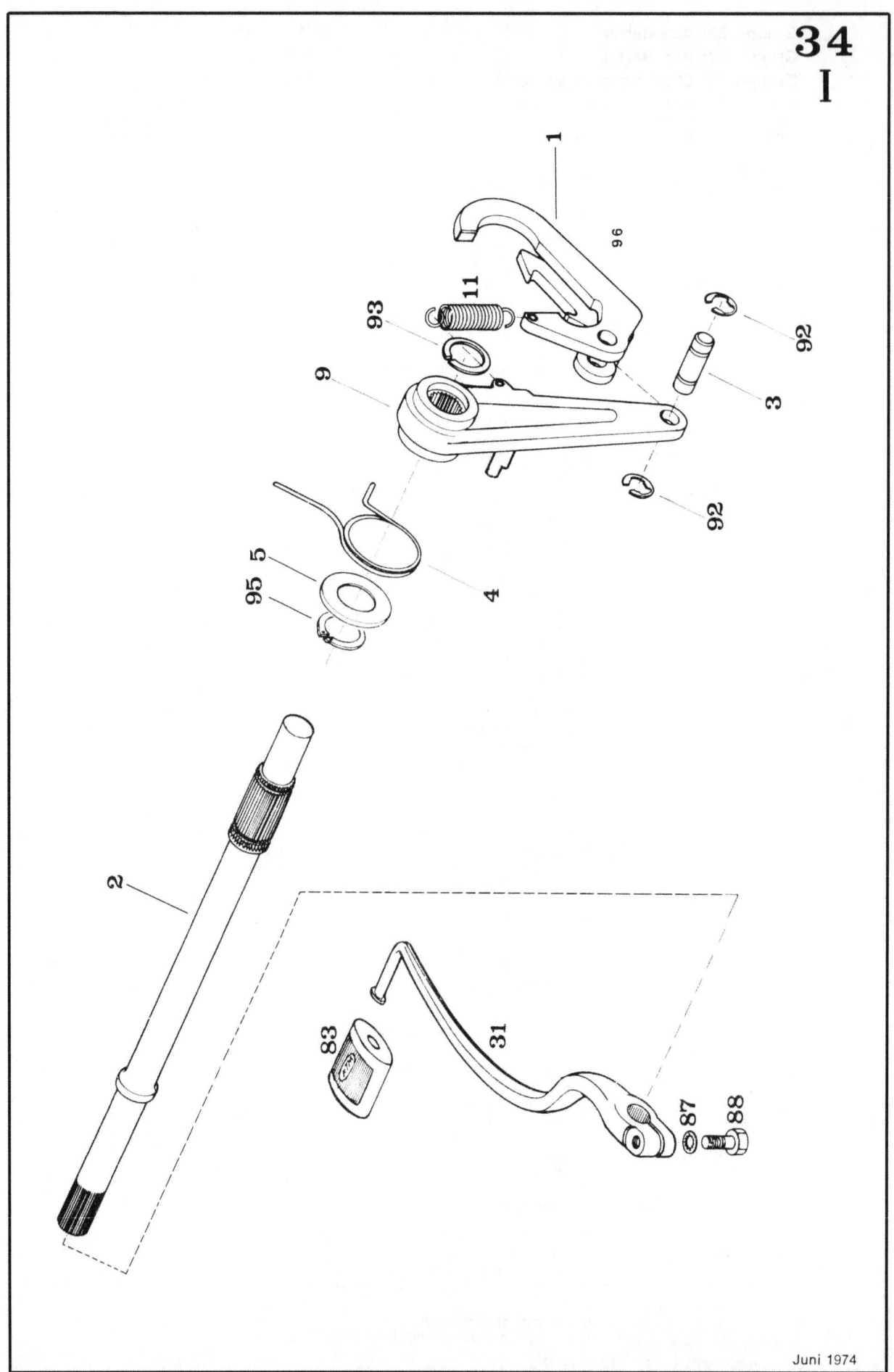

Gruppe 34: Schaltung I
Group 34: Shifting mechanism I
Gruppo 34: Cambiamento di marcia I

Bild Picture Foto	Teil-Nr. Part-No. Parte No	Benennung Description Descrizione	Stk./Motor Pos./Engine Pezzi/Motore
			175 / 250 / 400
1	51.34.001.400	Schaltstück kpl. Shifting quadrant Claw Only Quadrante di cambio marcia cpl.	1 1 1
2	51.34.002.500	Schaltwelle Shifting shaft Albero di cambio marcia	1 1 1
3	51.34.003.300	Bolzen Pin Perno	1 1 1
4	51.34.004.100	Rückholfeder Returning spring Molla di ritorno	1 1 1
5	51.34.005.300	Scheibe für Feder Washer for spring Rondella per molla	1 1 1
9	51.34.009.500	Schalthebel innen Shift lever internal Leva di cambio interna	1 1 1
11	51.34.011.000	Schalthebelfeder Shift lever spring Molla leva di cambio	1 1 1
31	51.34.031.400	Schalthebel außen mit Teil 83 und Schraube Shift lever with part 83 + screw Leva di cambio con parte 83 + vite	1 1 1
83	32.03.083.000	Pedalgummi Rubber — shift lever Gomma — leva di cambio	1 1 1
87	DIN 127/A6	Federring A 6 DIN 127 Lock washer A 6 DIN 127 Rondella di bloccaggio A 6 DIN 127	1 1 1
88	263.000	Sechskantschraube M 6x25 Hexagon head screw M 6x25 Vite M 6x25	1 1 1
92	DIN 6799/RS7	Sicherungsscheibe 7 DIN 6799 Retaining clip Anello di sicurezza	1 1 1
93	SW 17	Seegerring SW 17 (ohne Ösen) Circlip Anello di sicurezza	1 1 1
95	DIN 471/A17x1.5 SD	Seegerring A 17x1,5 SD DIN 471 Circlip Anello di sicurezza	2 2 2
96	51.34.001.500	Shifting quadrant cpl.	1 1 1

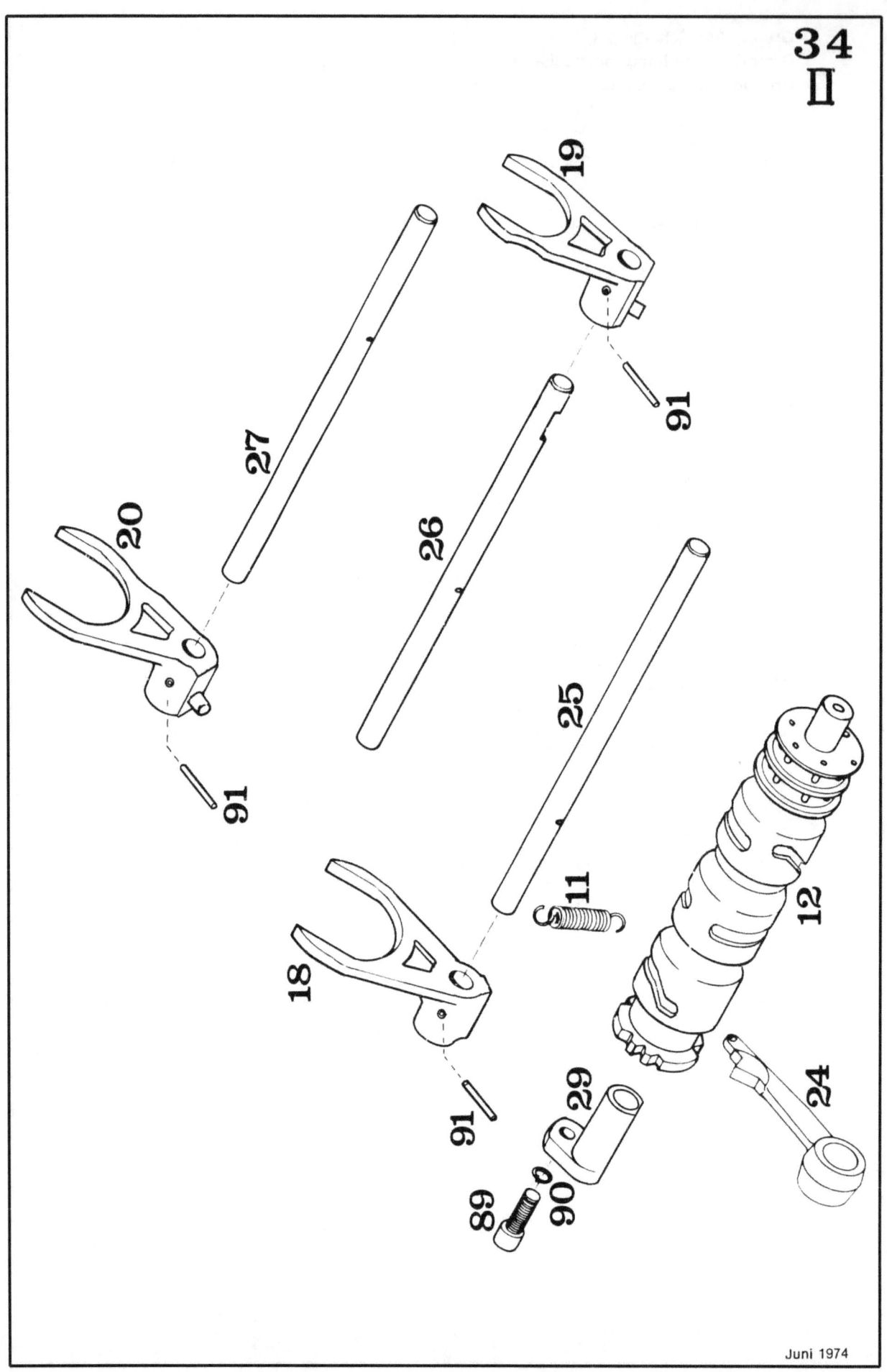

Gruppe 34: Schaltung II
Group 34: Shifting mechanism II
Gruppo 34: Cambiamento di marcia II

Bild / Picture / Foto	Teil-Nr. / Part-No. / Parte-No	Benennung / Description / Descrizione	Stk./Motor Pos./Engine Pezzi/Motore 175/250/400		
11	51.34.011.000	Schalthebelfeder / Shift lever spring / Molla leva di cambio	1	1	1
12	54.34.012.206	Schaltwalze 6-Gang kpl. GS / Shifting drum for 5-speed cpl. GS / Cilindro di cambio marcia 6 marce cpl. GS	1	1	1
–	54.34.012.205	Schaltwalze 5-Gang kpl. MC / Shifting drum for 5-speed cpl. MC / cilindro di cambio marcia 5 marce cpl. MC	1	1	1
18	54.34.018.000	Schaltgabel 1./3. Gang / Shifting fork 1st/3rd gear / Forcella di cambio 1a/3a marcia	1	1	1
19	54.34.019.000	Schaltgabel 2./4. Gang / Shifting fork 2nd/4th gear / Forcella 2a/4a marcia	1	1	1
20	54.34.020.000	Schaltgabel 5./6. Gang / Shifting fork 5th/6th gear / Forcella 5a/6a marcia	1	1	1
24	51.34.024.200	Arretierhebel / Locating lever / Leva di posizionamento	1	–	–
–	55.34.024.200	Arretierhebel / Locating lever / Leva di posizionamento	–	1	1
25	51.34.025.100 na	Schaltschiene 1./3. Gang / Shifting rod 1st/3rd gear / Asta di cambio 1a/3a marcia	1	1	1
26	51.34.026.200 na	Schatschiene 2./4. Gang / Shifting rod 2nd/4th gear / Asta di cambio 2a/4a marcia	1	1	1
27	51.34.027.100 na	Schaltschiene 5./6. Gang / Shifting rod 5th/6th gear / Asta di cambio 5a/6a marcia	1	1	1
29	54.34.029.100	Büchse für Schaltwalze / Bushing for shifting drum / Bussola per cilindro di cambio marcia	1	1	1
89	DIN 912/M6x15/86	Innensechskantschraube M 6x16 DIN 912 / Allen head screw M 6x16 DIN 912 / Vite a testa esagonale interna M 6x16 DIN 912	1	1	1
90	DIN 137/B6	Federscheibe B 6 DIN 137 / Spring washer B 6 DIN 137 / Rondella elastica B 6 DIN 137	1	1	1
91	RP 3x18	Spannstift 3x18 / Roll in pin / Perno di tensione	3	3	3
–	54.34.018.000	△ **Zsb.** Schaltschiene mit Schaltgabel 1./3. Gang / △ **Assembly:** Shifting rod with shifting fork 1st/3rd gear / △ **Compl.:** Asta di cambio con forcella di cambio 1a/3a marcia	1	1	1
–	54.34.019.000	△ **Zsb.** Schaltschiene mit Schaltgabel 2./4. Gang / △ **Assembly:** Shifting rod with shifting fork 2nd/4th gear / △ **Compl.:** Asta di cambio con forcella di cambio 1a/3a marcia	1	1	1
–	54.34.020.000	△ **Zsb.** Schaltschiene mit Schaltgabel 5./6. Gang / △ **Assembly:** Shifting rod with shifting fork 5th/6th gear / △ **Compl.:** Asta di cambio con forcella di cambio 5a/6a marcia	1	1	1

△ komplett montiert und ausgewinkelt
Completely assembled
Completamente montato e centrato

Gruppe 34: Schaltung II
Group 34: Shifting mechanism II
Gruppo 34: Cambiamento di marcia II

Bild Picture Foto	Teil-Nr. Part-No. Parte No	Benennung Description Descrizione	Stk./Motor Pos./Engine Pezzi/Motore
			175/250/400

Teile für alte Ausführung mit geschweißter Schaltwalze:
Parts for old style shifting mechanism with welded shifting drum:
Pezz iper tipo vecchio con cilindro di cambio marcia saldato:

—	51.34.012.200	Schaltwalze 6-Gang kpl. GS Shifting drum for 6-speed cpl. GS Cilindro di cambio marcia 6 marce cpl. GS	1	1	—
—	54.34.012.100	Schaltwalze 5-Gang kpl. MC Shifting drum for 5-speed cpl. MC Cilindro di cambio marcia 5 marce cpl. MC	1	1	—
—	1.51.34.018.300	△ **Zsb.** Schaltschiene mit Schaltgabel 1./3. Gang △ **Assembly:** Shifting rod with shifting fork 1st/3rd gear △ **Compl.:** Asta di cambio con forcella di cambio 1a/3a marcia	1	1	—
—	1.51.34.019.400	△ **Zsb.** Schaltschiene mit Schaltgabel 2./4. Gang △ **Assembly:** Shifting rod with shifting fork 2nd/4th gear △ **Compl.:** Asta di cambio con forcella di cambio 2a/4a marcia	1	1	—
—	1.51.34.020.400	△ **Zsb.** Schaltschiene mit Schaltgabel 5./6. Gang △ **Assembly:** Shifting rod with shifting fork 5th/6th gear △ **Compl.:** Asta di cambio con forcella di cambio 5a/6a marcia	1	1	—
—	51.34.029.100	Büchse für Schaltwalze Bushing for shifting drum Bussola per cilindro di cambio marcia	1	1	—

△ Komplett montiert und ausgewinkelt
  Completely assembled
  Completamente montato e centrato

VELOCEPRESS MANUALS – MOTORCYCLE BY MAKE

AJS 1932-1948 SINGLES & TWINS 250cc THRU 1000cc (BOOK OF)
AJS 1945-1960 SINGLES 350cc & 500cc MODELS 16 & 18 (BOOK OF)
AJS 1955-1965 SINGLES 350cc & 500cc (BOOK OF)
AJS 1957-1966 FACTORY WSM - ALL SINGLES & TWINS
AJS 1959-1969 FACTORY WSM G80CS G85CS & P11 OFF ROAD
ARIEL UP TO 1932 (BOOK OF)
ARIEL 1932-1939 PREWAR MODELS (BOOK OF)
ARIEL 1933-1951 (WORKSHOP MANUAL)
ARIEL 1939-1960 4 STROKE SINGLES (BOOK OF)
ARIEL 1958-1964 LEADER & ARROW FACTORY WSM & PARTS LIST
ARIEL 1958-1964 LEADER & ARROW (BOOK OF)
BMW R26 R27 (1956-1967) FACTORY WORKSHOP MANUAL
BMW R50 R50S R60 R69S (1955-1969) FACTORY WORKSHOP MANUAL
BMW R50/5 R60/5 R75/5 (1969-1973) FACTORY WORKSHOP MANUAL
BRIDGESTONE 90 SERIES FACTORY WSM & PARTS CATALOGUE
BRIDGESTONE 175 SERIES FACTORY WSM & PARTS CATALOGUE
BRIDGESTONE 350 SERIES FACTORY WSM & PARTS CATALOGUES
BSA SERVICE SHEETS MASTER CATALOGUE ALL MODELS 1945-1967
BSA BANTAM D1 TO D7 1948-1966 FACTORY SERVICE SHEETS MANUAL
BSA BANTAM ALL MODELS FROM 1948 ONWARDS (BOOK OF)
BSA BANTAM D14 FACTORY SERVICE MANUAL
BSA DANDY FACTORY WORKSHOP MANUAL (COMPILATION)
BSA SINGLES & V-TWINS UP TO 1926 inc. 1927 SUPPLEMENT (BOOK OF)
BSA SINGLES & V-TWINS UP TO 1930 (BOOK OF)
BSA SINGLES & V-TWINS UP TO 1935 (BOOK OF)
BSA SINGLES & V-TWINS 1936-1939 (BOOK OF)
BSA C10, C11 & C12 1945-1958 FACTORY SERVICE SHEETS MANUAL
BSA OHV & SV SINGLES 250-600cc 1945-1959 (BOOK OF)
BSA C15 & B40 1958-1967 FACTORY SERVICE SHEETS MANUAL
BSA OHV & SV SINGLES 250cc (ONLY) 1954-1970 (BOOK OF)
BSA B31, B32, B33 & B34 1945-60 FACTORY SERVICE SHEETS MANUAL
BSA OHV SINGLES 350 & 500cc 1955-1967 (BOOK OF)
BSA M20, M21 & M33 1945-1963 FACTORY SERVICE SHEETS MANUAL
BSA TWINS A7 & A10 1948-1962 FACTORY SERVICE SHEETS MANUAL
BSA TWINS A7 & A10 1948-1962 (BOOK OF)
BSA TWINS A50 & A65 1962-1965 FACTORY WORKSHOP MANUAL
BSA TWINS A50 & A65 1962-1969 (SECOND BOOK OF)
BULTACO 125cc to 37cc SINGLES 1968-1979 WORKSHOP MANUAL
CZ 125cc to 380cc SINGLES 1967-1974 WORKSHOP MANUAL
DOUGLAS 1929-1939 PREWAR ALL MODELS (BOOK OF)
DOUGLAS 1948-1957 POSTWAR ALL MODELS FACTORY SHOP MANUAL
DUCATI 160cc, 250cc & 350cc OHC MODELS FACTORY SHOP MANUAL
HONDA 50cc ALL MODELS UP TO 1970 INC MONKEY & TRAIL (BOOK OF)
HONDA 90cc ALL MODELS UP TO 1966 (BOOK OF)
HONDA TWINS & SINGLES 50cc THRU 305cc 1960-1966 (BOOK OF)
HONDA TWINS ALL MODELS 125cc THRU 450cc UP TO 1968 (BOOK OF)
HONDA C100 50cc SUPER CUB O.H.C. 1959-1962 FACTORY WSM
HONDA C110 50cc SPORT CUB O.H.C. 1960-1962 FACTORY WSM
HONDA 50-65-70-90cc O.H.C. SINGLES 1959-1983 WSM
HONDA 100-125cc SINGLES CB/CD/CL/SL/TL 1970-1984 FACTORY WSM
HONDA 125-150cc TWINS C/CS/CB/CA 1959-1966 FACTORY WSM
HONDA 125-160-175-200cc TWINS 1965-1978 WORKSHOP MANUAL
HONDA 250-305cc TWINS C/CS/CB 1961-1968 FACTORY WSM
HOHDA 250-350cc TWINS CB/CL/SL 1968-1973 FACTORY WSM
HONDA 250-360cc TWINS CB/CL/CJ 1974-1977 FACTORY WSM
HONDA 350F & 400F 4-CYLINDER 1972-1977 FACTORY WSM
HONDA 450cc TWINS CB/CL 1965-1974 K0 TO K7 WORKSHOP MANUAL
HONDA 500cc & 550cc 4-CYL 1971-1978 FACTORY WORKSHOP MANUAL
HONDA 750cc SHOC 4-CYL 1969-1978 K0~K8 WORKSHOP MANUAL
HUSQVARNA 125cc to 450cc SINGLES 1965-1975 WORKSHOP MANUAL
INDIAN PONYBIKE, BOY RACER & PAPOOSE ILL PARTS LIST & SALES LIT

J.A.P. ENGINES 1927-1952 & MOTORCYCLES 1934-1952 (BOOK OF)
MATCHLESS 1931-1939 ALL MODELS 250cc THRU 990cc (BOOK OF)
MATCHLESS 1945-1956 350 & 500cc SINGLES (BOOK OF)
MATCHLESS 1955-1966 350 & 500cc SINGLES (BOOK OF)
MATCHLESS 1957-1966 FACTORY WSM - ALL SINGLES & TWINS
NEW IMPERIAL ALL SV & OHV FROM 1935 ONWARDS (BOOK OF)
NORTON 1932-1939 PREWAR MODELS (BOOK OF)
NORTON 1932-1947 (BOOK OF)
NORTON 1938-1956 (BOOK OF)
NORTON 1945-1963 MODELS 16H, Big4, ES2, 19 & 50 WSM'S & PARTS
NORTON 1955-1963 MODELS 19, 50 & ES2 (BOOK OF)
NORTON 1948-1970 DOMINATOR TWINS FACTORY WSM'S & PARTS
NORTON 1955-1965 DOMINATOR TWINS (BOOK OF)
NORTON 1960-1970 TWIN CYLINDER FACTORY WORKSHOP MANUAL
NORTON 1970-1975 COMMANDO 850 & 750cc FACTORY WSM
NORTON 1975-1978 MK 3 COMMANDO 850 cc FACTORY WSM
PANTHER 1932-1958 LIGHTWEIGHT MODELS 250 & 350cc (BOOK OF)
PANTHER 1938-1966 HEAVYWEIGHT MODELS 600 & 650cc (BOOK OF)
PENTON-KTM-SACHS 1968-1975 100cc & 125cc WORKSHOP MANUAL
PENTON-KTM 1972-1975 175cc, 250cc & 400cc WSM & PARTS MANUALS
RALEIGH MOTORCYCLES 1919-1933 (BOOK OF)
ROYAL ENFIELD 1934-1946 SINGLES & V TWINS (BOOK OF)
ROYAL ENFIELD 1937-1953 SINGLES & V TWINS (BOOK OF)
ROYAL ENFIELD 1946-1962 SINGLES (BOOK OF)
ROYAL ENFIELD 1948-1962 350cc & 500cc PRE-UNIT BULLET WSM
ROYAL ENFIELD 1948-1963 500cc TWINS FACTORY WORKSHOP MANUAL
ROYAL ENFIELD 1952-1963 700cc TWINS FACTORY WORKSHOP MANUAL
ROYAL ENFIELD 1956-1966 250cc CRUSADER & 350cc NEW BULLET WSM
ROYAL ENFIELD 1958-1966 250cc & 350cc SINGLES (SECOND BOOK OF)
ROYAL ENFIELD 1962-1970 INTERCEPTOR WSM'S & PARTS (Compilation)
RUDGE 1933-1939 (BOOK OF)
SACHS 1968-1975 100cc & 125cc ENGINES WSM & M/CYCLE PARTS LIST
SUNBEAM 1928-1939 (BOOK OF)
SUNBEAM 1946-1957 S7 & S8 (BOOK OF)
SUZUKI 50cc & 80cc UP TO 1966 (BOOK OF)
SUZUKI T10 1963-1967 FACTORY WORKSHOP MANUAL
SUZUKI T20 & T200 1965-1969 FACTORY WORKSHOP MANUAL
SUZUKI TWINS 1962 ONWARDS 125-500cc WORKSHOP MANUAL
TRIUMPH 1935-1949 SINGLES & TWINS (BOOK OF)
TRIUMPH 1937-1961 SINGLES SV & OHV 250cc-600cc + TERRIER & CUB
TRIUMPH 1945-1955 PRE-UNIT 350cc, 500cc & 650cc TWINS WSM No.11
TRIUMPH 1945-1959 TWINS (BOOK OF)
TRIUMPH 1956-1969 TWINS (BOOK OF)
TRIUMPH 1956-1962 PRE-UNIT 500 & 650cc TWINS WSM No.17
TRIUMPH 1957-1963 UNIT CONSTRUCTION 350-500cc WSM No.4
TRIUMPH 1963-1974 UNIT CONSTRUCTION 350-500cc FACTORY WSM
TRIUMPH 1963-1970 UNIT CONSTRUCTION 650cc FACTORY WSM
TRIUMPH 1968-1974 TRIDENT T150 & T150V FACTORY WSM
TRIUMPH 1971-1973 650cc OIL-IN-FRAME FACTORY WSM
TRIUMPH 1973-1978 750cc BONNEVILLE & TIGER FACTORY WSM
TRIUMPH 1979-1983 750cc T140, TR7 & TR65 FACTORY WSM
VELOCETTE 1925-1970 ALL SINGLES & TWINS (BOOK OF)
VELOCETTE 1933-1952 MOV-MAC-MSS RIGID FRAME FACTORY WSM
VELOCETTE 1953-1960 MAC SPRING FRAME WSM & ILL PARTS LIST
VELOCETTE 1954-1971 MSS-VENOM-THRUXTON-VIPER FACTORY WSM
VILLIERS ENGINE UP TO 1959 INC. 3 WHEELERS (BOOK OF)
VILLIERS ENGINE UP TO 1969 (BOOK OF)
VINCENT 1935-1955 (WORKSHOP MANUAL)
YAMAHA 1961-1967 YA5 & YA6 (WORKSHOP MANUAL & ILL PARTS LIST)
YAMAHA 1968-1971 DT1 & MX SERIES Inc. GYT WORKSHOP MANUAL
YAMAHA 1971-1972 JT1 & JT2 (WORKSHOP MANUAL & ILL PARTS LIST)

VELOCEPRESS MANUALS – SCOOTERS BY MAKE

BSA SUNBEAM SCOOTER WORKSHOP MANUAL 1959-1965
BSA SUNBEAM SCOOTER 1959-1965 (BOOK OF)
LAMBRETTA 1947-1957 ALL 125 & 150cc MODELS (BOOK OF)
LAMBRETTA 1957-1970 LI & TV MODELS (SECOND BOOK OF)
NSU PRIMA 1956-1964 ALL MODELS (BOOK OF)
TRIUMPH TIGRESS SCOOTER WORKSHOP MANUAL 1959-1965
TRIUMPH TIGRESS SCOOTER (BOOK OF)
VESPA 1951-1961 (BOOK OF)
VESPA 1955-1963 125 & 150cc & GS MODELS (SECOND BOOK OF)
VESPA 1955-1968 GS & SS (BOOK OF)
VESPA 1963-1972 90, 125 & 150cc (THIRD BOOK OF)

VELOCEPRESS MANUALS – MOPEDS & MOTORIZED BICYCLES

CYCLEMOTOR (BOOK OF)
NSU QUICKLY 1953-1963 ALL MODELS (BOOK OF)
PUCH MAXI N & S MAINTENANCE & REPAIR (3 MANUAL COMPILATION)
RALEIGH MOPEDS 1960-1969 (BOOK OF)

VELOCEPRESS MANUALS - THREE WHEELER'S

BOND MINICAR THREE WHEELER 1948-1967 (BOOK OF)
BMW ISETTA FACTORY WORKSHOP MANUAL
BSA THREE WHEELER (BOOK OF)
RELIANT REGAL THREE WHEELER 1952-1973 (BOOK OF)
VINTAGE MORGAN THREE WHEELER (BOOK OF)

VELOCEPRESS TECHNICAL BOOKS – MOTORCYCLE

1930'S BRITISH MOTORCYCLE CARBS & ELEC COMPONENTS (BOOK OF)
1930'S BRITISH MOTORCYCLE ENGINES (OVERHAUL & MAINTENANCE)
1930'S BRITISH MOTORCYCLE GEARBOXES & CLUTCHES (BOOK OF)
CATALOG OF BRITISH MOTORCYCLES (1951 MODELS)
LUCAS ELECTRONICS BRITISH M/CYCLES REPAIR & PARTS (1950-1977)
MOTORCYCLE ENGINEERING (P.E. Irving)
MOTORCYCLE ROAD TESTS 1949-1953 (Motor Cycle Magazine UK)
SPEED AND HOW TO OBTAIN IT (Motor Cycle Magazine UK)
TUNING FOR SPEED (P.E. Irving)
WIPAC (COMBO) MANUAL NUMBER 3 + M/CYCLE & SCOOTER MANUAL

www.VelocePress.com

VELOCEPRESS MANUALS – AUTOMOBILE BY MAKE

ALFA ROMEO GIULIA WORKSHOP MANUAL 1300 TO 2000cc 1962-1975
ALFA ROMEO GIULIA TECH MANUAL CARBURETED CARS FROM 1962
ALFA ROMEO GIULIA TECH MANUAL FUEL INJECTED CARS FROM 1969
ALFA ROMEO GIULIETTA & GIULIA 750 & 101 SERIES 1955-1965 WSM
AUSTIN-HEALEY SPRITE & MG MIDGET WORKSHOP MANUAL 1958-1971
BMW 600 LIMOUSINE FACTORY WORKSHOP MANUAL
BMW 600 LIMOUSINE OWNERS HAND BOOK & SERVICE MANUAL
BMW 2000 & 2002 1966-1976 WORKSHOP MANUAL
BMW 2500, 2800, 3.0 & BARVARIA WORKSHOP MANUAL
CORVAIR 1960-1969 WORKSHOP MANUAL
CORVETTE V8 1955-1962 WORKSHOP MANUAL
FERRARI HANDBOOK ROAD & RACE CARS (SERVICE/SPECS) 1948-1958
FERRARI 250GT SERVICE & MAINTENANCE by JIM RIFF 1956-1965
FERRARI 250GT & 250GTE FACTORY PARTS AND REPAIR MANUALS
FIAT 500 FACTORY WORKSHOP MANUAL 1957-1973
FIAT 600, 600D & MULTIPLA FACTORY WORKSHOP MANUAL 1955-1969
FORD MUSTANG 1965-1973 TRANSMISSION WORKSHOP MANUAL
JAGUAR E-TYPE 3.8 & 4.2 SERIES 1 & 2 WORKSHOP MANUAL
JAGUAR MK 7, 8, 9 & XK120, 140, 150 WORKSHOP MANUAL 1948-1961
MERCEDES-BENZ 230 SERIES 1963-1968
MERCEDES-BENZ 280 SERIES 1968-1972
METROPOLITAN FACTORY WORKSHOP MANUAL
MGA & MGB OWNERS HANDBOOK & WORKSHOP MANUAL
MG MIDGET TC, TD, TF & TF1500 WORKSHOP MANUAL
PORSCHE 356 1948-1965 WORKSHOP MANUAL
PORSCHE 911 2.0, 2.2, 2.4 LITRE 1964-1973 WORKSHOP MANUAL
PORSCHE 911 2.7, 3.0, 3.2 LITRE 1973-1989 WORKSHOP MANUAL
PORSCHE 912 WORKSHOP MANUAL
PORSCHE 914/4 & 914/6 1.7, 1.8, 2.0 LITRE 1970-1976 WSM
TRIUMPH TR2, TR3, TR4 1953-1965 WORKSHOP MANUAL
VOLKSWAGEN TRANSPORTER, TRUCKS & WAGONS 1950-1979 WSM
VOLVO 1944-1968 ALL MODELS WORKSHOP MANUAL

VELOCEPRESS TECHNICAL BOOKS - AUTOMOBILE

HOW TO BUILD A FIBERGLASS CAR
HOW TO BUILD A RACING CAR
HOW TO RESTORE THE MODEL 'A' FORD
MASERATI OWNER'S HANDBOOK
PERFORMANCE TUNING THE SUNBEAM TIGER
SOUPING THE VOLKSWAGEN
SOLEX CARBURETORS (EMPHASIS ON UK & EU AUTOMOBILES)
SU CARBURETORS (EMPHASIS ON UK AUTOMOBILES)
WEBER CARBURETORS (EMPHASIS ON ALFA & FIAT)

VELOCEPRESS BOOKS & GUIDES - AUTOMOBILE

COMPLETE CATALOG OF JAPANESE MOTOR VEHICLES
FERRARI 308 SERIES BUYER'S AND OWNER'S GUIDE
FERRARI BROCHURES AND SALES LITERATURE 1968-1989
FERRARI SERIAL NUMBERS PART I - ODD NUMBERS TO 21399
FERRARI SERIAL NUMBERS PART II - EVEN NUMBERS TO 1050
HENRY'S FABULOUS MODEL "A" FORD
MASERATI BROCHURES AND SALES LITERATURE

VELOCEPRESS BOOKS – AUTO RACING

BOOK OF THE 1950 CARRERA PANAMERICANA - MEXICAN ROAD RACE
DIALED IN - THE JAN OPPERMAN STORY
VEDA ORR'S NEW REVISED HOT ROD PICTORIAL
LIFE OF TED HORN – AMERICAN RACING CHAMPION

www.VelocePress.com

www.ingramcontent.com/pod-product-compliance
Lightning Source LLC
Chambersburg PA
CBHW080745300426
44114CB00019B/2652